D0717286

WHO
DID WHAT
WHEN

PEOPLE AND EVENTS IN
WORLD HISTORY
Edited by Chris Parker

MITCHELL BEAZLEY LIMITED

ISBN 0 85533 198 4

Typesetting by G.A. Pindar & Son Ltd., Scarborough.

Printed and bound in England.

Contents

Introduction

This book of historical facts, figures and personalities can be used in two ways. If the name of a particular person is known, it can be found easily in the alphabetically-arranged articles that occupy the upper parts of pages 5 to 208. If, on the other hand, a particular period is of interest, that too can quickly be found by reference to the time chart, which is arranged chronologically along the lower parts of the same pages. In addition, a cross-referencing system leads from one to the other. Thus more information about a historical figure appearing in the time chart can be obtained by following the cross-reference instruction by his or her name. This instruction takes the form of an A in the margin opposite the proper noun in question. Modern countries such as England, Spain etc have no articles on them, so any cross-reference instruction against them can be taken as referring to another proper noun occurring in the same line. In the rare event of two cross-references occurring in the same line, only one symbol has been used. Names should be looked up under their surname. Conversely, more background information about the historical context of a particular figure or event can be obtained by referring in the time chart to the date in question. At the end of the book is a list of countries, with their location, population, form of government and present and past rulers.

In the A–Z section, priority has been given to political figures (such as monarchs and statesmen) and to important historical events (wars, declarations of independence and treaties). Also included are articles on musicians, writers, inventors, explorers and religious leaders. These are more thoroughly covered in the time chart section, where their contributions in various fields are assessed in a historical context.

The time chart itself covers the years 4000 BC to 1978. All history's great empires, inventions, artistic achievements and religious movements have been described in an easy-to-assimilate, readable manner designed to complement the A–Z section. The length of the period covered by each section has been carefully matched with its importance. Thus each of the last few years has a section to itself, whereas the first pages of the time chart cover periods up to 400 years each.

The tables which complete the book contain many countries' current rulers, and complete lists of past rulers of the more prominent countries such as the USSR and the USA. Commonwealth and western European countries are also dealt with in more detail. The United Kingdom tables, for instance, list all monarchs of Scotland and England, the kings and queens of the United Kingdom after 1603, and all the Prime Ministers.

In this way, the figures and events historically responsible for the way things are today can be identified and studied. The book thus provides an extremely handy quick reference tool and an excellent solid basis for the further more detailed study of history.

Abbasids, Muslim dynasty that held the Caliphate from 750 to 1258. They traced their descent from al-Abbas, the uncle of Mohammed, and came to power by defeating the Umayyads. The Abbasids moved the Caliphate from Damascus to Baghdad in 862, where it achieved great splendour, particularly under Harun ar-Rashid and al-Mamun. After the family's downfall in 1258, one member was invited by the Mameluke sultan to Cairo, where the dynasty was recognized until the 16th century.

Abd al-Malik (646–705), fifth Umayyad Caliph (685–705). He united Islam by defeating the rival Caliph, Abdullah ibn-al-Zubayr, and also fought against the Byzantines. He reformed the government and made Arabic the official language.

Abdul-Hamid II (1842–1918), Sultan of Turkey (1876–1909). He suspended the constitution and formed an alliance with Germany after the Treaty of San Stephano (1878) when Russia threatened the continuation of the Ottoman Empire. He was deposed in 1909 after a revolt of the Young Turks.

Abélard, Pierre (1079–1142), French philosopher and monk. In his famous work *Sic et Non (Yes and No)* he attempted to reconcile differences between the Fathers of the Church by the use of the Aristotelian method of dialectic. His views were condemned by the Council of Sens (1140). He is perhaps best known for his tragic love for Héloise, which inspired his work *A History of Misfortunes.*

Abolitionists, people who sought to end slavery. William Wilberforce headed the movement that led to the abolition of Britain's role in the slave trade in 1807. Slavery was abolished throughout the British Empire by 1833. In the USA, Abolitionists were particularly active between 1820 and 1860, when they worked against the Fugitive Slave Law and helped slaves escape (through the "Underground Railroad", a series of hiding places).

Abu Bakr (573–634), first Muslim Caliph, successor to Mohammed. He accompanied Mohammed on the Hegira,

---

4000–3600 BC

A **Sumerians** settled the site of
A **Babylon** and developed a pictographic script, communicating ideas by the use of pictures. Simplification of this script's characters later led to the use of symbols to represent sounds rather than ideas. Their culture also produced sledges for land transport.
A **Egypt** saw the growth of a New Stone Age culture of stone tools, flint sickles and reed and wattle buildings.
In **Mesopotamia**, the wheel was invented during the period of the establishment of city states.
In **Britain**, hunting and gathering were gradually replaced by farming from 3700 onwards.
Religion took the form of burial cults and fertility cults based on the seasons.

and his daughter married the Prophet. After Mohammed's death, he became Caliph. He subdued the hostile Arabian tribes, made conquests in Iraq, Iran (Persia) and Syria, and united the Arabian peninsula. He also began the extension of Islam as a major world religion.

Achaemenids, *See* **Cyrus the Great, Darius the Great** *and* **Persian Empire.**

Actium, Battle of, *See* **Augustus, Cleopatra** *and* **Mark Antony.**

Adams, Samuel (1722–1803), American revolutionary patriot and signatory of the Declaration of American Independence. As a member and clerk of the Massachusetts legislature (1765–74) he was the chief radical spokesman for revolution. He helped form several radical organizations and led the Stamp Act (1765) protest and helped to plan the Boston Tea Party of 1773. He was a delegate to the Continental Congress until 1781.

Addison, Joseph (1672–1719), English poet, essayist and politician. His outstanding essays were published in the periodicals the *Tatler* (1709–11) and the *Spectator* (1711–12 and 1714) and cover the fields of literature, philosophy, politics and morals. He worked closely in collaboration with his schoolfriend Richard Steele. His poetry includes the verse tragedy *Cato* (1713). A Member of Parliament after 1708, he was appointed secretary of state in 1717 by the Whig government.

Adenauer, Konrad (1876–1967), politician, Chancellor of West Germany (1949–63). He was Lord High Mayor of Cologne from 1917 to 1933 and was later twice imprisoned by the Nazis. He helped to create the Christian Democratic Union, the dominant post-war party of West Germany, and was its leader (1946–66). In 1949 he was elected the first chancellor of the Federal Republic of Germany. As Chancellor he promoted German reconstruction, led Germany to membership of NATO (1955), and campaigned for European unity and the establishment of the Common Market (EEC).

3600–3200 BC

A **Sumerians**, their culture centred on the early city state of Uruk, built a network of canals for irrigation. In Susa, they produced fine pottery, facilitated by the introduction of kilns (c. 3400). They also prfected the shadow clock (c. 3500).

A **In Egypt**, heiroglyphic script representing sounds and ideas developed (c. 3400), possibly through contact with the Sumerians. Egyptians also produced ploughs, made of branches, and cylindrical jars hewn out of solid blocks.

In Britain, animals were domesticated and crops cultivated. Megalithic tombs and standing stones were also erected.

Religion in Egypt centred on Re the sun god. The Mesopotamian 'council' of gods reflected their politics.

Aeschylus (*c.* 525–456 BC), Greek dramatist. The earliest of the great Greek playwrights, he is said to have been responsible for the development of tragedy as a dramatic form by his addition of a second actor to the older tradition of one actor and a chorus. He was also the first to introduce scenery. His work is best remembered for its lofty and grandiloquent verse. Among his surviving works are *The Suppliants*, *The Persians*, *The Seven against Thebes* and *Prometheus Bound*, but his best-known work was the trilogy *Oresteia*, comprising *Agamemnon*, *The Choephoroe* and *The Eumenides*. These plays, on the subject of the house of Atreus, were first performed in 458 BC.

Aesop (*c.* 620–560 BC), semi-legendary Greek fabulist. A former slave, he was the reputed creator of numerous short tales about animals, all illustrating human virtues and failings (although they were almost certainly written by several people). Aesop supposedly died at Delphi, where he angered citizens and was thrown off a cliff. Most of the fables are simple tales in which animals symbolize human characteristics to convey a moral lesson, eg *The Hare and the Tortoise* teaches "slow and steady wins the race", and *The Fox and the Crow* cautions against trusting flatterers. The fables attributed to Aesop were preserved principally through Babrius, Phaedrus and Maximus Planudes.

Agincourt, *See* **Hundred Years War.**

Ahmad Shah Durrani (*c.* 1722–73), Emir of Afghanistan (1747–73) and founder of the Durrani dynasty. He united the Afghan tribes and is sometimes known as the founder of modern Afghanistan. He invaded India, taking Delhi twice, in 1757 and 1760. But he was unable to hold on to the territory gained and in the 1760s he lost the Punjab to the Sikhs.

Albigensians, followers of the Catharist heresy in Languedoc, southern France, in the 12th and 13th centuries. They believed in a Manichaean division between the forces of good and evil, and practised extreme asceticism. Innocent III called for a crusade against them

---

3200–2800 BC

A **Sumerians**, their cities ruled by hereditary kings from 2900, had by 3200 evolved cuneiform script, consisting of strokes made by a stylus on a clay tablet. They also practised metal moulding, producing copper and bronze axes.

A **Egypt**, united under its conqueror Menes (*c.* 3100), was producing boats made of reeds by 3000; canal-building and other public works led to the growth of bureaucracy and of a national government. **Mesopotamia** had made bronze alloys by 2800. **Religion** there, concerning itself with four main gods, was centralized and hierarchical, reflecting social structure. In Egypt, the Memphite theology was established.

Alexander

(started in 1209) which was led by Simon de Montfort, who mercilessly persecuted the heresy. The French crown then conquered Languedoc in 1229.

Alexander, name of three Russian tsars. Alexander I (1777–1825) came to the throne in 1801, and with his chief minister Michael Speranski introduced administrative and educational reforms. He repelled Napoleon's invasion of Russia in 1812 and led his troops across Europe and into Paris in 1814. After the war, influenced by Alexis Ararchev, he introduced many reactionary measures. His mystical interests led him to help form the Holy Alliance. He was named constitutional monarch of Poland in 1815 and annexed Finland, Georgia and Bessarabia. Alexander II (1818–81), who became Tsar in 1855, was best known for his emancipation of the serfs in 1861. Although he ended the Crimean War in 1856, his Pan-Slavist affiliations led him to declare war on Turkey in 1877 and the Russian victory in 1878 resulted in the independence of Bulgaria from Turkey. He expanded his empire to the east despite selling Alaska to the USA in 1867. He was assassinated by revolutionaries in 1881.

Alexander the Great, Alexander III of Macedonia (356–323 BC), the greatest general in ancient history. Tutored by Aristotle, he became king at the age of 20, destroying rivals and consolidating power in Greece. In 334 BC he began the Persian expedition, conquering western Asia Minor and storming the island of Tyre in 332 BC, his greatest military achievement. He subdued Egypt and occupied Babylon, marching north in 330 BC to Media and then conquering central Asia in 328 BC. In 327 BC he invaded India and set about consolidating his empire. While planning a voyage around Arabia he caught a fever and died at the age of 33.

Alexander Nevski (c. 1220–63), Russian ruler, national hero, Grand Duke of Novgorod from 1236, and from 1252 Grand Duke of Vladimir (the political centre of Russia at that time). He submitted to Mongol rule following their

---

2800–2400 BC

A **Sumerian** records of kings begin with Mebaragesi of Kish (c. 2700) but include the legendary hero Gilgamesh of Uruk (c. 2750), who inspired mankind's first epic poem.
Akkadians in Sumeria devised a simplified 550-symbol script.

A **Egyptian** agricultural skill fed a growing population, and social stability led to cultural growth; the

pyramids, the Great Sphinx of Khafre, the first 365-day calendar and wooden boats.
Chinese Neolithic culture flourished (c. 2500).
The Indian subcontinent had the Indus script (c. 2500).

A **Minoan civilization** developed in Crete, a sea-going culture making stone artefacts.
In Britain, chieftains probably emerged in Wessex at this time.

invasion of Russia and the Great Khan appointed him Grand Duke of Kiev. He defeated the Swedes on the Neva in 1240 (hence the name 'Nevski') and the Teutonic Knights in 1242. He was canonized in 1547.

Alfred (849-99), King of Wessex (871–99), called Alfred the Great. Warrior and scholar, he saved Wessex from the Danes and laid the foundations of a united English kingdom. Youngest of four successively reigning sons of King Ethelwulf, he became king at a time when the Danes threatened to overrun the kingdom. After the Danish invasion of Wessex in 878, he escaped to Athelney in Somerset, returning later to defeat the Danes at Edington and recover the kingdom. The legend in which he is reprimanded by a peasant woman for letting her cakes burn probably derives from this period. To strengthen Wessex against future attack he built a fleet of ships, constructed forts and reorganized the army. He instituted political reform by publishing a code of laws, translated several Latin works into English and founded several schools.

Ali (c. 600–61), 4th Muslim Caliph (656–61), son of Abu Talib, the Prophet Mohammed's cousin. Ali married Mohammed's daughter Fatima and was expected to become Caliph on the Prophet's death but had to wait 24 years before succeeding Othman. Ali crushed a revolt in Iraq but was unable to suppress Muawiya, Mohammed's former secretary who governed Syria. When Ali was murdered by fanatics his son Husan was persuaded to forgo his claim to the throne by Muawiya. The division in Islam between the Sunni and Shi'ite sects dates from this time. Ali and his wife are venerated by the Shi'ites, who believe Ali to have been the rightful heir of Mohammed.

Allende Gossens, Salvador (1908–73), President of Chile (1970–73). He died in a military coup in Sept. 1973. Candidate of the Popular Unity coalition, he was the first democratically elected Marxist head of state in Latin America. A doctor and active member of the Chilean Socialist Party since its formation in 1933, he was a senator

---

2400–2000 BC

A **Sumerians**, conquered by Sargon the Great (c. 2350), later had some commercial prosperity restored by Gudea of Lagash. An artistic revival under Ur-Nammu produced the Temple of Ur, a fine example of a ziggurat, a Mesopotamian building later used both as a grain storehouse and as a primitive astronomical observatory.

A **Egyptian civilization** produced the first literature, in the form of prayers (c. 2300). In 2181, central government collapsed, to be reinstated by Mentuhotep of Thebes.

A **In Babylon** a library of clay tablets was established. **The Indus Valley civilization** emerged around Harappa, a brick-built city with efficient drainage and sewage systems. **Britain** produced Stonehenge.

from 1945 and unsuccessfully ran for the presidency in 1952, 1958 and 1964.

Almohads, *See* **Moors.**

Almoravids, *See* **Moors.**

American Civil War (1861–65), the war fought in the USA between the Unionist forces of the federal government and the forces of the southern secessionist states, the Confederate States of America. It began on 12 April 1861 at Fort Sumter, South Carolina, and ended with the surrender of the Confederate commander Robert E. Lee at Appomattox, Virginia, on 9 April 1865. The Confederacy collapsed and the Union was restored.

American Independence, War of (1775–83), the successful revolt by the British colonies in America against imperial rule from London. A number of issues produced the conflict – the restrictions on trade and manufacturing imposed by the Navigation Acts, imperial control of land settlement in the virgin West, and the British attempt to raise revenue in America by such means as the Sugar Act (1764), the Stamp Acts (1765), the Revenue Act (1767) and the Tea Act (1773) – leading to the Boston Tea Party. "No taxation without representation" became the colonial radicals' rallying cry. Each dispute narrowed to one question, whether the colonies ought to be self-governing. The British parliament's rigid adherence to at least the principle of the supremacy of parliament, embodied in the Declaratory Act (1766), made war inescapable. Shots were fired first at Lexington and Concord, Massachusetts, in April 1775. In May the second Continental Congress met at Philadelphia, established an army under George Washington and assumed the role of a revolutionary government. On 4 July 1776 the Declaration of Independence was proclaimed. The first decisive colonial victory, at Saratoga in 1777, brought France into the war against Britain. Spain also entered the lists on the colonial side in 1779. When Gen. Cornwallis surrendered to the Americans at Yorktown in 1781 the war was effectively ended. It was formally ended by the Peace of

---

2000–1840 BC

A **Sumerians** (*c.* 1950) were overrun by Amorites, sparking off a long period of Mesopotamian unrest, later becoming a conflict between Isin and Larsa, and resulting in the area's breakdown into independent city states. Their language was also superseded by the Amorites' Semitic language.

A **Egyptian** civilization flourished with the suppression of

the nobility of Amenemhet I who claimed divine descent. The economy and the arts revived and devices such as the shaduf aided agriculture. Under Senusret III (1887–1849) royal authority was consolidated. **In Britain,** Wessex flourished by controlling trade routes. **Canaanite religion,** centred on El (possibly a forerunner of Yahweh), flourished in Palestine.

Paris (1783) which granted independence to America.

Ampère, André-Marie (1775–1836), French physicist and mathematician. He was professor of chemistry and physics at Bourg and later of mathematics at the École Polytechnique in Paris. He founded electrodynamics (now called electromagnetism) and performed numerous experiments to investigate the magnetic effects of electric currents. He was the first to devise techniques for measuring electricity, and constructed an early type of galvanometer. Ampère's law – proposed by him – is a mathematical description of the magnetic force between two electric currents. His name is also commemorated in the fundamental unit of current, the ampere (A), used in the SI system of units. The ampere is defined as the current in a pair of straight and parallel conductors of equal length one metre apart that produces a force of 2×10^{-7} newton per metre of their length. This force may be measured on a current balance, which becomes the standard against which current meters such as ammeters and galvanometers are calibrated.

Anne (1665–1714), Queen of Great Britain and Ireland (r. 1702–14). The second daughter of James II, she was the last reigning Stuart, and after the Act of Union of 1707 the first monarch of the United Kingdom of England and Scotland. She was dependent on her favourites, Sarah Churchill, Duchess of Marlborough, and Abigail Masham, but presided over an age of military success and cultural distinction. Despite 18 pregnancies, no child survived her.

Anschluss, the unification of Austria and Germany. Prohibited by treaty at the end of WWI, expressly to limit the strength of Germany, the Anschluss was nevertheless favoured by Germans and Austrians of all political persuasions. Unification finally took place through a show of force under Hitler (1938). The union was dissolved by the Allies in 1945, and Austria, after ten years' Allied occupation, again became an independent state.

Apollo programme, US project to land men on the Moon.

1840–1680 BC

A **The Babylonian Empire** under Hammurabi the Great was ruled with a complex law code based on principles absorbed from Sumerian culture. Art flourished; the ritual poem *The Epic of Creation* reached a classic form as part of New Year ceremonies; old palaces and buildings were strengthened and new cities built under Zimrilin.

A **Egypt's** Middle Kingdom ended c. 1786, weakened by the Hyksos, a Syrian Semitic people who adopted Egyptian culture and established a dynasty of pharaohs by 1700.
The Indus civilization was destroyed by Aryans (c. 1760).

A **Minoan civilization** produced grand palaces with efficient sanitation.

A **Hittites** powerful in Anatolia.

Aquinas, Saint Thomas

Initiated in May 1961 by President John Kennedy, it achieved its objective on 21 July, 1969, when Neil Armstrong set foot on the lunar surface. The programme terminated with the successful Apollo-Soyuz linkup in space during July 1975, having placed more than 30 astronauts in space and 12 on the moon.

Aquinas, Saint Thomas (1225–74), Roman Catholic theologian and philosopher. He played a leading part in the 13th-century movement of Scholasticism. Aquinas joined the Dominican Order and followed the Aristotelian Albertus Magnus to Paris in 1245. Thereafter Thomas refused ecclesiastical positions in order to preach and work on his most important treatise, *Summa Universae Theologica* (1266–73). Reconciling Aristotelianism with Christian theology, he argued that revelation could not conflict with reason, and while separate, both rested on the one absolute Truth – the existence of God. He provided five proofs of God's existence. He was canonized in 1323.

Arab-Israeli Wars (1948–49, 1956, 1967, 1973–74), conflicts between Israel and the Arab states. After being established in 1945 Israel made substantial gains from the Palestinians; Israeli independence (14 May 1948) saw troops from Egypt, Iraq, Lebanon, Syria and Transjordan (modern Jordan) invade the country. Initial Arab gains were halted and armistices arranged at Rhodes (Jan.–July 1949). UN security forces upheld the truce until Oct. 1956 when Israeli forces under Dayan attacked the Sinai Peninsula, supported a few days later by France and Britain, alarmed at the nationalization of the Suez Canal. International opinion forced a ceasefire in Nov. when Israel surrendered gains after being guaranteed access to the Gulf of Aqaba. In 1967 guerrilla raids led to an Israeli mobilization. In the ensuing Six Days War, Israel captured Sinai, the Golan Heights on the Syrian border and the Old City of Jerusalem. In 1973, after intermittent hostilities, the Arabs again began to prepare for war; Egyptian and Syrian forces invaded on 6 Oct. 1973, on Yom Kippur, a Jewish

---

1680–1520 BC

AHittites, having overthrown **A**Babylon (*c.* 1550) under Mursilis I, had as another subject people the Chalybes, who made cementation steel by hammering red-hot iron together with charcoal.

AEgyptian civilization flourished again with the expulsion of the Hyksos (*c.* 1570). Love songs developed into a sophisticated literary form, and art underwent a classical flowering during the New Kingdom (*c.* 1570–1085). Metalwork, involving copper, iron, gold etc. also reached a new standard.

AMinoans established a maritime empire under King Minos. Their culture approached its golden age, producing fine art and influencing ship design.

In China, the Shang dynasty developed urbanization.

holiday. Israel pushed back their advance after severe losses. Fighting continued until 1974. Egypt and Israel signed a peace treaty in 1979. This was not countenanced by the rest of the Arab world.

Archimedes (287–212 BC), Greek mathematician and engineer. He developed a method for expressing large numbers and made outstanding discoveries about the determination of areas and volumes, which led to a new accurate method of measuring π (pi). In his work *On Floating Bodies* he enunciated "The Principle of Archimedes", which states that a body in a fluid is buoyed up by a force equal to the weight of the fluid it displaces. An Archimedian screw is a machine used for raising water, thought to have been invented by Archimedes. It consists of a cylindrical pipe enclosing a revolving helix, with its lower end in the water.

Aristotle (384–322 BC), Greek philosopher, Plato's disciple for 20 years. His work on logic founded the science and has until recently remained unchallenged. In direct opposition to Plato's idealism, Aristotle's philosophical work is based on the principle that all knowledge and theorizing must proceed directly from observation of the particular. Among his works are the *Organon*, in which he defines the syllogism and logic, *Politics*, on the conduct of the state and *Nicomachean ethics*, in which he describes the virtuous life. His work was the basis of medieval Scholasticism.

Armstrong, Neil Alden *See* **Apollo Programme.**

Ashoka (*c*. 274–*c*. 236 BC), Emperor of India, the first to unite most of the Indian subcontinent under a single authority. After the violent conquest of Kalinga in *c*. 261 he turned to Buddhism, which he promulgated throughout his realm in edicts which are preserved in rocks and pillars.

Ashurbanipal (Assurbanipal), last great King of Assyria (668–*c*. 627 BC). During his reign Assyria reached its highest level in art, architecture, literature and science.

Asquith, Herbert Henry (1852–1918), First Earl of Oxford and Asquith, British Liberal Prime Minister (1908–16); MP

1520–1360 BC

A **Hittites**, still growing as a military power (1600–1200), produced much literature, a law code, decrees and treaties.

A **Egyptian civilization** under Thutmose I began building the tombs of the kings at Thebes; Molten glass technology produced bottles in *c*. 1500. Amenhotep III (1417–1379) extended the empire. Monotheistic religious reforms of Akhenaton brought internal dissension. Water clocks appeared; also a system of measurement using the cubit.

A **Minoan civilization** reached its peak, influencing the growing Mycenaean civilization on mainland Greece, until destroyed by an earthquake in Thera (*c*. 1450). **Mitanni** conquered Assyria (*c*. 1440).

---

for East Fife (1886–1918). His second cabinet appointment was as Chancellor of the Exchequer (1906–08), when he made the first provision for old-age pensions. His government, faced with House of Lords opposition to reforms such as Lloyd George's welfare budget of 1909, saw the passing of the Parliament Act (1911), which ended the Lords' power of veto. In 1916 he was replaced as Prime Minister by Lloyd George; he resigned as head of the Liberal party in 1926.

Assad, Hafez al- (1928–), President of Syria. He attended the Syrian Military Academy and rose through the ranks to become a general. From 1965 to 1970 he was Minister of Defence and Commander-in-Chief of the air force, positions he used to gain power and influence. In 1970 he seized power through a coup. His policies have been militantly anti-Zionist.

Atatürk, Kemal (1881–1938), *b.* Mustafa Kemal, founder of modern Turkey. As a youth he joined the Young Turks, a liberal movement that sought to establish a government independent of Ottoman rule. He fought against the Italians in Tripolitania in 1911 and served with distinction in WWI. In 1919 he organized a Turkish Nationalist party in E Anatolia and formed an army. He also announced the aims of an independent Turkish state and in 1921–22 he expelled the Greeks from Anatolia. He abolished the sultanate in 1922 and proclaimed the republic in 1923. Elected President in 1923 and re-elected in 1927, 1931 and 1935, he instituted sweeping reforms aimed at Westernizing Turkey.

Attila (*c.* 406–53), King of the Huns (434–53), co-ruler with his elder brother Bleda until he murdered him in 445. Theodosius II, eastern Roman emperor, was compelled to pay him tribute. Attila invaded Gaul in 451, although his motives for this action are unclear. His army suffered heavy losses, but he was still able to invade Italy the next year. But with his army suffering from disease and lack of provisions, he recrossed the Alps and died before he could again invade Italy.

1360–1200 BC

A **Hittites** built an empire in the Near East, conquering North Syria and Aleppo, but after this collapsed (c. 1200) their ironsmiths' skills slowly spread throughout East Europe.

A **Egyptian** King Ramesses I re-established a Near Eastern Empire (c. 1319). Currency appeared and chariots improved.

A **Mycenaean** civilization, reaching its height (c. 1320), seems to have received the origins of the Greek alphabet, maybe from the Phoenician Cadmus. The Trojan War (c. 1200), however, reflected growing stress. **Assyrians**, a military power under Ashur-uballit I, took Babylon from the Cassites. **Religion** under Moses became monotheistic for the Israelites, who fled Egypt, establishing worship of Yahweh.

Attlee, Clement Richard, 1st Earl (1883–1967), British Labour politician, Prime Minister 1945–51. He began as a social worker in London's East End in 1907 and joined the Fabian Society the same year. He was elected MP for Limehouse in 1922, and served in the first Labour government of 1924. He was Postmaster-General in Macdonald's government of 1929, but resigned in 1931 over the formation of the National Government. Elected Labour leader in 1935, he served as deputy prime minister in Churchill's wartime cabinet (1940–45). As Prime Minister he was responsible for the establishment of the National Health Service, an extension of national insurance, and the nationalization of the Bank of England, the railways, the coal, iron, steel, gas and electricity industries. Attlee was also involved in the granting of Indian independence. His government's majority was substantially reduced in the election of 1950 and at the next election (in Oct. 1951) Labour was narrowly defeated. Attlee continued to be Labour leader until he retired in 1955.

Augustine of Hippo (354–430), Christian theologian and philosopher. Augustine's *Confessions* provide an intimate psychological self-portrait of a spirit in search of ultimate purpose. This he believed he found in his conversion to Christianity in 386. As Bishop of Hippo, North Africa (396–430), he defended Christian orthodoxy against Manichaeanism, Donatism and Pelagianism. In his *Enchiridion* (421) he tended to emphasize the corruption of human will and the freedom of the divine gift of grace. *The City of God* (426), perhaps his most enduring work, is a model of Christian apologetic literature. Of the Four Fathers of the Latin Church, who also included Ambrose, Jerome and Gregory I, Augustine is considered the greatest.

Augustus, Gaius Julius Caesar Octavianus (Octavian) (63 BC–AD 14), Emperor of Rome after 27 BC. He was the adopted son of Julius Caesar, and returned to Rome to avenge Caesar's assassination in 44 BC. He was elected consul and formed the Second Triumvirate with Mark

1200–1100 BC

Mesopotamian stability was restored by Nebuchadrezzar I (1124–1103), ending in the final coalescing of the *Gilgamesh* epic.

A Egypt under Ramesses III repelled the invasion of the Sea Peoples, who had previously destroyed the Hittites. Economic and political stagnation set in, however, with Re's priests' rise to power.

A Greece was invaded by the Dorians (*c.* 1200), who brought Aryan gods (Zeus, etc.) to re-

A place Mycenaean nature gods. Food technology, including drying, smoking and salting fish, was instituted.

A Phoenician sea-trade replaced

A Minoan by 1200.

Olmec art forms included large stone monuments, found in Central Mexico; San Lorenzo (*c.* 1150) was the earliest site.

Antony and Lepidus. With Antony he defeated Brutus and Cassius, who had murdered Caesar, at the battle of Philippi in 42 BC. With the assistance of Agrippa he beat Pompeius in 36 BC and after Agrippa's victory over Antony at the battle of Actium in 31 BC, Octavian's power at Rome was assured. The Senate voted him the title of "Augustus" in 27 BC, but he himself preferred to be called "First Citizen". As emperor, he sought to stabilize the power of Rome and to foster colonization in the empire. He rebuilt much of Rome, particularly the Forum, took general censuses of his subjects and tried to make taxation more equitable. He set up fire and police services, and was an important patron of the arts and of learning. His only defeat occurred when his legions under the command of Varus were massacred by the German troops of Arminius in AD 9. He was succeeded by his stepson Tiberius.

Avon, Lord (1897–1977), previously Robert Anthony Eden, British politician. He served in WWI as a captain in the King's Royal Rifle Corps, winning the Military Cross, and took a first-class degree in Oriental languages at Oxford (1922). He entered the House of Commons in 1923 and in 1935 became the youngest man ever to be made Foreign Secretary. He resigned in February 1938 in protest against the appeasement policy of Neville Chamberlain. He served again as Foreign Secretary in 1940–45 and 1951–55. He was Prime Minister 1955–57, when ill health and the dissatisfaction with his handling of the Suez crisis forced him to resign.

Aztecs, Indian civilization that rose to a position of dominance in the central valley of Mexico in about AD 1450. A warlike group, the Aztecs (also called Tenochca) settled on islands in Lake Texcoco in about 1325 and there founded their capital Tenochtitlan (now Mexico City). They established an empire that included most of modern Mexico and extended southwards as far as Guatemala. The state was theocratic, with a number of deities whose worship included human sacrifice. The Aztecs built temples,

---

1100–1000 BC

Assyrians, having conquered Mesopotamia under Tiglath-Pileser I, mass-produced iron tools until defeated by the Aramaeans after 1077.

A Greece, containing monarchical city states like Athens, Thebes and Sparta, developed an alphabet after 1050, modi-

A fied from Phoenician script.

Israelites, settling down and consolidating under their mono-

theistic religion, were conquered by the Philistines. Under their first king, Saul, they continued fighting non-Semitic enemies.

Chinese philosophy under the

A Chou dynasty (c. 1122–221) dealt with man's increasing control over nature, clarifying thought. Artistic traditions of the Shang dynasty were continued.

---

pyramids and palaces and adorned them with stone images and symbolic carvings. At the time of the Spanish conquest, Aztec society was based on the exploitation of labour. As a result, Hernán Cortés was able to use disaffected Indians to help him defeat the Aztecs in 1521.

Babylonia, ancient region and empire of Mesopotamia, based on the city of Babylon. The Babylonian empire was first established in the early 18th century BC by Hammurabi the Great, but it soon declined under the impact of Hittite and Kassite invaders in about 1595 BC. After a long period of weakness and confusion, the empire eventually fell to the Assyrians in the 8th century. Babylon's greatness was restored as part of the Assyrian empire, and in about 625 BC its independence was won by Nabopolassar, who captured the Assyrian capital Nineveh, with the help of the Medes and Persians. This New Babylonian, or Chaldaean, Empire defeated Egypt and took the Jews to captivity in Babylon in 586 BC; but in 538 BC it fell to the Persians, under whom it remained until the rise of Alexander the Great.

Bach, German family of composers, the most outstanding of whom were Johann Sebastian (1685–1750) and four of his sons, Wilhelm Friedemann (1710–84), Carl Philipp Emanuel (1714–88), Johann Christoph Friedrich (1732–95) and Johann Christian (1735–82).

In J. S. Bach, the greatest of the family, the style of Baroque counterpoint reached its highest expression. He was renowned as a virtuoso on organ and harpsichord, and composed prolifically for these instruments and for orchestra and choir. Bach's musical career began with a short time as court musician at Weimar, after which he was organist at Arnstadt (1703–07) and at Mühlhausen (1707–08). He served again at Weimar, as court organist and chamber musician (1708–17), and was the Prince of Anhalt-Köthen's musical director (1717–23). From 1723 until his death Bach was *Kapellmeister* at the church of St Thomas, Leipzig. Much of his work was therefore sacred music – more than 200 Cantatas, more

---

Jews, under David (1000–961), defeated the Philistines. Solomon (961–922) built the temple at Jerusalem and wrote the famous *Song of Songs*. On his death, the kingdom divided into the Israelites' kingdom in the north and Judah in the south.

Egypt reconquered Palestine. **Assyrian** military technology involved efficient war chariots, siege weapons and battering rams, and under Assurdan II their authority was briefly restored. In 912, however, Assyria was at its weakest.

Japanese religion, Shinto, was based on love of nature, whose powers were seen as beneficent. Divination was practised. **Greek** oral poetry dealt with the Trojan War.

than 300 four-part chorales, the great *Passions* and the monumental *Mass in B Minor*. His secular works include the Brandenburg Concertos, the four orchestral suites and several concertos for solo instrument and orchestra. His keyboard works include 18 preludes and fugues for organ and the harpsichord compositions, the *Well-Tempered Clavier*, the French and English suites and the two-part and three-part inventions.

Bacon, Francis (1561–1626), British philosopher, statesman and early advocate of the scientific method. He is also a literary figure of the first rank, especially in his essays. Successively Attorney-General, Lord Keeper and Lord Chancellor, he was forced to resign his offices in 1621 on charges of venality. None of this interrupted his efforts to break the hold of Aristotelian Logic and establish an inductive empiricism. He entertained the idea of cataloguing all useful knowledge in his *Advancement of Learning* (1605) and *Novum Organum* (1620). *The New Atlantis* (1627) discusses his philosophy as practised in an imaginary nation.

Baird, John Logie (1888–1946), Scottish engineer, the first man to transmit moving pictures. He demonstrated the first true television to members of the Royal Institution, London, in 1926; he transmitted television to a ship at sea in 1928 and was granted experimental broadcasting facilities by the BBC, London, in 1929. His mechanical television system was used alternately with an electronic system for the world's first public television service set up by the BBC in 1936.

Bakunin, Mikhail Alexandrovich (1814–76), Russian political philosopher. He became a believer in violent revolution while in Paris in 1848, and was active in the First Communist International until expelled by Marx in 1872. His approach, known as revolutionary anarchy, repudiates all forms of governmental authority as fundamentally at variance with human freedom and dignity. In *God and the State* (1882) Bakunin recognized natural law alone as consistent with liberty.

900–800 BC

Israelites with the Aramaeans, defeated the Assyrians (854). Their king Ahab, and his wife, Jezebel, were overthrown soon after by followers of Yahweh under Elisha. They were later (c. 820) subdued by Damascus. Egypt, having fought Assyria (900–830), had developed an advanced method of tanning and hardening leather by c. 800. Phoenicians established Byblos (c. 900), the centre of the cult of Baal, and Carthage (c. 814). A Greece saw a shift from monarchies to oligarchies almost everywhere except Sparta. The Bacchus cult also arrived from Thrace and Phrygia. A Medes, a horse-rearing people, appear in Babylonian records. Hindu wisdom appeared in the *Upanishads* as a teacher-pupil dialogue.

Baldwin, Stanley, 1st Earl Baldwin of Bewdley (1867-1947), British Conservative statesman. He ran the family iron and steel business before entering Parliament in 1908. He became Chancellor of the Exchequer(1922-23), and although his handling of the US debt was criticized, he succeeded Bonar Law as Prime Minister (1923-24). He was Prime Minister again in 1924-29. Prime Minister for a third time (1935-37) as leader to the National Government, he had to deal with the abdication crisis (1936).

Balfour, Arthur James Balfour, 1st Earl of (1848-1930), British Conservative statesman b. Scotland. His time as Prime Minister (1902–05) was marked by party friction. He was an energetic leader of the opposition (1906–11) and First Lord of the Admiralty (1915–16). In 1917, as Foreign Minister, he issued the Balfour Declaration in favour of founding a Jewish nation in Palestine. He played a major role in various post-war European agreements.

Banda, Hastings Kamuzu (c. 1902–   ), President of Malawi (1966–   ). He studied medicine in the USA and practised in England before returning to Africa in 1953. He became a nationalist political leader, guiding Nyasaland to independence as Malawi within the British Commonwealth (1964) and establishing an autocratic Presidency (1966). He has been criticized by other black African leaders for maintaining amicable relations with South Africa.

Bandaranaike, Sirimavo (Ratwatte Dias) (1916–   ), Prime Minister of Sri Lanka (formerly Ceylon). She became the world's first woman Prime Minister in 1960 after her husband, the former premier, was assassinated in 1959. Her Sri Lanka Freedom Party was defeated in 1965, but returned to power in 1970. In 1971 she put down an uprising led by the Marxist People's Liberation Front. In 1972 a republican constitution was adopted and the country's name was officially changed to Sri Lanka. Mrs Bandaranaike and her party were resoundingly defeated by J.R. Jayawardene's United National Party in the July 1977 general election.

800–700 BC

Assyrian military power, after a decline (c. 800), revived under Tiglath-Pileser III (745–727) and his successors, aided by the development of siege towers and A biremes. Babylon was conquered and art flourished.

Israelites, prosperous under Jeroboam (780–740), were castigated by their prophets for their syncretist tendencies, and were conquered by the Assyrians (721).

A **Greece** reacted to
A the stimulus from Phoenician trade, producing the *Iliad* and the *Odyssey*, much pottery and bronze work. Colonies were founded in south Italy (c. 750). **India** established the caste system. **Rome** was founded (753). **Kushite kingdom**, in Nubia, was founded, (c. 800), and A overran Egypt (725).

Barras, Paul François Jean Nicolas, Vicomte de
(1755–1829), French revolutionary leader. He joined the
Jacobins and was a member of the Convention. He was a
leader in the coup which brought down Robespierre in July
1794 (which, in the Revolutionary Calendar, was 9
Thermidor). By turning over his troops to the command of
Napoleon during a royalist uprising in Paris in 1795, he
helped advance Napoleon's career. He was a member of the
Directory (1795–99).

Bastille, 14th-century fort and prison in Paris. Political
prisoners were often incarcerated there and it became a
symbol of royal oppression in the 18th century. On 14 July
1789 a Parisian mob stormed it, captured the ammunition
store and released its prisoners (only seven, none of whom
was political). Its governor was killed, its troops
surrendered and the fort was pulled down. The incident
marked the beginning of the French revolution and its
anniversary (14 July) is celebrated as the major holiday in
France.

Batista y Zaldivar, Fulgencio (1901–73), Cuban political
leader. A sergeant in the army, he led a successful coup in
1933. From then until 1940 he ruled through figurehead
presidents. In 1940 he was elected president. He retired in
1944 and moved to Florida, but in 1952 a military coup
returned him to power. In 1959 he was overthrown by Fidel
Castro.

Bay of Pigs Invasion (1961), unsuccessful effort by Cuban
exiles to overthrow Fidel Castro by invading the s coast of
Cuba near the Bay of Pigs. About 1,500 Cubans, trained ,
equipped and transported by the USA, were involved. John
Kennedy, the US president, initially denied but then
accepted US involvement in the invasion attempt.

Becket, Thomas à (c. 1118-70), English clergyman and
statesman. He was appointed Chancellor of England
(1155), became a friend of Henry II and vigorously pursued
the interests of the Crown. In 1162 he became Afchbishop
of Canterbury. Resigning the Chancellorship that year he

700–620 BC

Assyria, after rebuilding under
Sennacherib II (704–681) and
his successor, declined sud-
denly. In Babylon, the Chaldean
Nabopolassar led a successful
revolt, Josiah did the same in
Judah, and Phoenicia won her
A independence. Ashurbanipal
(668–627) established a library
of 20,000 tablets at Nineveh.
A **Greece**'s city states were ruled
by tyrants (rich and powerful

merchant classes), and her art
flourished. Terpander (*fl.* 675)
founded classical Greek music,
Thales of Miletus' theories
greatly influenced Greek
thought, and silver coinage was
A established there. Sparta
dominated the Peloponnese.
A **Etruscan** cities flourished in
central Italy (*c.* 675).
A **Zoroaster** proclaimed a dualistic
cosmology in Iran (*c.* 600).

---

devoted all his energies to Church affairs. Conflict with Henry over clerical privileges and the independence of ecclesiastical courts followed and Becket fled from England and sought support from the Pope. Returning to Canterbury after six years' exile, he was murdered there by four of Henry's knights. He was acclaimed a martyr and canonized in 1173.

Bede, Saint (*c.*673-735), the Venerable Bede, monk and scholar from Northumbria who spent his entire life in the monasteries of Wearmouth at Sunderland and Jarrow. The most important of his many works on science, grammar, history and theology is the *Ecclesiastical History of the English Nation*, which remains an indispensable primary source for English history from 54 BC-AD 597.

Beethoven, Ludwig van (1770–1827), German composer who exerted a profound influence on the development of musical styles. Despite the onset of deafness, which finally became total, he wrote many masterpieces that are among the finest and most popular of their type. He provides a link between the formal classical style of Haydn and Mozart and the romanticism of Wagner, Brahms and Bruckner. Born in Bonn, Beethoven visited Vienna in 1787 and was taught briefly by Mozart; he made Vienna his home from 1792 and took lessons from Haydn. He was a proud, determined and independent man. Unlike his predecessors he was never directly employed by a European ruler, aristocrat or Church; he did get support from men of means, but he wrote to satisfy his own inclinations. As a result he liberated music from many of the conventions then current. His music is ultimately optimistic, although sometimes involving dark, gloomy struggle. With the onset of deafness from about 1800 Beethoven became difficult, unpredictable and suspicious, alternately cheerful and moody, tender and boisterous. He composed nine symphonies, five piano concertos, a violin concerto, one opera (*Fidelio*), more than 30 piano sonatas and a sizeable body of chamber music. He is best known for having made the symphony a dramatic

620–540 BC

Babylon, under Nabopolassar, took Nineveh (612) and under Nebuchadrezzar II built an empire in Syria-Palestine, producing the famous Hanging Gardens. A **Greece** saw Sparta introduce military education and found the Peloponnesian League (560). In Athens, tensions grew between merchants and the aristocracy. Anaximander produced A a map of the world, Aesop his famous *Fables*, and Attic black-figure pottery dominated Greek A vases. Pythagoras studied medicine, astronomy, musical scales and mathematics.
Persian Empire was founded by A Cyrus the Great (*d.* 529).
China saw the rise of Taoism, A stemming from Lao-tze's work.
India produced the *Bhagavad Gita*; Jainism also developed through Mahavira's work.

form; he also expanded the size of the orchestra and wrote compositions that were considered long. His output is often divided into three periods. Until 1800 he generally followed the convention of Haydn and Mozart; from about 1800–14 he wrote passionate works, now among his most popular, including the third and fifth symphonies, the violin concerto and *Appassionata* piano sonata; and from 1814 date his most sublime compositions, among them the last five string quartets, the ninth symphony and the *Missa Solemnis*.

Bell, Alexander Graham (1847–1922), inventor of the telephone. Born in Scotland, he first worked with his father, inventor of a system for educating the deaf. The family moved to Canada in 1870, and Bell taught speech at Boston University (1873–77). His work on the transmission of sound by electricity led to the first demonstration of the telephone in 1876. A year later he founded the Bell Telephone Company. His many other inventions included the photophone (an instrument for transmitting sound by light vibrations) and the wax cylinder for phonographs.

Ben Bella, Ahmed (1919–   ), Algerian statesman. After WWII, he joined the movement for Algerian independence from France. After helping to found the *Front de Libération Nationale* (1954), he was imprisoned (1956–62). Following independence in 1962, he became Algeria's first premier. He was overthrown in a coup in 1965.

Bentham, Jeremy (1748–1832), British philosopher, jurist and social reformer. He trained as a lawyer but never practised. Bentham developed the theory of Utilitarianism based on the premise that "the greatest happiness of the greatest number" should be the object of individual and government action. This philosophy was defined in his *Introduction to the Principles of Morals and Legislation* (1789). His followers were responsible for much of England's early reform legislation.

Bernini, Gianlorenzo (1598-1680), Italian architect and sculptor, one of the fathers of Roman Baroque. By the age of 22 he had startled Rome with his sculpture, eg such

---

540–460 BC

Persian Empire expanded when
A Cyrus took Babylon (538) and
A Egypt (525). Darius' invasion
A of Greece, however, was checked
at Marathon (490), and Xerxes'
at Salamis (480).
Greece saw the foundations of
democracy laid by Cleisthenes
in Athens (508) and the beginnings of classical tragedy
by Aeschylus and Sophocles.
Heraclitus, Zeno and Anaxagoras

were prominent in philosophy
and science. Athenian power
in eastern Greece was shown
by the Delian League (478), and
Greeks defeated Carthage (480)
A and the Etruscans (474) at sea.
China saw the social ethics
A of Confucius, and much art in
A the Chou dynasty.
Religion in India was revo-
lutionized by Siddhartha Gau-
tama's founding Buddhism.

---

psychological portrait studies as the *Vigevano* bust (1617-18) and the *Montoya* (c. 1621). He was also a skilful painter. His architecture was splendid in conception, lavish in use of marble and dramatic lighting, and often grand in scale, giving Rome its Baroque character.

Bismarck, Otto von (1815-98), German statesman. He was born into a wealthy Prussian family and in 1862 Wilhelm I named him Chancellor of Prussia. Victory in the Franco-Prussian War (1870-71) brought the southern German states into the Prussian-led confederation, and in 1871 Wilhelm I was proclaimed German Emperor and Bismarck the first Chancellor of the Empire. In 1882 he formed the Triple Alliance with Austro-Hungary and Italy. Bismarck encouraged industrialization and a paternalist programme of social welfare at home, and colonization overseas. He found it difficult to work with Wilhelm II, and in 1890 the "Iron Chancellor" was forced to resign.

Black Power, doctrine of radical Black movements in the USA, probably first used by Stokeley Carmichael in 1965. Its principal organizations have been SNCC, the Black Muslims, the Organization of Afro-American Unity and the Black Panther party. The Black Power movement rejects the policy of non-violent civil disobedience associated with Martin Luther King and advocates armed preparedness and Black nationalism.

Blücher, Gebhard Leberecht von, *See* **Waterloo.**

Boccaccio, Giovanni (1313–75), Italian poet. His early work, the *Filocolo* (c. 1340) is sometimes considered the first European novel, but he is best known for the *Decameron* (1348–53), a series of stories of contemporary mores, and for *La Fiammetta*, a romance. He knew and imitated Dante, and with his friend Petrarch he is considered to be one of the founders of the Italian Renaissance.

Boer War, *See* **South African War.**

Bolívar, Simón (1783–1830), Venezuelan soldier and statesman whose experiences in Napoleonic Europe

---

460–380 BC

Greece saw Athenian power and culture flourish under Pericles. The Peloponnesian War with Sparta ended with defeat for Athens at Aegospotami (405). Socrates and Democritus in philosophy, Euripides in drama and Herodotus and Thucydides in history were all prominent at this time. Hippocrates founded medicine, and Greek art reached its High Classical per-iod. Plato founded the Academy and Aristophanes wrote comic drama. The Late Classical period (400–323) brought new naturalism to art. Rome expanded into central Italy capturing Veii (396) from the Etruscans. China saw the development of cast iron (c. 400), and in music, of the chromatic scale. The *I Ching* was finally formed.

influenced his persistent attempts to free South America of Spanish rule. He achieved no real success, however, until he established an inland base in 1819 from where he succeeded in liberating New Granada (later Colombia) in 1821. The liberation of Venezuela (1821), Ecuador (1822), Peru (1824) and Upper Peru (1825) followed, the latter renaming itself Bolivia in his honour. Despite this complete removal of Spanish hegemony from the continent, his hopes of uniting South America into one continental alliance were dashed by the inevitable nationalistic rivalry between the new states.

Bolsheviks, Marxists led by Lenin who obtained and held power by the Russian revolution. Their name ("the majority") distinguished them from the Mensheviks ("the minority"), whom they narrowly defeated at the Second Congress of the All-Russian Soviet Democratic Workers' Party in London in 1903. The split, on tactics as much as doctrine, centred on the means of achieving revolution, the Bolsheviks believing it could be obtained only by professional revolutionaries leading the Proletariat, their more liberal Menshevik opponents led by Julius Martov holding a less doctrinaire, more democratic approach which included cooperation with other parties including those in the Duma. Numerically in a minority in 1917, the Bolsheviks were nevertheless able to overthrow the Provisional government of Kerensky through their support in the Soviets of Moscow and Petrograd led by Trotsky.

Boone, Daniel (1734–1820), US pioneer. In 1775 he blazed the famous Wilderness Road from Virginia to Kentucky and founded the settlement of Boonsborough. During the American War of Independence he was captured by Shawnee Indians but escaped and reached Boonsborough in time to prevent its capture.

Boston Tea Party (1773), protest by a group of American colonists, disguised as Indians and led by Sam Adams, against the British policy of taxing tea and, more generally, against "taxation without representation". Tea from ships

---

380–300 BC

Greece saw the alliance of Thebes with Athens to defeat Sparta (371). The Cynics flourished under Diogenes; Aristotle, re-
A jecting Plato's idealism, tried to systematize knowledge and even nature; Eudoxus developed a mathematical method which was a forerunner of calculus.
A Later (333) Alexander the Great, assured of authority in Greece, defeated Darius of Persia,

crossed the Indus (327) and established a large empire, which collapsed by 306. Zeno founded Stoicism, Epicurus championed pleasure, and Menander produced good examples of New Comedy.
Persian rule was re-established in Egypt by Artaxerxes III, (359–38).
Rome had effectively destroyed
A Etruscan power by 300.

---

was thrown into Boston harbour after Governor Thomas Hutchinson had refused to let the ships leave without paying tax.

Boumédienne, Houari (c. 1925–78), Algerian politician. In the Algerian war for independence from France he commanded guerrilla forces around Oran in 1955–60. He served as Vice-President from the achievement of independence in 1962 to 1965, when he overthrew President Ben Bella, his former ally, and became President and Prime Minister himself. He has maintained a strongly anti-Israel policy.

Boxer Rebellion (1900), violent Chinese uprising to oust all foreigners from China. Forces led by the secret society of Boxers (Righteous and Harmonious Fists) that attacked Europeans and Chinese Christians besieged Peking's foreign legations enclave for two months. An international expeditionary force put down the uprising.

Boyle, Robert (1627–91), Anglo-Irish scientist, often regarded as the father of modern chemistry. Working at Oxford (1656–68), he made an efficient vacuum pump and used it in 1662 to establish that the volume of a gas is inversely proportional to its pressure at a constant temperature; this relationship is known as Boyle's law. An advocate of experimental methods, he freed chemistry from Aristotelian theory and formulated the chemical definitions of an element and a reaction. He also researched into the calcination of metals, combustion, acids and bases, the nature of colours and the propagation of sound in air. He later worked in London (1668–91) and was a founding Fellow of the Royal Society.

Brahms, Johannes (1833–97), German composer. Encouraged by his friends Robert and Clara Schumann, he began to earn his living as a composer at the age of 30. He followed classical models of form and was a master of contrapuntal harmony. He composed in all major musical forms except opera. Among his works are the *German Requiem* (1868), the *Variations on a Theme by Paganini*

300–220 BC

A **Greece** saw the disintegration
A of Alexander's empire into the Hellenistic kingdoms of Macedonia and Thrace,
A the Seleucid dynasty in Syria and the Ptolemaic in Egypt.
A **Euclid** founded geometry in Alexandria (a centre of learning)
A in 300; **Archimedes** discovered the laws of fluid displacement and was a prolific inventor; and art entered its Hellenistic period.

Rome, controlling southern Italy, defeated Carthage in the
A first Punic War (264–241) and produced Latin literature.
India was almost united by Ashoka under Buddhism.
China produced the yin-yang school of philosophy under Tsou Yen, based on the principle of complementary but opposing forces in nature.

Braille, Louis

(1863), the *Violin Concerto in D* (1878) and two piano concertos (1858 and 1881). His best-known works include the orchestral *Hungarian Dances* (1873) and the *Lullaby* (1868). He wrote four symphonies between 1876 and 1885.

Braille, Louis (1809–52), French inventor of the Braille system of reading for the blind (he was himself blinded at the age of three). A scholar, and later a teacher, at the National Institute of Blind Youth in Paris, Braille developed a system of embossed dots to enable the blind to read by touch. This was first published in 1829, and a more complete form appeared in 1837. There are also Braille codes for music and mathematics.

Brandt, Willy (1913–), German Social Democrat politician. His real name was Karl Herbert Frahm. He fled to Norway and then Sweden during the Nazi era and adopted the name "Willy Brandt". He returned to Germany after WWII and was elected Mayor of West Berlin in 1957. In 1969 he became Chancellor of West Germany. He initiated a programme of co-operation with the Communist bloc nations. In 1971 he was awarded the Nobel Peace Prize. He resigned in 1974 after a close aide was exposed as an East German spy.

Brezhnev, Leonid Ilyich (1906–), Soviet political leader. In 1952 he became secretary to the central committee of the Soviet Communist Party. In 1957 he became a member of the presidium (later politburo) of the central committee. He helped to plan the downfall of Nikita Khrushchev in 1964 and soon emerged as one of the two chief rulers of the USSR, sharing power with Alexei Kosygin. Brezhnev was named First Secretary and Kosygin became Premier. By the late 1960s, Brezhnev was acknowledged as the sole ruler, although Kosygin remained as premier.

Britain, Battle of (July-Oct. 1940), series of air battles fought over Britain during WWII between the German Luftwaffe and the Royal Air Force (RAF). The Germans hoped to destroy Britain's industry and military installations and shatter morale by bombing, as a prelude to invasion.

220–140 BC

A **Roman Empire** was established in
A this period, despite Hannibal
invading Italy (218). Roman
nobility controlled wealth, and
a standing army was kept. Stress
A of the second Punic War
resulted in mystery religions
and Stoicism taking hold of
Roman thought; and Latin drama
was exemplified by the work of
Plautus and Terence. Rome an-
A nexed Greece (147) and destroyed

Carthage (146).
China, under Huang-Ti
completed the Great Wall and
A burnt Confucian texts to end
the Classical period. Cast iron
production was aided by piston
A bellows in the Han dynasty.
Greek architecture was in-
fluenced by town planning;
Alexandria produced an
improved map of the world.
Glassblowing was started.

Although outnumbered, the defending RAF fighter pilots inflicted such heavy losses that the strategy was abandoned.

Brown, John (1800–59), American anti-slavery leader who, with 21 cohorts, took possession of the US arsenal at Harper's Ferry, Virginia. He was captured, tried and hanged. The trial raised North–South tensions on the eve of the Civil War. He is the hero of the song *John Brown's Body*.

Bruce, Robert (1274–1329), Robert I of Scotland and securer of Scotland's independence from the English. He was crowned at Scone on 27 March 1306, and immediately began a campaign to wrest from Edward I those Scottish castles and towns in English hands. Bruce's victory at Bannockburn in 1314 marked the defeat of the English.

Brutus, Marcus Junius (*c.* 85-42 BC), Roman republican politician, one of the principal assassins of the dictator Julius Caesar. He sided first with Pompey against Caesar, but Caesar forgave him and made him governor of Cisalpine Gaul in 46 BC and city praetor in 44 BC. After Caesar's murder in 44 BC, he went to Greece where he raised an army. He was defeated at Philippi in 42 BC, by Mark Antony and Octavian (Augustus), and committed suicide.

Burke, Edmund (1729–97), British statesman and writer. He played a major part in the reduction of royal influence in the House of Commons. With Charles James Fox he sought better treatment for the Catholics and Americans. He instigated the impeachment of Warren Hastings in an attempt to reform India's government in 1788. Burke believed in liberty based on order, with change being gradual; his horror at the radicalism of the French revolution is shown in *Reflections on the Revolution in France* (1790).

Burnham, Forbes (1923–), Prime Minister of Guyana (1964–). Leader of the People's National Congress (1957–), Burnham was chief executive when British Guiana attained independence in 1966 and became a republic (1970). His party increased its majority in 1973.

Byzantine Empire, known also as the Eastern

140–60 BC

Rome, led by the Gracchus brothers, reformed land laws and defied the wishes of the Senate (133). Cicero (106–43) upheld the republic's constitutional basis to prevent any individual gaining power. Pompey and Julius Caesar both rose to power in this period. Latin poetry flourished with Lucretius and Catullus, Roman arches were used for tenement houses and theatres, and art generally projected realism, asceticism and authority. Their technology, however, could not yet produce a furnace which melted iron.

China, under Wu Ti established Confucianism as the basis of civil administration, beginning 2,000 years of stable imperialism. Fu poetry was perfected by 100; musical notation had also been devised.

Byzantine Empire

Roman Empire, or Medieval Greek Empire. The history of the Byzantine Empire spanned the long period from AD 330 when its capital city of Constantinople (Istanbul) was established by the Roman Emperor Constantine the Great (as part of the attempt to modify the structure of the Roman Empire to deal with barbarian invasions), to the year 1453, when the same city was overrun and captured by the Ottoman Turks.

Constantinople, a well-fortified city on the Bosporus, commanded one of the most important routes between the European and Asian continents. The city was the heart of the Byzantine empire, the outer boundaries of which were constantly changing, as the empire annexed foreign territories and was in turn invaded. It generally comprised large parts of Anatolia, or Asia Minor, and the Balkans, as well as (for varying lengths of time during periods of expansion) southern Italy and Ravenna, Greece, Syria, Egypt and portions of Spain and the N African coast. Although the Byzantines referred to themselves as "Romans", their society was made up of many other elements. The traditions of Imperial Rome shaped their governmental institutions; the language and customs of Classical Greece moulded their cultural life; and orthodox Christianity, within which a series of heresies occurred, determined their religion.

The Byzantine state was, in theory, a continuation of the Roman Empire. While the Roman Empire in the W had fallen into decline after the Germanic invasions, the E provinces remained a centralized state. The Emperor Justinian I (r. 527–65) reconquered much of the Mediterranean territory of the old Roman Empire and codified Byzantine law. Under the Heraclian emperors (610–717), the empire defeated its Persian enemies, but also faced the rise of Arab power, which continued to threaten its control of the Middle East. During the age of the Iconoclastic controversy (717–843), the Isaurian and Amorian rulers dealt with severe internal crises. The

---

60 BC–AD 20

Rome took Gaul (58–51 BC) and Britain (54 BC) through Julius
A Caesar, who defeated Pompey to become dictator (45 BC). Civil war followed his assassination
A (44 BC). Octavian (Augustus) took imperial authority (27 BC) and prevented unrest. Egypt was
A taken in 30 BC. Tiberius consolidated the imperial position, although dependent on the Praetorian Guard. Judea was

taken (AD 6). In literature, Titus Lucretius wrote *De Rerum Naturae*, Roman history was idealized in Virgil's *Aeneid*, Horace (65–8 BC) wrote his famous *Odes*, Caesar his history of the Gallic wars, and Ovid (43 BC–AD 17) developed erotic verse. The Julian calendar was introduced (45 BC).
Judea saw the birth of Jesus
A Christ (c. 4 BC).

Macedonian epoch (867–1025) is known as the Golden Age of the Byzantine Empire; it was a time of territorial consolidation and cultural flowering. The emperors of the Comnenian and Angelian dynasties (1081–1204) had to deal with the unpredictable and rapacious Crusaders, who besieged and stormed Constantinople in 1204. These crusaders ruled Byzantium during the dominion of the Latin empire of the east (1204–61). Michael VIII, restorer of the Greek Empire, founded the Palaeologan dynasty (1261–1453). The area of the empire shrank rapidly under the attacks of the Ottoman Turks, who finally took Constantinople itself in 1453.

Caesar, Gaius Julius (100–44 BC), Roman general and statesman. He married Cornelia, daughter of Cinna, an associate of Marius, and after the death of Sulla Caesar became military tribune and leader of the popular party against the Senate. As *pontifex maximus* he directed reforms in 63 BC that resulted in the Julian calendar. He formed the first Triumvirate in 60 BC with Pompey and Crassus, and instituted agrarian reforms, created a patrician-plebeian alliance and successfully conquered Gaul for Rome in 58–49 BC. In 54 BC Caesar led a successful military campaign in Britain. He refused Senate demands that he disband his army and engaged in civil war with Pompey, defeating him at Pharsalus in 48 BC. He pursued Pompey to Egypt where he met Cleopatra. He returned to Rome in 45 BC using the title of *dictator*, but refusing that of king. He was assassinated in the Senate on 15 March 44 BC by a conspiracy led by Cassius and Marcus Brutus, and he bequeathed his wealth and power on his grandnephew Octavian (later Augustus) who, with Mark Antony, avenged his murder.

Callaghan, Leonard James (1912–   ), British Labour politician. He entered Parliament as member for Cardiff South in 1945 and sat for Cardiff South-East from 1950. He was elected leader of the Labour party and became Prime Minister in April 1976. He has held all three of the

---

AD 20–100

A Roman Empire expanded under Tiberius and Claudius and imperial power was consolidated. Nero rebuilt Rome after a fire (64); a civil war ensued on his death until Vespasian took over. Scotland was taken on Boadicea's defeat (62). In art, Seneca the Younger (4 BC–AD 65) adapted Greek tragedies and architecture flourished, best exemplified by buildings like the Villa Albani. In technology, brass was manufactured, a mountain tunnel and aqueducts supplied Lead piping supplied Rome with water.

China officially accepted Buddhism. Technology there produced paper and mirrors.

Religion in Christian form spread throughout the Roman Empire after Jesus Christ's crucifixion (30).

Calvin, John (Jean)

major offices of state: Chancellor of the Exchequer (1964–67), Home Secretary (1967–70) and Foreign Secretary (1974–76). His government fell in 1979.

Calvin, John (Jean) (1509–64), French theologian of the Reformation. He first prepared for a career in the Catholic Church but then turned to the study of classics. Around 1533 he became a protestant and began work on his *Institutes of the Christian Religion*. In this work he presented the basics of what came to be known as Calvinism. To avoid persecution, he went in 1536 to stay in Geneva, where he advanced the Reformation.

Canute, or Cnut, name of two kings of Denmark and England. Canute I (994– 1035) began his conquest of England with his father Sweyn in 1013, and was accepted as sole ruler of the country in 1016. He became king of Denmark in 1018, and led several expeditions to Norway. He established a code of laws, and upheld the traditional Anglo-Saxon society and Church. He was succeeded by his son, Canute II.

Capone, Alphonse (1899–1947), Italian-born US gangster of the Prohibition era. He grew up in Brooklyn, New York City, and was bodyguard to the gang leader Johnny Torio from whom he inherited a vast crime empire. He was eventually convicted of income tax evasion (1931) and imprisoned.

Carlyle, Thomas (1795–1881), Scottish philosopher, critic and historian. His most successful work, *Sartor Resartus* (1836), combined philosophy and autobiography. His histories include *The French Revolution* (three vols 1837), and a study of Frederick II of Prussia (six vols 1858–65). He studied Goethe and the German Romantics. He was anti-democratic in his political thought and expressed his preference for strong heroes or leaders in a series of lectures *On Heroes, Hero Worship and the Heroic in History* (1841).

Carter, James Earl (1924–   ), US politician and 39th president. He graduated from the US Naval Academy and served in the navy until 1953. He then devoted himself to

---

AD 100–160

A Roman Empire expanded into Dacia. Hadrian stabilized the empire and consolidated his own power, a policy continued by Antonius Pius (138–61). In literature, Lucullus produced satires later perfected by Juvenal, and Tacitus (*c.* 55–*c.* 120) wrote the definitive history of the period. The Pantheon (*c.* 118) is an architectural realization of imperial grandeur.

Surgical instruments were produced.
China saw the popularization of Taoism and (*c.* 100) the invention of the wheelbarrow.
A Greek astronomer Ptolemy produced the *Almagest* (*c.* 150), a definitive work on stars, and his *Geography*.
Religion in the Buddhist world was influenced by Brahmanism; Christianity by Gnosticism.

managing his family's extensive peanut farms. He was a senator for the state of Georgia (1962–66) and governor of the state (1971–74). He was elected President as the Democratic candidate in 1976, when he defeated the Republican incumbent, Gerald Ford. He is the first President since the Civil War to come from the "Old South".

Casanova de Seingalt, Giovanni Giacomo (Jacopo) (1725–98), Italian adventurer. From 1750 he travelled through Europe leading a dissolute existence. In 1755 he was imprisoned in Venice but made a daring escape to Paris, where he amassed a fortune and mixed with the leading men and women of the day. After 1785 he became a librarian. He is remembered for his memoirs, which were not published in unexpurgated form until 1960.

Castro, Fidel (1926–   ), Cuban revolutionary leader and prime minister (1959–   ). In 1953 he was sentenced to 15 years' imprisonment after an unsuccessful coup against Batista's regime. Two years later he was granted an amnesty and began, in Mexico, his association with Che Guevara. In 1959, barely two years after Castro's return to Cuba, his guerrilla forces deposed Batista and he became *de facto* ruler. He collectivized agriculture, dispossessed foreign companies and established close connections with communist countries. In 1961 he declared himself a Marxist-Leninist, aligning his country with the Third World nations.

Catherine II, the Great (1729–96), Empress of Russia (1762–96), *b*. Germany. She married Peter III in 1745 and in 1762 organized a rebellion ending in his assassination. She began as an "enlightened autocrat", with ambitious plans for reform, but few were carried out. She became rigidly conservative after the Pugachev peasant revolt (1773–74) and French Revolution, and gave the nobility absolute power over the peasants (1785). She increased Russia's territory and international prestige but was a notorious libertine.

AD 160–220

A **Roman Empire**, depopulated by plague (166–7), embraced Stoicism and increased its persecution of Christians (*c.* 170). Severus (193–211) reformed the army and reinforced provincial administration. Caracella (211–
A 17) expelled the Goths and bestowed citizenship on most of the empire's free inhabitants. Literature increasingly took the form of prose romance exemplified by the popularity of Petronius' *Satyricon* (*c.* 60) and Apuleius' *Golden Ass.*

A **China** saw the fall of the Han dynasty (220) and was split into three kingdoms. The abacus was used by 190.

A **Greek** surgeon Galen founded physiology, writing 500 works. **Religion** was influenced by Origen (185–254) synthesizing Gospels and philosophy.

Cato the Younger, Marcus Porcius Cato Uticensis

Cato the Younger, Marcus Porcius Cato Uticensis (95–46 BC), Roman patriot; great-grandson of Cato the Elder. He supported republican government and his opposition to Julius Caesar led to the foundation of the first triumvirate. He became military tribune of Macedonia in 67 and quaestor in 65; he was made tribune in 62 and praetor in 54. He favoured Pompey against Caesar in 49 and, after Pompey's defeat, committed suicide.

Caxton, William (c.1422–91) the first English printer. Following a period in Cologne (1470–72), where he learned printing, he set up his own printing press in 1476 at Westminster. He published more than 100 items, many of them his own translations from French, Latin and Dutch. His books, carefully edited, are fine examples of superb craftmanship.

Ceausescu, Nicolae (1918–   ), Romanian politician. He became a member of the politburo (1955), general secretary of the Romanian Communist Party (1965) and head of state (1967). He has aimed at fostering Romanian nationalism, achieving greater independence from the USSR and encouraging trade with the West.

Chaitanya (Caitanya) (1485–1533), Hindu mystic and theistic reformer, worshipped as the incarnation of Krishna. Moved by a religious experience at Bodh-Gaya calling him to a life of total commitment, he founded a cult devoted to the worship of the God Vishnu in his form as Krishna and played an important part in the Vishnuism (Vaishnavism) movement in Bengal. His cult was characterized by the performance of chanting and eurhythmic movements and for its emphasis on equality of treatment to all castes. Temples were built after his death at the traditional site of Vishnuism at Brindaban, which he visited and which is still the site of pilgrimages and festivals.

Chamberlain, Arthur Neville (1869–1940), British politician, son of Joseph Chamberlain and half-brother of Austen Chamberlain. He turned from business to local politics in 1911 and in 1915 became mayor of Birmingham.

AD 220–280

Rome, after the murder of Alexander Severus (222–35) was the scene of factional troop warfare. After the Goths took Dacia (257) capable emperors reigned. Claudius II (268–70) defeated the Goths and settled them in the Danubian provinces. Aurelian (270–5) drove out the invading Alemanni, but abandoned Dacia.
China, reunited under the Western Ch'in dynasty produced a treatise on acupuncture. **Persian Sassanid Empire** reached its zenith under Shapur I. **Greek** mathematician Diophantus produced the *Arithmetica* (c. 250), introducing algebraic symbols. A **Mayan culture** grew in America. **Religion** saw the rise of neo-Platonism and Manicheanism.

In 1918 he was elected to Parliament as a Conservative. He was chancellor of the exchequer (1923–24) and minister of health (1924–29). At the latter office he distinguished himself by a thorough reform of the social services which brought about a simplification of local government. As prime minister (1937–40) he conducted the policy of Appeasement and signed the Munich agreement in 1938. German successes at the beginning of WWII led to criticism of his leadership and he resigned in May, 1940.

Charlemagne (742–814), King of the Franks, (768–814) and Holy Roman Emperor (800–14). The eldest son of Pepin the Short, he inherited Neustria, the NW half of the Frankish kingdom, in 768 and annexed the remainder on his brother Carloman's death in 771. Responding to Lombard threats against the papacy, he led two armies into Italy and took the Lombard throne in 773. He undertook a long (772–804) and brutal conquest of Saxony, which he forcibly converted to Christianity. He also annexed Bavaria in 788 and defeated the Avars of the middle Danube (791–96, 804). After regular campaigns against the Muslims, he had established the Spanish march in N Spain by 811. He was crowned Emperor of the West by Pope Leo II in 800, thus reviving the concept of the Roman Empire, and completing the West's split with the Byzantine Empire. A man of great forcefulness, he initiated the intellectual awakening of the Carolingian Renaissance. He set up a strong central authority and kept control of his lands by means of regular visits by his officials, but the empire lacked sufficient coherence to maintain its unity after his death.

Charles I (1600–49), King of England, Scotland and Ireland (r. 1625–49). Charles was the second son of James I of England and became heir apparent on the death of his brother Henry in 1612. He inherited his father's reliance on the counsel of the unpopular Buckingham, and was attacked for his marriage in 1625 to the Catholic Henrietta Maria. Charles' unpopular foreign policy and his literal interpretation of the divine right of kings made him mistrust

---

AD 280–340

A **Roman Empire**, divided by Diocletian (284–305) into eastern and western spheres (285), captured Armenia and Mesopotamia and restored imperial authority in Britain (297). Roman taxation crippled Mediterranean economy (c. 300). Freedom was granted to
A all religions by Constantine (313), himself interested in Christianity. The old St Peter's Church in Rome was built (330) specifically for Christians, and numerous buildings exemplified the Roman preference for the massive. Horse-breeding flourished and interest in alchemy revived. **In Europe** the Franks, Alemanni and Burgundians crossed the Rhine, runes were used and clinker-built boats developed. **Religion** saw monasticism rise and the Council of Nicaea (325).

Charles II

Parliament, and led him to rule without it for 11 years (1629–40) and to resort to feudal impositions to raise revenue. The attempt of his minister Laud to impose High Church liturgy on Scotland led to a rebellion in that country in 1639, which necessitated the recall of Parliament. Charles allowed Parliament to impeach Laud and to execute his chief adviser Strafford in 1641, but he attempted a coup against the Commons in 1642 when he tried to arrest the five leading members of his opposition. The incident was the trigger for English Civil War. Charles took command of the royalist army and made his headquarters in Oxford. Following his defeat at Naseby in 1645, Charles surrendered and was imprisoned by the parliamentary army which tried to establish a constitutional monarchy. Disputes over its form, and plots by Charles, led in Dec. 1648 to a purge of Parliament of all but those most hostile to Charles; he was tried for treason and executed on 30 Jan. 1649.

Charles II (1630–85), King of England, Scotland and Ireland (r. 1660–85). When his father Charles I was defeated in 1646 he fled to France where Thomas Hobbes acted as his tutor. He was crowned King of Scots in 1651, but after the failure of his Scottish uprising in that year he again went into exile in France and Holland. He issued a declaration at Breda in 1660 that included an indemnity for all those involved in the civil wars, and he was invited to return to the throne the same year. His reign was marked by his attempts to manoeuvre towards a more autocratic monarchy and to introduce greater religious toleration. Initially he relied on the advice of the Earl of Clarendon; in the late 1670s his harmonious relationship with Parliament broke up as fears arose that he sympathized with Roman Catholicism. Parliamentary opposition reached a peak during the Popish Plot and Exclusion Crisis of 1679–81, when attempts were made to exclude Charles's brother, the Catholic Duke of York (later James II) from the succession. Charles survived the crisis and in the last years of his reign rooted out much of the opposition in the boroughs.

AD 340–400

A Rome under Julian (331–63) campaigned against the Franks, tried to organize a pagan church and to absorb Germanic tribes. A Visigoth invasion was repelled and withdrawal from Britain began (383).

A Mayan civilization, having developed mathematics, produced superior calendars and advanced astronomy.

China produced Hsieh Ho's work on art theory and foreign-influenced music.

India, under Samudra Gupta, conquered Nepal and Bengal. Art and classical Sanskrit flourished with the rule of the Guptas (320–535).

Japan conquered Korea (c. 360).

Religion saw Buddhism in China, the Nestorian Church develop, and monasticism furthered.

Charles the Bold

Charles, name of seven Holy Roman emperors. For Charles I *see* Charlemagne. Charles V (1500–58), the greatest of the Hapsburg kings, was King of Spain 1516–56 and Emperor 1519–56, and also controlled The Netherlands, Sicily and Naples and Spanish America. He was constantly thwarted in his attempts to unify his empire by his rivalry with the Valois kings of France, and by the emergence of the Reformation in the 1520s. He became leader of the Catholic cause, but after constant opposition within the empire, he abdicated his various thrones in the mid-1550s and retired to the monastery of Yuste in Spain.

Charles, name of ten kings of France. For Charles I, *see* Charlemagne; Charles VII (1403–61), took the title of king on his father's death and ruled s of the Loire. He was prompted to oppose the English by Joan of Arc in 1429. He signed the Treaty of Arras in 1435 and won Paris the next year. By 1453 he finally secured the complete withdrawal of English troops from France, thus ending the Hundred Years War. Charles VIII (1470–98) came to the throne in 1483. He invaded Italy in 1494 to capture Naples but was driven out of Naples the next year. This expedition was important in introducing the Italian Renaissance to France. Charles X (1757–1836) fled France in 1789, went into the Austrian Netherlands, Turin, Prussia and Russia, and finally went into exile in England until 1814. After the assassination of Louis XVIII in 1824 Charles succeeded to the throne. In 1830 he abolished the liberal chamber of deputies and restricted press freedom. He was forced to abdicate in the ensuing July revolution.

Charles Martel (*c.* 688–741), Frankish ruler, grandfather of Charlemagne. Upon the death of his father in 714, he seized control of the Frankish kingdoms of Austrasia and Neustria. He later conquered Burgundy, Aquitaine and Provence and subjugated many German tribes E of the Rhine. In 732 at Poitiers he halted the advance of the Muslims from Spain.

Charles the Bold (1433–77), last reigning Duke of Burgundy (*r.* 1467–77). He was allied with England by

AD 400–460

Rome had its western capital Ravenna (402) sacked by Visigoths (410), repelled Atilla the Hun's invasion (452). Vandals attacked Rome (455) and annexed the Mediterranean islands. Theodosius II (401–50) founded the university of Constantinople (425) and produced the Theodosian Code (438). Japan, assimilating Chinese civilization, evolved a complex writing system and adopted foreign music and dance forms. China produced compasses and armillary spheres. Britain saw the destruction of Roman life by Saxon invaders. Franks and Burgundians created a barbarian kingdom. Religion saw the Augustine produce the *City of God* and Councils at Ephesus (431) and Chalcedon.

marriage and was ruler of the Low Countries, Luxembourg, Burgundy and Franche-Comté. He seized Nancy in 1475, and subsequently attacked the Swiss, who killed him in 1477. Burgundy's resistance to France ended with his death.

Chartism, British working-class movement 1838–48. Combining the discontent of the industrial workers in a period of depression with the demands of radical artisans, the movement was united under the People's Charter, drawn up in 1838 by William Lovett, which demanded electoral reform including universal male suffrage. As well as local riots and strikes, the Chartists organized three mass petitions (1839, 1842, 1848), but after a period of national organization led by the Irishman Feargus O'Connor, the movement became quiescent until 1848 when it briefly revived in the wake of the European revolutions of that year.

Chatham, William Pitt, 1st Earl of (1708–78), English statesman also known as William Pitt the Elder. He became known in Parliament after 1735 for his speeches advocating that England should concentrate on commerce and colonial development. He became secretary of state in 1756 following a crisis in the Seven Years War, and the next year headed a coalition with the Duke of Newcastle. He subsidized Frederick the Great, expanded the navy and continually harassed the French. His main effort was devoted to the successful capture of much of India and Canada. He resigned in 1761 when George III refused to declare war on Spain, and opposed the Treaty of Paris as inadequate. He denounced the prosecution of Wilkes in 1763 and attacked the Stamp Act in 1765. He was created Earl of Chatham in 1766 and nominally headed a ministry in 1766–68, but it was weak and divided, partly on account of his physical and mental illnesses. He retired from active politics in 1768 but continued to argue for any peace settlement with the American colonies short of granting independence.

Chaucer, Geoffrey (1345–1400), the greatest English

AD 460–520

A **Roman Empire** in the west ended (467) with Odoacer's barbarian invasion of Italy.

Ostrogoths under Theodoric (489–526) invaded Italy (488), defeated Odoacer (493) and set up a kingdom.

Franks under Clovis I (481–511) set up the Merovingian dynasty in Gaul (486). Baptized (497), Clovis was supported by the papacy and drove the Visigoths into Spain (507).

India saw the rise of the Shakta and Tantra cults, emphasizing divine fertility and energy. Vaishnaism flourished as did the Yogacara school. Astronomy developed.

China was politically fragmented. **Britain** saw the Anglo-Saxon invasion go westwards and the foundation of the kingdom of Wessex under Arthur (c. 495).

medieval poet. He was the son of a wine merchant and served at court and on diplomatic missions before being appointed controller of customs in London (1374–86). His writings are remarkable for their range, narrative sense, power of characterization and humour. They include *The Book of the Duchesse*, (1369), *The House of Fame*, (c.1375) *The Parliament of Fowls*, (c.1385) *Troilus and Criseyde*, (c.1385) and *The Canterbury Tales* (c.1385–1400).

Chiang Kai-shek (1887–1975), Chinese politician. After training in a Japanese military academy (1909) he joined the Chinese Kuomintang (Nationalist Party), and succeeded Sun Yat-sen as its leader in 1925 and in 1927 violently purged the KMT of Mao's Communist followers. Although Chiang managed to maintain some unity his leadership had led to civil war. His international status rose during WWII when he led the fight against Japan, and he was elected president of China in 1948. By 1949 Communist victories drove his government to Taiwan, where he accepted US aid and launched a series of attacks on mainland China.

Ch'in dynasty (221–207 BC), ruling Chinese house whose main achievement was the establishment of a unified sovereign state which survived as an empire until 1911. Originating in NW China, the Ch'in led by Shih Huang Ti conquered the feuding states of the Chou dynasty and maintained an effective administration along feudal lines to govern their vast territory. Two dynasties with the name "Chin" ruled from 265 to 419 and from 1122 to 1234 AD.

Ch'ing dynasty (1644–1912), also known as the Manchu dynasty, the last dynasty of imperial China. The Manchus were a tribe from Manchuria who, by capturing Peking in 1644, established control over the whole country. Their rule was consolidated by K'Ang Hsi and for a long time they retained their cultural identity, encouraging the development of the arts, in particular the production of porcelain which was popular in 18th-century Europe. In the

---

AD 520–580

A **Byzantine Empire** under Justinian the Great reconquered North Africa (534) and Italy (554). Law was codified and an alliance concluded with the papacy. Architecture and mosaics flourished, but the Athenian university closed. Silk production was instituted.

Persian Empire under Chosroes I (531–79) fought Byzantium and took southern Arabia.

India saw the Guptas fall (535). **China** saw the development of palaeontology and, in music, A of Confucian ceremonies involving dance and poetry.

Japan, absorbing Buddhism (552), developed artistically during the Asuka period (552–645).

Britain saw the founding of the kingdom of Bernicia (c. 547).

Religion was revolutionized by Mohammed's birth in Mecca.

Chola

20th century the dynasty's failure to deal adequately with Western imperialism and to institute reforms led to its overthrow by nationalists led by Sun Yat-sen.

Chola, medieval dynasty of s India. The Cholas established a kingdom around Tenjore in the 2nd century AD, but did not rise to prominence until the 9th century. They replaced the Pallavas on the E coast of s India in 888, and between 985 and 1024 established an empire that included Ceylon, Bengal, parts of Sumatra and Malaya. The dynasty declined and ended in 1279. The Cholas brought a great period of Hindu culture to s India.

Chou dynasty (c. 1030–221 BC), Chinese dynasty responsible for the creation of much of the Chinese society and culture. It overthrew the Shang dynasty, after the Chou people had moved out of their homelands N of the Hwang-Ho river. Chinese civilization spread under the Chou to most parts of modern China, but the dynasty never established effective control over the regions. Confucius and Lao tze achieved the greatest of the many cultural glories of Chou China.

Chou En-lai (1898–1976), Chinese politician. He was educated in Japan and Europe and worked for the nationalist Kuomintang (1924–27), after which he joined the Communist Party. He participated in the Long March, and acted as second-in-command to Mao Tse-Tung. He negotiated the eventual Communist victory, and became prime minister (1949–76) and foreign minister (1949–58). He was the country's chief international spokesman until his death.

Christina (1626–89), Queen of Sweden (1632–54). After the regency of Oxenstierna (1632–44) she ruled eccentrically, giving away Crown lands. She attracted foreign scholars, including Descartes, to her court. She abdicated in 1654 and travelled widely, trying unsuccessfully to obtain the crown of Poland on John Casimir's abdication in 1667.

Christophe, Henri (1767–1820), Haitian revolutionary

AD 580–640

Persia at war with Byzantium (602–28), developed the windmill, possibly from wind-driven prayer-wheels. Persian art developed intricate metalwork.
Papal authority was assisted by Gregory I's defence of Rome against the Lombards. He also gave his name to plainsong (c. 600).
China, reunified by the Sui dynasty (589), was bureaucratized by the T'ang dynasty (618).

Disease-diagnosis was documented by Chao Yuan Fang (c. 610) and surgery developed.
Japan saw the rise of the Soga clan (587), introducing a Chinese, paternalist constitution.
Indian Sanskrit poetry flourished.
Religion was profoundly affected by Mohammed's flight to Medina (620) and by the institution of the concept of jihad (holy war).

leader, president (1806–11) and king (1811–20). Born a free black on the island of Grenada, he participated in the armed struggle against the French in Haiti and fought a civil war with the partisans of the mulatto Pétion. Christophe ordered the construction of the citadel of La Ferrière, a fort overlooking Cap Haitien, the building of which cost many Haitian lives.

Churchill, Sir Winston Leonard Spencer (1874–1965), British statesman, son of Lord Randolph Churchill. As a reporter in the South African (Boer) War he was captured in 1899 but escaped. He was elected to Parliament in 1900 as a Conservative, but joined the Liberals in 1904. As home secretary (1910–11) he introduced important pension Acts, but suppressed labour unrest. He was first lord of the admiralty (1911–15), minister of munitions (1917–18), secretary of state for war and for air (1919–21) and colonial secretary (1921–22). He was chancellor of the exchequer (1924–29) and was out of office 1929–39, but spoke constantly against the rising threat of Nazi Germany. He was first lord of the admiralty (1939–40), and acted as prime minister and minister of defence in the War Cabinet (1940–45). His inspiring oratory made him a great war leader. He established close contact with US president F. D. Roosevelt, and was principal architect of the grand alliance of Britain, the USA and the USSR. He was prime minister again 1951–55, after which he retired from politics. He wrote extensively, his major works being *The World Crisis* (1923–31), *The Second World War* (1948–54) and the *History of the English-Speaking Peoples* (1956–58). He was awarded the Nobel Prize in literature in 1953.

Cicero, Marcus Tullius, or Tully (106–43 BC), Roman politician, philospher and orator. A leader of the senate, he exposed Catiline's conspiracy and prosecuted his supporters. He opposed Julius Caesar but took no part in his assassination. He criticised Mark Antony in the senate and when Octavian came to power, Antony persuaded him to have Cicero executed. Among Cicero's greatest speeches

---

AD 640–700

Islamic world suffered disputes about the succession of the caliphate under Othman (*d.* 656) and Ali. Civil war ensued, leading to the establishment (661) of the Umayyad dynasty. Muslims took Iran and Egypt (642), Armenia (653) and Afghanistan (664). Later fragmentation led to the emergence of the Sunni, Shi'ite and Khawarij sects. *The Koran* was finished (651–2).

Britain saw the victory of Roman Christianity in Northumbria and the Sutton Hoo ship burial (*c.* 650). Book illustration flourished with *Lindisfarne Gospels* (*c.* 700)

Byzantine Empire produced Greek fire for naval warfare.

Religion saw the condemnation of the Monothelites in the Ecumenical Council of Constantinople (681).

were *Orations Against Catiline* and the *Phillipics*. He also wrote a number of books on rhetoric and philosophical works including *De Amicitia* and *De Officiis*.

Cid, Rodrigo Díaz de Vivar, "El Cid" (*c.* 1043–99), Spanish national hero in the wars against the Moors. He was a knight in the service of the king of Castile, but was banished in 1081 and joined the Moorish king of Saragossa. He conquered Valencia in 1094 and ruled it until his death, but the Moors took the kingdom in 1102. His various exploits have been romanticized in Spanish legend.

Clarendon, Edward Hyde, 1st Earl of (1609–74), English statesman and historian. He was initially critical of Charles I, but became a leading royal adviser in 1641 and negotiated the Restoration in 1660. As Charles II's chief minister, his caution made him unpopular. He was forced into exile in 1667, where he wrote his *History of the Rebellion* about the English Civil War.

Claudius I (10 BC–AD54), Roman emperor (*r.* 41–54), nephew of Tiberius, the first emperor chosen by the army. He had military successes in Germany, conquered Britain in 43, and built both the harbour at Ostia at the mouth of the Tiber and the Claudian aqueduct. Agrippina, his fourth wife, poisoned him and made her son Nero emperor.

Cleopatra (69–30 BC), Queen of Egypt (51–30 BC). In 48 BC, with the aid of Julius Caesar, she overthrew her husband, brother and co-ruler Ptolemy XIII. She became Caesar's mistress, but returned to Egypt after his assassination in 44 BC. In 41 BC she won Mark Antony's love and they married in 37 BC. Octavian Caesar (later Augustus) determined to destroy them and in 31 BC their fleet was defeated at Actium. They fled and Antony killed himself. Cleopatra surrendered and, after she failed to win Octavian's affections, killed herself with an asp. These events assured Octavian of supreme power in Rome and are the subject of numerous dramas, notably Shakespeare's *Antony and Cleopatra*.

Clive, Robert, Baron Clive of Plassey (1725–74), British

AD 700–760

Islamic world, having taken Spain (715), was repulsed by Eastern Emperor Leo III (717–41) at Constantinople (718). Al Mansur (745–75) founded the Abbasid Caliphate (750). A Frankish king Charles Martel thwarted Muslim invaders at Poitiers (732) and his son Pepin donated land to the papacy, establishing its temporal power (756).

China underwent a poetic golden age in the T'ang dynasty, and saw the invention of gunpowder. Mayan science reached its peak. Britain, almost completely ruled by Ethelbald (716-57), produced Bede's *History of the English Church and People*. Religion saw the beginnings of the Iconoclasm movement (726), with Leo III's prohibition of icons.

soldier and colonial administrator. He went to India as an official of the British East India Company (1743) and successfully resisted growing French power in India with his capture of Arcot (1751). By taking Calcutta and defeating the pro-French Nawab of Bengal at Plassey in 1757 he effectively assured British control of northern India, and was Governor of Bengal 1757–60 and 1765–67. He was acquitted of embezzling state funds in 1773.

Colbert, Jean Baptiste (1619–83), French statesman, the principal exponent of Mercantilism in economic policy. He became controller-general to Louis XIV in 1665, and tried to reform the taxes. His major effort was to encourage the growth of French industry and trade; his tariffs led to economic conflict with the Netherlands.

Columbus, Christopher (1451–1506), Italian-born explorer often, although erroneously, credited with the discovery of America. After seeking Portuguese sponsorship he went to Spain in 1484, where he found support for a voyage in search of a western route to China. In Oct. 1492 he landed in the Bahamas, the first European to reach the Americas, and called the people found there "Indians". He had made three other journeys by 1503, but without reaching the North American mainland. He died in poverty, still thinking he had found a route to the East.

Commune of Paris (1871), insurrection against the French national government, which was accepting a humiliating peace following the Franco-Prussian war. The Parisians, spurred on by radicals, anarchists and Marxists, decided to continue the fight and organized their own defences. The French government, based in Versailles, besieged the city (March–May 1871) and put down the revolt with great brutality.

Comte, Auguste (1798–1857), French philosopher, the founder of Positivism. Comte proposed the law of the three stages – theological, metaphysical and positive – that represent the development of the human race. In the first two stages the human mind finds religious or abstract causes

---

AD 760–820

A Frankish king Charlemagne united France, conquered Italy (774), northern Spain (777), Saxony (785) and Bavaria (788). Crowned Holy Roman Emperor (800), he instituted the Carolingian Renaissance with Alcuin (732–804). Islamic world, extended to Cordoba with the Umayyad dynasty (756), made Baghdad the Abbasid capital (762). Their art produced sophisticated music, under Harun ar-Rashid (764–809), and the Great Mosque at Cordoba. Japan under Emperor Kammu introduced feudalism, replacing Chinese-based social order. Printing with blocks was also in use there.
Bulgar kingdom reached a peak under Krum (808–14).
Britain saw Offa's dyke built, A the beginning of Viking raids and Egbert ruling Wessex.

to explain phenomena, while in the third, explanation of a phenomenon is found in a scientific law. His philosophy influenced British thinkers such as J. S. Mill and Frederick Harrison. His works include *Positive Philosophy* (1830–42) and *System of Positive Polity* (1851–54).

Confucius (*c.*551–479 BC), founder of Confucianism. Born in the Chinese province of Lu of aristocratic parents, he was largely self-educated. An excellent scholar, he became an influential teacher of the sons of wealthy families and is said to have been prime minister of Lu but resigned when he realized the post carried no real authority. In his later years he sought a return to the political morality of the early Chou Dynasty, but found no support. He died a frustrated man, but his ethical concepts dominated Chinese society for 2,000 years. Some of his teachings are recorded in the *Analects*.

Constantine I, or Constantine the Great (*c.*285-337), Roman Emperor (*r.*305-37). In the early part of his reign he had to contend with rivals for his throne, and during the decisive battle of Milvian Bridge against Maxentius he was said to have indicated his conversion to Christianity (312). In 313 he extended toleration to the Christians of the Empire by the Edict of Milan, perhaps seeing it as a means to achieve political unity. In 324 Constantine at last won sole control of the Empire, and he convened the Council of Nicaea in 325. He rebuilt Byzantium, which was dedicated in 330, and renamed it Constantinople. He introduced legal reforms but ruled autocratically. He was baptized on his deathbed.

Cook, James (1728–79), British naval officer and explorer. In 1768–71 he led a scientific expedition to Tahiti to observe the transit of Venus, and also surveyed the coast of New Zealand. On the same voyage he charted the E coast of Australia, naming it New South Wales and claiming it for England. On a second expedition to the s Pacific (1772–75), Cook mapped much of the s Hemisphere and sailed further south than anyone before him. On his last voyage

---

AD 820–850

Carolingian Empire was divided into three at the Treaty of Verdun (843).
Islamic world (Abbasid) moved its capital to Samarra (836), having experienced its most glorious epoch under Al Mamum the Great (813–33). Lyrical desert poetry re-emerged and constructional and geometric skills were perfected. Al-Farghani (*d.* 850) summarized

A Ptolomeian astronomy in his treatise the *Elements*. Within the Sunni branch, Ahmad ibn Hanbal (780–855) founded a school of Islamic law.
England was ruled by Egbert. Danes sacked London (836).
A **Mayan** skill produced the great Pyramid of the Sun, 66m high.
Scandinavians absorbed
A Byzantine culture through trading contacts.

(1776–79) he discovered the Sandwich (Hawaiian) Islands, where he was killed.

Copernicus, Nicholas, or Mikotaj Kopernik (1473–1543), Polish astronomer. He studied initially at Cracow and also in Italy, where he studied law and medicine as well as astronomy. He was appointed canon of the cathedral at Frauenberg, E Prussia, in 1497. His work *De Revolutionibus Orbium Caelestium*, which laid the foundations of modern astronomy, was probably written in 1530 but not published until 1543.

Corn Laws, series of acts regulating the import and export of grain in Britain. Records mention their existence as early as the 12th century. The most important was the 1815 act, which virtually prohibited the entry of foreign corn. It was thus held to keep British food prices high and led to a 30–year campaign for free trade, which ended with the repeal of the Corn Laws in 1846.

Cornwallis, Charles Cornwallis, 1st Marquess (1738–1805), British soldier and administrator. At first a successful commander for the British in the American Revolution, he was forced to surrender at Yorktown (1781). As governor-general of India (1786–93, 1805), he reformed the administration, law and army and suppressed Tippoo Sahib's revolt. Cornwallis was also viceroy of Ireland (1798–1801), where he defeated the 1798 revolt and carried through reforms and parliamentary union with Britain.

Cortés, Hernán (1485–1547), central figure in the Spanish conquest and colonization of Mexico. Under the patronage of Diego de Valásquez, Cortés sailed for central America with 550 men in 1518. He declared himself independent of Valásquez, gave himself the official standing and legal authority to colonize and marched inland towards the Aztec capital. Converting many of the local American Indians into allies of his cause, Cortés was able to capture Tenochtitlán in 1521. Cortés's personal power, symbolized by his titles and estates, was gradually eroded by the crown. He died in

---

AD 850–880

Carolingian states, weakened by invasion, were increasingly controlled by provincial nobility, and in Italy, papal authority declined.

A Byzantine Empire, its Christianity split from Rome (867) until the Fourth Council of Constantinople (870), under Basil I (867–86) attacked the Muslims in Mesopotamia and revived Byzantine civilization.

Pre-Iconoclastic churches were redecorated and figurative representation became increasingly stylized. The university of Constantinople's teaching of science was suppressed by Basil II. Islamic world saw the rise of scientific enquiry through Al Khindi (d. 873) and Al-Rhazi. English opposition to the Danes,

A organized by Alfred, produced peace and literary chronicles.

Spain, but his remains were transferred to Mexico fifteen years later.

Cosgrave, William Thomas (1880–1965), Irish nationalist. He fought in the 1916 rebellion against Britain and helped win independence. Cosgrave was president of the Irish Free State (1922–32). His party, Cumann na nGaedheal, lost the election of 1932 to the Eaman de Valera's Fianna Fáil. Soon after, Cosgrave helped found the moderate Fine Gael Party, from which he resigned in 1948.

Counter-Reformation, revival of the spiritual and theological life of the Roman Catholic Church in Europe during the 16th and early 17th centuries. It began as a reaction to the Protestant Reformation. The Counter-Reformation strove to remove many of the abuses that had crept into the late medieval Church and won new prestige for the papacy and the Church. A leading part was played in the movement by new monastic orders, particularly by the Society of Jesus (Jesuits), founded by St Ignatius of Loyola. The Council of Trent (1545–63) clarified Roman Catholic teaching on the major theological controversies of the period and initiated internal Church reforms.

Cranmer, Thomas (1489–1556), English prelate and religious reformer. He was a distinguished theologian, and was appointed Archbishop of Canterbury by Henry VIII in 1533. He secured the annulment of Henry's marriage with Catherine of Aragon despite opposition from the pope. Cranmer, a friend of Thomas Cromwell, promoted the introduction of Protestantism into England, encouraging the translation and dissemination of the "Great Bible" in 1539 and compiling the first Book of Common Prayer in 1548. After the accession of Mary in 1553, Cranmer was burnt at the stake.

Crassus, Marcus Licinius (c. 116–53 BC), Roman politician. He commanded an army for Sulla in 83 BC and amassed a vast personal fortune in urban and rural property. He suppressed the slave rebellion led by Spartacus in 71 BC, financing six new legions. Crassus served as consul with his

AD 880–910

Norse raiders disrupted urban development in north Europe.

A Byzantium warred constantly with Bulgarians under Symeon I.

A India saw the Chola dynasty replace the Pallavas (888).

China witnessed the fall of the

A T'ang dynasty (907).

England regained much of the Danelaw under Edward (899–925).

Cambodia, in its Angkor period (889–1434), had Phnom Bakheng as

its administrative centre.

Japan saw the emergence of classical literature during its Heian period (794–1192).

Islamic world introduced cotton and silk manufacture into Spain and Sicily and lateen sails into the West.

Religion saw a revival of monasticism at Cluny, France (910), and the foundation of the Cluniac Reform Movement.

rival Pompey in 70 BC, and in 60 BC Julius Caesar formed with them the first triumvirate. He acted mainly in alliance with Caesar, and became governor of Syria in 54 BC. He was killed fighting the Parthians at Carrhae.

Crazy Horse, *See* **Little Bighorn.**

Crécy, *See* **Hundred Years War.**

Crimean War (1853–56), war fought by Britain, France and Turkey, with later support from Sardinia-Piedmont, against Russia. Russian ambitions for expansion in the Middle East led the other powers to fear for the future independence of the Ottoman Empire. They occupied the Crimean Peninsula in 1854 to capture Sevastopol, after the Russians had claimed a protectorate over Orthodox Christians in the Holy Land and seized two Turkish dependencies. The war was marked on both sides by incompetent leadership and organization. There were many deaths from disease and infection, despite the pioneering work of Florence Nightingale in introducing modern nursing methods. Most of the war was centred on the capture of Sevastopol, which was finally evacuated in 1855. On the accession of Alexander II, Russia sued for peace, which was achieved at the Congress of Paris in 1856. The war ended Russian dominance in SE Europe.

Crockett, David (1786–1836), US frontiersman. He served in the US Congress (1827–31, 1833–35) as a Whig, and shrewdly cultivated the image of a rough frontiersman. He moved to Texas in 1835 and died at the Alamo.

Cromwell, Oliver (1599–1658), English politician, Lord Protector (1653–58). He was a landowner from Huntingdon, and an MP after 1628. He rose to prominence as a commander of the parliamentary army in the Civil War, and after the war he was a key figure in the negotiations about a new constitution, since he had the confidence of the army leaders, He eventually supported Pride's Purge and led the demand for the execution of Charles I. After the proclamation of the Commonwealth, he was unofficially ruler of the country, and commanded the

---

AD 910–940

Normandy was founded (911) by Rollo, a Viking invader. He was baptized in 912.

Saxon king Henry I (919–36) was first to rule a unified Germany.

Islamic world (Umayyad) reached a cultural zenith under Abd ar-Rahman III (912–61). Cordoba became a centre of science. Sufism, a mystical literary movement within Islam, developed in opposition to orthodox interpretations of the *Koran*.

Japan experienced strife in the provinces as a result of the rise of a military class, (935–41).

England was completely won back by Athelstan; local government was organized in shires and hundreds. Lyric and elegaic poetry was produced, surviving in the *Exeter Book*, and including *The Dream of the Rood*.

army in campaigns in Ireland (1649) and Scotland (1650–51). He attempted various constitutional measures until 1653, when he accepted the title of Lord Protector. In 1657 he refused the offer of the throne. His domestic policy was typified by an attempt to restore social stability although relying on the radical army, and his foreign policy was aggressively anti-Spanish. He was succeeded on his death by his son Richard. This arrangement, however, only lasted until 1659, when Richard was ousted from power.

Cromwell, Thomas, Earl of Essex (c. 1485–1540), English statesman. He was originally a wool merchant, and came to Henry VIII's attention as secretary to Wolsey. After his master's fall, he became the king's chief adviser in 1532, and was responsible for the achievement of the break with Rome and the dissolution of the monasteries. He also reorganized the royal administration. He fell from power after the failure of Henry's marriage with Anne of Cleves, which he had promoted, and he was executed in 1540.

Crusades, series of military enterprises undertaken by western Christendom to capture Palestine from the Seljuk Turks. The First Crusade (1096–99), which followed a chaotic Peasants' Crusade (1095–96) from France and Germany, captured much of the E Mediterranean coast and took Jerusalem in 1099. The second Crusade (1147–49) failed to capture Damascus. The Third Crusade (1189–91) was jointly commanded by Philip II of France and Richard I of England; the latter negotiated with the Turkish leader Saladin for Christians to have access to Jerusalem. The Fourth Crusade (1202–04) sacked Constantinople and set up the Latin empire of the east. The Children's Crusade (1212) was followed by the unsuccessful Fifth Crusade (1218–21) which attacked Egypt. The Sixth Crusade (1228–29) was not a military expedition, but the Emperor Frederick II negotiated a new truce with the Turks. The Seventh Crusade (1248–50) was ineffectual, led by Louis IX of France, who was killed on the Eighth Crusade (1270).

AD 940–970

Saxon king Otto I became Holy Roman Emperor (962) after ending the recurrent Magyar invasions at Lechfeld (955).

China under the Northern Sung dynasty (960) was more humanistic in government, social organization and thought. *Tzu* poetry was irregular and colloquial. An Imperial Academy of painting was founded in the Ten Kingdoms period (907–80).

Islamic world set up a Ghaznavid dynasty in Afghanistan (962) and continued its exploration of chemistry.

England saw a clerical revival (c. 940), establishing a useful network for the spreading of royal authority.

Religion in the Jewish academy in Babylon was monotheistic orthodox Judaism, championed by Sa'adia ben Joseph.

After the Ninth Crusade (1271–72), Acre, the last crusader kingdom in the Middle East, was taken by the Turks in 1291.

Cuban Missile Crisis (1962), USA–USSR confrontation over the installation in Cuba of Soviet nuclear rockets. Photographs taken by US reconnaissance aircraft revealed the construction of missile bases in Cuba, and a study was made of photographs of the cargo being carried on the decks of Cuba-bound Soviet ships. President John Kennedy protested to Premier Nikita Khrushchev about the threat that such bases posed to the Western Hemisphere and, after increasingly hostile exchanges, Khrushchev ordered the bases to be dismantled.'

Culloden, Battle of (1746), decisive battle of the Second Jacobite rising, in which the army of Charles Edward Stuart (Bonnie Prince Charlie) was defeated by forces under the Duke of Cumberland. Culloden ended the Stuart attempts to regain the throne by force. The battle was followed by a ruthless subjugation of the Scottish Highland clans who had provided most of Prince Charles Edward's army.

Cultural Revolution, The, officially the Great Proletarian Cultural Revolution, campaign led by Mao Tse-Tung to purge the Chinese Communist Party of his opponents and to instil correct revolutionary social and political attitudes in the population. It was intended to combat the counter-revolution in domestic affairs which, in the early 1960s, had introduced incentives meant to promote efficiency in Chinese industry. It began with an attack on the moderates written by Mao and published in a Shanghai newspaper in November 1965. Senior party officials were removed from their posts and a series of open-air rallies, attended by millions of Mao's new youth corps, the Red Guards, was begun in August 1966. The revolution then spread throughout China and became a mass movement to defend the revolution against "bourgeois revisionism". It reached its peak in the autumn of 1968, when Liu Shao-Chi, previously Mao's second-in-command, was relieved of all

AD 970–1000

French king Hugo Capet (987–96) reasserted royal authority over the nobility, pope and emperor. Romanesque architecture there was grandiose, involving stone vaults below the roofs. Gerbert (940–1003) introduced the astrolabe and Arabic numerals from Cordoba.

A **Byzantine Empire** granted trading privileges to Venice (992), and under Basil II (976–1025) took Greece from the Bulgarians (996).

A **Viking** invasions of Europe reached a peak (c. 1000), threatening southern France and Italy. They worshipped tribes of warlike gods led by Odin.

England, again overrun by

A Danes in Ethelred II's reign, experienced an artistic revival in Winchester as a result of the monastic movement.

his posts. It was then that Lin Piao was raised to the position of second most important official in China's political hierarchy. Throughout 1967 and 1968 the established local Communist Party authorities were replaced by Maoist Revolutionary Committees.

Custer, George Armstrong, *See* **Little Bighorn.**

Cyrus the Great (*c.* 600–529 BC), King of Persia, founder of the Achaemenid dynasty and the Persian Empire in 549 BC. He took over Media, defeated and captured King Croesus of Lydia (*c.* 546 BC), captured Babylon in 539 BC and the Greek cities in Asia Minor, but failed to conquer Egypt. He delivered the Jews from captivity, giving them Palestine to rule. While fighting the Massagetae, a tribe NW of the Caspian Sea, he was killed.

Danby, Thomas Osborne, Earl of (1632–1712) (subsequently Marquess of Carmarthen, Duke of Leeds), English Tory politician who was Charles II's treasurer and chief minister (1673–78). He built up an Anglican court party in Parliament, but was impeached and imprisoned (1679–84) by them when a secret subsidy he had negotiated with Louis XIV was made public. Danby organized Tory support for William and Mary, invited them to seize the crown and became their chief minister (1690–95) until he was again impeached on a charge of bribery.

Danes, North Germanic peoples who first settled in the Jutland peninsula about 10,000 BC. Their history is vague until about AD 800 when they played an important part in the Viking raids on Western Europe. In the 9th–11th centuries they invaded England and established kingdoms in Yorkshire and in East Anglia. Unification of Denmark was completed by Harold Bluetooth, and his grandson Canute added Norway and England to his kingdom.

Dante Alighieri (1265–1321), Italian poet famous for the *Divine Comedy*, written in *terza rima*. In his early years he wrote many *canzoni* to Beatrice Portinari, whom he admired from afar. In 1300 he became one of the rulers of the city-state of Florence, and during this time was

---

AD 1000–1025

Byzantine authority was restored by Basil II to Syria, Crete and southern Italy. The Bulgarian army was destroyed. **Islamic world** in Afghanistan under Mahmud (997–1030) plundered and annexed the Punjab. Persian encyclopedist Avicenna (980–1037) wrote seminally on astronomy, physics and medicine. Al-Biruni (943–1048), a countryman, wrote on many subjects and was the first to analyse flower structure by methods important to plant classification.

A England accepted Canute as king (1016); he appointed his supporters earls and his empire included Norway and Denmark.

A India under the Chola dynasty took Ceylon and Bengal. **Religion** saw the Pope prohibit clerical marriage.

responsible for the exile of his friend, Guido Cavalcanti, who had been a great influence on his early writing. Later Dante himself was exiled and wrote his inspired and majestic works under the patronage of various nobles until he died in poverty in Ravenna.

Danton, Georges Jacques (1759–94), French statesman and controversial official of the revolution. He played the role of moderate in the turbulent 1790s, seeking conciliation between the Girondins and Montagnards. Briefly leader of the Jacobins (1793) and a member of the Committee of Public Safety, he was arrested during the Reign of Terror and guillotined.

Darius the Great (548–486 BC), Achaemenid king of Persia (r. 521–486), also known as Darius I. He divided his lands into satrapies (provinces) with a degree of regional autonomy but responsible to Darius himself. He also fixed an annual taxation, consolidated his frontiers in both India and Thrace, and linked the Nile with the Red Sea by canal. He invaded Greece to punish the Greeks for aiding an Ionian revolt (499–494 BC), but he was defeated at Marathon (490 BC). He also restored much of the power of the kingdom of Judah.

Darwin, Charles Robert (1809–82), British naturalist, originator of a firm theory of organic evolution. In 1831 he joined an expedition in HMS *Beagle*, which explored the South American coast. The observations made of the flora and fauna there, and in particular on the Galapagos Islands, formed the basis of his future work on animal variations. He considered various earlier theories on the subject of evolution and compared them with his own research. The development of a theory similar to Darwin's own by A. R. Wallace led Darwin to present his ideas to a meeting of the Linnean Society in 1858, and he published *The Origin of Species*, a detailed exposition of evolution, in 1859. His ideas reached a wider public with the publication of *The Descent of Man* (1871), and other works.

David, name of two kings of Scotland. David I (1084–1153)

AD 1025–1050

A **Normandy** was organized (1035) by William I along totally feudal and military lines.

A the **Islamic** world saw the fall of the Umayyad dynasty in Spain (1031) as a result of racial and religious pressures. Muslims raided west India (1000–26) defacing temples. Their science continued to flourish with Alhazen's study of the eye.

Russia reached a peak during the reign of Yaroslav (1019–54).

China during the Sung period (960–1279) produced great prose writers and many illustrated botanical texts, medically useful.

A **England** under Edward the Confessor was ruled through earls. Normans visited the court.

Religion saw the establishment of Buddhism in Tibet and, in accordance with Cluniac reform, papal decrees against simony.

---

came to the throne in 1124. His interests in Cumbria and Northumbria involved him in the English civil war on the side of Matilda against Stephen, who defeated him in 1138. He introduced Anglo-Norman feudalism to Scotland and strengthened the towns. David II (1324–71) became king in 1329 and was defeated by Edward III of England at Halidon Hill in 1333. He was exiled to France, and was again defeated in England in 1346 following his return to Scotland in 1341. He was released on ransom in 1357.

Davis, Jefferson (1808–89), President of the Confederate States of America (1861–65). He was elected to Congress in 1845 but resigned to fight in the Mexican War in 1846. He was made secretary of war in 1853 but resigned from the Senate when Mississippi seceded from the Union, and he became president of the Confederate States. He served two years in prison and was indicted for treason in 1866, but never tried.

Decembrists, *See* **Nicholas I.**

Declaration of the Rights of Man and Citizen (1789), statement of the principles of the French revolution. It was adopted by the National Assembly, accepted by Louis XVI, and included in the constitution of 1791. Influenced by the American Declaration of Independence and the ideas of Rousseau, it established the sovereignty of the people and the restrictions for social consideration embodied in "liberty, equality, and fraternity".

Defenestration of Prague (May 1618), event that marked the outbreak of the Thirty Years War. The Protestant Bohemian subjects of the Hapsburg Ferdinand resented his Catholic rule. Two Hapsburg regents were thrown from the windows of the Prague council chamber; the Bohemian throne was offered to the Protestant Frederick, the Elector Palatine.

De Gaulle, Charles André Joseph Marie (1890–1970), French general and politician. A graduate of the *Ecole Spéciale Militaire* of Saint-Cyr, he fought in WWI and was wounded and captured in 1916. In 1924 he graduated from

---

AD 1050–1075

Islamic world lost Portugal (1055) to Ferdinand of Castile (1035–65). In Algeria and Morocco the Berber dynasty, the
A **Almoravids**, built a kingdom
A (1054). Seljuk Turks took Georgia and Armenia (1063–72). Persian scientist, poet and mathematician Omar Khayyam (*c.* 1048–1122) wrote the *Rubáiyát* expressing a rational, pessimistic and hedonistic philosophy

unacceptable to Islam. He also solved cubic equations by geometric methods and reformed the Muslim calendar.
A **Normans** under William I conquered England (1066) and southern Italy (1068). Cluniac reform and a feudal society were introduced into England. **Religion** saw a final schism between the papacy and the Greek Christian Church (1054).

the *Ecole Supérieure de Guerre* and served in the occupation of the Rhineland and in Lebanon. He was made a brigadier-general in charge of the fourth Armoured Division in 1940. When the Vichy government was created, he went to England as the self-declared head of the Free French forces and was sentenced to death by court martial in France. He was later head of the French Committee of National Liberation in Algiers. After the war, he made two partially successful attempts to reorganize the French government (1945–46) and following a period of retirement was elected president of the Fifth Republic in 1958. He settled the Algerian crisis and made France a nuclear power. He resigned after defeat in the referendum on administrative reform in 1969.

Desai Morarji Ranchodji (1896–   ), Indian politician. From 1930 he devoted himself to the movement for Indian independence and was jailed by the British several times. After independence (1947) he was chief minister of Bombay (1952–56), minister of commerce and industry (1956–58), minister of finance (1958–63, 1967–69) and deputy prime minister (1967–69). In 1969 he was ousted by Prime Minister Indira Gandhi but became Prime Minister in 1977.

Descartes, René (1596–1650), French philosopher and mathematician who was educated by Jesuits. He founded analytic geometry; he introduced Cartesian coordinates in the treatise that prefaced the *Discourse on Method* (1637). Here, and in his *Meditations* (1641), Descartes' method of deduction and intuition, later known as Cartesianism, led to modern metaphysics. By doubting all his ideas, he found that he reached one indubitable proposition: "I am thinking" and from this it followed that he existed, hence *cogito, ergo sum* – "I think therefore I am". Although mind and matter are distinct so that only ideas can be perceived, Descartes deduced the existence of an external world from his proofs of the existence of a perfect and consequently undeceiving God.

AD 1075–1100

Islamic world (Almoravids) annexed Moorish Spain until Alfonso VI (1072–1109) retook Toledo. Jerusalem was taken from the Seljuk Turks by the First Crusade (1099).

Byzantine Empire under Alexius I (1081–1118) recovered some of Asia Minor.

England saw William I order the production of the Domesday Book (1086), recording land use and tenure for taxation purposes. Stone castles were built and towns grew. The Bayeux Tapestry (c. 1080) described the Conquest.

China continued to produce medical pharmacopoeias; doctors had to pass qualifying exams.

Indian medicine involved yoga.

Religion saw Pope Gregory VII and Emperor Henry IV clashing over the appointment of bishops.

Dessalines, Jean Jacques (1758–1806), Haitian revolutionary and leader of the independence movement after the capture of Toussaint l'Ouverture. In 1803 he drove out the French and declared independence in 1804, changing the country's name from St Domingue to Haiti. As Emperor Jacques, his despotic rule lasted from 1804–06.

De Valera, Eamon (1882–1975), US-born Irish statesman. He was active in the movement for Irish independence and after the Easter Rebellion of 1916 was elected president of the Sinn Fein Party while imprisoned in England. He opposed William Cosgrave's Irish Free State ministry and founded the Fianna Fáil Party in 1924. He defeated Cosgrave in 1932 and remained head of Ireland's government (with two brief interruptions) until 1959, when he became president of the Republic of Ireland. He retired in 1973.

Dickens, Charles (1812–70), British novelist. He began his writing career as a parliamentary reporter for the *Morning Chronicle*. His first great success was the series of satirical pieces which appeared in the press after 1833, collected in 1836 as *Sketches by Boz*. They were followed by the sporting sketches collected as *The Posthumous Papers of the Pickwick Club* (1836–37). His first novel was *Oliver Twist* (1838); his other novels include *Dombey and Son* (1848), *David Copperfield* (1850), *Bleak House* (1853) and *Great Expectations* (1861).

Diderot, Denis, *See* **Encyclopedists** *and* **Enlightenment, The**.

Diggers, millenarian social and religious sect in England in 1649–50, an extreme group of the Levellers, who emerged in the New Model Army. They formed an egalitarian agrarian community at St George's Hill, Surrey, in 1649; it was destroyed the following year by local farmers. The main Digger theorist was Gerrard Winstanley, who proposed an immediate communalization of property to establish social equality in his book *Law of Freedom* (1652).

Disraeli, Benjamin, 1st Earl of Beaconsfield (1804–81),

AD 1100–1125

Islamic world saw the Seljuk Empire split into separate regencies (1100–25).
French king Louis VI (1108–37) granted many urban charters.
China helped the Jurchen tribes overthrow the Khitai (1116); they later destroyed the Sung dynasty (1136). Landscape painting reached its zenith there under Hui Tsung (1101–25).
Cambodia's Khmer Empire reached A

its peak *c.* 1100.
England saw Henry I (1100–35) stimulate economic development and expand and classify the A rule of law. Normans and Saxons were integrated by 1125.
Religion saw a compromise in the bishop-investiture controversy at the Concordat of Worms (1122), and the philosophical breakthroughs of Anselm A and Peter Abelard.

British Conservative politician and novelist. He helped to overthrow Robert Peel when the Corn Laws were repealed in 1846. As Conservative leader in the House of Commons (1849–68), Disraeli was several times Chancellor of the Exchequer and guided the 1867 Reform Act through Parliament. He was Prime Minister in 1868 and again in 1874–80. He secured Britain's half-share in the Suez Canal in 1875 and at the Congress of Berlin (1878) forced Russia to surrender Turkish lands and gained Cyprus for Britain. His most famous novels are *Coningsby, Sybil* and *Tancred*.

Dissolution of the Monasteries (1536–40), abolition of English monasticism in the reign of Henry VIII, devised and carried out by Thomas Cromwell. The dissolution completed the break with the Church of Rome, but the main motive was financial, the confiscated property reverting to the king's possession. By an Act of Parliament of 1536, Cromwell sent commissioners to close the smaller monasteries and the larger ones were closed piecemeal, 1538–40. The dissolution caused some social disruption, since the monasteries were the greatest landowners in the country, but it is probable that the contemporary stories of ex-monks starving were exaggerated. New secular schools were set up to replace the education formerly provided by the monks and much of the land was sold by the king to the newly wealthy rural middle class.

Dollfuss, Englebert (1892–1934), Austrian chancellor (1932–34) who took office at a time when his country was close to economic collapse. In 1933 he dissolved the National Socialist Party, which had been calling for union with Nazi Germany. In 1934 he crushed the Social Democratic Party and assumed dictatorial powers. He was assassinated by Austrian Nazis.

Domesday Book, two-volume village-by-village account of the population and wealth of England ordered by William the Conqueror in 1085 and completed the following year. The book is a unique record of medieval economic conditions and survives almost intact in the Public Record

---

AD 1125–1150

Islamic world suffered Alfonso VII (1126–57) reclaiming Spain while the Muslim dynasties of Spain and north Africa fought each other. Seljuk Turks took the Frankish kingdom of Edessa (1144); the Second Crusade failed to stop their advance (1147–9).

North Europe saw towns claiming independence from royal authority. Rouen did this (1145).

France saw trouvères in the north developing along similar lines to the earlier southern troubadours.

England experienced civil war over the sucession between Stephen (1135–54) and Matilda.

Religion saw the encouragement of mysticism by Saint Bernard of Clairvaux (1090–1153) in opposition to the prevalent scholastic rationalism, and the collection of canon law (*c.* 1140).

Office, London. The survey was intended to provide an accurate record of land ownership and of the value of each village and manor for the purposes of taxation, although some counties escaped it. The values of estates are compared with their values in the reign of Edward the Confessor; the social status of their inhabitants and number of plough-teams or value of the crops are also included. The survey was carried out by royal agents, each covering a hundred (division of the shire).

Dostoevsky, Fyodor Mikhailovich (1821–81), Russian novelist. After writing *Poor Folk* (1846) and *The Double* (1846) he joined a revolutionary group, was arrested, and sentenced to death in 1849. He was reprieved just before the time set for his execution and sentenced to four years' hard labour. He returned to St Petersburg in 1859 where he wrote *Notes from the Underground* (1864). After *Crime and Punishment* (1866) appeared, he left Russia and travelled in Europe, partly to escape his creditors. While abroad, he wrote *The Idiot* (1868) and *The Possessed* (1871–72). His last major work was *The Brothers Karamazov* (1879–80).

Drake, Sir Francis (*c.* 1540–96), English admiral and navigator, the first Englishman to sail round the world. He achieved fame raiding Spanish shipping and colonies in the Caribbean (1570–72). In 1577–80 he sailed west around the world in his ship the *Golden Hind*. He was knighted by Elizabeth I and made mayor of Plymouth in 1581. He made further raids against Spain (1585–87) and his seamanship and daring contributed greatly to the defeat of the Spanish Armada.

Dreyfus Affair (1894), French scandal in which Alfred Dreyfus, an army officer and a Jew, was charged with treason. Convicted under forged evidence of sending military information to the Germans, Dreyfus was deported for life. Evidence incriminating a Major Esterhazy was suppressed, but under pressure from Dreyfus' supporters, Major Hubert Henri, an accomplice, confessed to the forgeries and committed suicide. After a second trial

---

AD 1150–1175

Islamic world saw Saladin unite Muslim tribes in Egypt and Syria. At his court, Maimonides (1135–1204) the Jewish thinker, wrote on psychosomatic medicine, theology and philosophy. Averrhoës (1126–98) wrote commentaries on Aristotle (1169).

England's Henry II added Aquitaine and Gascony to the Angevin Empire in France. He had Thomas à Becket, the

Archbishop of Canterbury, murdered (1170).

French troubadour music encouraged the growth of lyrical poetry in Provençal dialect.

Japan underwent civil war between local clans (1156–81).

Religion saw the foundation of the Waldenses (1170), rejecting corruption and embracing simplicity; they also elected their own priests.

Dreyfus was pardoned in 1899, but it was not until 1906 that he was fully cleared.

Druses, or Druzes, Middle Eastern religious sect. An offspring of the Isma'ili Muslims, it includes elements of belief from other religions. The Druses originated in the reign of al-Hakim (996– 1021), the sixth Fatimid Caliph of Egypt. Al-Hakim claimed to be divine, and a cult grew up about him of which the Druses are a continuation. They are named after al-Darazi, the first to proclaim the cult publicly. Stressing pure monotheism, they maintained that al-Hakim would live in hiding until his re-appearance for the Last Judgment. They also emphasized, however, the possibilities of direct communication with divinity as a living presence. They were persecuted in Egypt and fought many wars against both Turks and local Christians, and revolted against French rule in Syria in the 1920s. Their number in the mid-1970s was estimated at about 320,000.

Dubček, Alexander (1921–), Czechoslovak Communist Party secretary, leader of liberal reform movement during the late 1960s. He earned enthusiastic national support with his commitment to "the widest possible democratization". The USSR, however, viewed the reform programme as a threat to their economic domination of the country, and on 20–21 Aug. 1968 Warsaw Pact forces occupied Czechoslovakia. A purge of party leaders followed and Dubček was removed from office.

Dunkirk, *See* **World War II.**

Duvalier, François ("Papa Doc") (1907–71), President of Haiti (1957–71), whose prominence as a public health specialist was a springboard to politics. Once elected, Papa Doc declared himself president-for-life and used voodoo worship and the feared Tontons Macoutes (an extra-legal vigilante group) to consolidate his dictatorship. Under his ruthless regime, the longest in Haiti's history, the country's economy severely declined.

Easter Rising, rebellion by Irish nationalists against British rule, launched on 24 April 1916 (Easter Monday). Led by

---

AD 1175–1200

Islamic world saw the Seljuks take Anatolia (1176), Saladin take Jerusalem (1187) until the
A Third Crusade retook the city (1191), and Muhammed of Ghur (1176–1206) take Delhi and Bihar in India.

A **Holy Roman Emperor** Frederick Barbarossa was defeated by the Lombard league when he invaded Italy in 1176.

Japan was inaugurated into the Kamabura period by Yorimoto's defeat of the Taira clan (1185). Zen Buddhism was introduced by the monk Eisai (1191).

A **England** under Henry II saw a reformed common law and the introduction of a jury system.

A **Richard I** did not develop these policies.

Styria introduced blast furnaces of a primitive type which burned charcoal.

Eden, Anthony

Patrick Pearse, Joseph Plunkett and James Connolly, about
1,200 men from para-military groups, chiefly the Irish
Citizen Army, seized the General Post Office and other
buildings in Dublin and proclaimed Ireland a republic. The
British crushed the rising within a week and executed 15 of
the ringleaders. Nationalist sentiment upsurged; renewed
guerrilla fighting led to the establishment of the Irish Free
State in 1921.

Eden, Anthony, *See* **Avon, Lord.**

Edison, Thomas Alva (1847–1931), US inventor. Although
he received little formal education, he made many
important inventions, including the telegraph, the
phonograph (1877), the first commercial electric light
(1879), and many improvements to the electricity
distribution system.

Edward I (1239–1307), King of England (*r.* 1272–1307).
He won influence and fame suppressing the baronial revolt
of 1263–65 against his father, Henry III, and on a crusade
(1270–72). He carried out important administrative,
judicial and financial reforms, and contributed greatly to the
development of Parliament by summoning frequent sittings
and including commoners in them. Edward conquered
Wales and incorporated it into England (1275–84).
Although he conquered Scotland in 1296, the remainder of
his reign was occupied with further Scottish revolts.

Edward II (1284–1327), King of England, (*r.* 1307–27).
Edward's weak rule and reliance on favourites alienated his
barons, who increasingly took control of the government,
especially after the Scots decisively defeated Edward at
Bannockburn in 1314. He regained control in 1322 only to
rely on new favourites. He alienated his queen, Isabella,
who became the mistress of the exiled baron Roger
Mortimer. These two invaded England in 1326, deposed
and murdered Edward, and crowned his son Edward III.

Edward III (1312–77), King of England (*r.* 1327–77). He
became involved in unsuccessful wars with Scotland at the
start of his reign, and his claim to the French throne after

AD 1200–1225

Islamic world lost Constantinople
A to the Fourth Crusade (1204). The
Latin Empire of the East was set
A up (1204–61). The Almohads were
defeated (1212) by Alfonso VIII
(1170–1214). They later declined
in both Africa and Spain.
India embraced Islam with the
establishment of the Delhi
kingdom (1206).
Mongols under Genghis Khan
had invaded China, Persia and

southern Russia by 1225.
Peruvian Tiahuanaco culture was
subdued by the Chimu (*c.* 1200).
A **England** under John lost French
lands (1204). He flagrantly
ignored baronial interests and
had to sign Magna Carta,
subjecting the monarchy to the
rule of law. Oxford University
was founded.
Italy produced Leonardo Fibo-
nacci's algebra textbook (1200).

1328 led to the outbreak of the Hundred Years War in 1337. Edward led several campaigns to France during which he took part in the battle of Crécy and the siege of Calais in 1346–47.

At home, he rallied the nobility behind his wars; he increased the scope of Parliament to improve its administration; and he enacted legislation limiting the powers of the papacy in 1351–53. Towards the end of his reign he fell under the influence of his mistress Alice Perrers; government was increasingly in the hands of Edward's sons John of Gaunt and the Black Prince.
Edward IV (1442–83), King of England (r. 1461–70; 1471–83). He became leader of the Yorkist faction in the Wars of the Roses in 1460 and became king the following year after defeating the Lancastrians at the battle of Mortimer's Cross. He relied on the support of Warwick, who allied with the exiled Henry VI in 1470 and forced Edward himself into exile. Edward returned to defeat Warwick and Henry at Barnet in 1471, and kept his throne thereafter in relative peace. He was responsible for the reorganization of the Crown lands and attempted to build up the power of the Crown independently of the nobility.
Edward VIII (1894–1972), King of Britain and Ireland, subsequently Duke of Windsor. In WWI he served in the army. Soon after becoming king in 1936 he abdicated in order to marry an American divorcee. During WWII he was governor of the Bahamas.
Edward the Black Prince (1330–76), outstanding English military commander, eldest son of Edward III. He distinguished himself in France at Crécy (1346) and led the English to victory at Poitiers (1356). He led several other expeditions in France, but as viceroy in Aquitaine (1362–71), he proved an unsuccessful ruler. In the 1370s he built up a faction against his brother John of Gaunt, but he died before he could ascend the throne.
Edward the Confessor (c. 1002–66), King of England (r. 1042–66). Edward was the half-Norman son of Ethelred

---

AD 1225–1250

Islamic world regained Jerusalem (1244) and was not weakened
A by the Seventh Crusade (1248–50).
India saw a fusion of Muslim and Hindu culture by 1230.
Mongols annexed the Chin Empire (1234), overran eastern
A Europe and set up the Tatar state of the Golden Horde on the lower Volga (1242).
A **Russian** prince Alexander Nevsky
A defeated the Teutonic Knights.

England saw national sentiment develop in opposition to the pro-papal attitudes of Henry III (1216–72).
A **Holy Roman Emperor** Frederick II (1212–50) wrote a learned treatise on falconry.
Religion saw the spread of the Franciscan and Dominican orders (1225–30) and the addition of a nationalistic element to Japanese Buddhism.

Egypt, ancient

II, and spent much of his life in Normandy before succeeding to the throne. He suffered a serious revolt from earl Godwin in 1051–52. He also introduced many Normans to the English court and may have offered the throne to William of Normandy who later certainly claimed the offer had been made. He supervised the rebuilding of Westminster Abbey.

Egypt, ancient, civilization that emerged in the region of the Nile valley in the 4th millenium BC and continued until 30 BC, when the region was annexed to the Roman empire. The region comprised two separate kingdoms: Lower Egypt, in the Nile delta, with its capital at Heliopolis, and Upper Egypt, on the Nile N of the 2nd Cataract, with its capital at Thebes. The two kingdoms were united by Menes in c. 3100 BC.

Eichmann, Adolf (1906–62), Austrian Nazi, head of subsection IV-B-4 of the Reich Central Security Office in WWII. He supervised fulfilment of the Nazi policies of deportation, slave labour, and mass murder in the concentration camps, which led to the death of some 6,000,000 Jews during the war. He escaped to Argentina in 1945, but was abducted by Israelis in 1960, tried and executed in Israel.

Einstein, Albert (1879–1955), German-American physicist, *b.* Germany. He published three important theoretical papers; the first contained a mathematical analysis of Brownian movement: the second concerned the application of quantum theory to photoelectricity, for which he was awarded the Nobel Prize for physics in 1921; and the third contained the first publication of the Special Theory of relativity – a paper that completely revolutionized physics and led, through its equation of mass and energy, to the discovery of the atomic bomb. In 1916 Einstein produced his General Theory of Relativity, but died before completing his work on a unified field theory. Being a Jew, he left Germany when Hitler came to power, spending the rest of his life in the USA, becoming a US citizen in 1940.

AD 1250–1265

Italy saw the introduction of gold currency in Florence and Genoa (1252) and the establishment of successful bankers. **Mongols** opened up a trade route to Europe for Chinese silk (1257) and Kublai Khan set up the Yuan dynasty in China. **Islamic world** employed the first cannons (1250); they were buckets charged with gun-

powder and filled with stones. **French** encyclopedist Vincent of Beauvais (*d.* 1264) was a major scholar. His *Speculum Majus* summarized the scientific and philosophic views of the time. **English** opposition to Henry III led to civil war (1264). De Montfort, the rebel leader, organized Parliament. **A Religion** saw Saint Thomas Aquinas' *Summa Contra Gentiles*.

Eisenhower, Dwight David (1890–1969), 34th US president (1953–61). A professional soldier, he commanded the invasion of N Africa (1942) and the victorious Allied offensive in Europe (1944) to become a national hero. He was later appointed US army chief of staff, then NATO commander. As president he shared Harry S. Truman's global view of US responsibilities, often clashed with Russian leaders and presided over rising affluence at home. He used troops to force school integration in Arkansas and although he was humiliated by the U-2 incident (1960) and bequeathed the abortive Bay of Pigs invasion of Cuba (1961) to his successor, he left office one of the most popular of all presidents.

Elizabeth I (1533–1603), Queen of England (r. 1558–1603). She was the daughter of Henry VIII and Anne Boleyn. During the reigns of Edward VI and Mary she was careful to avoid implication in political disputes and ascended the throne peacefully on Mary's death. She reintroduced Protestantism in 1559, broadly interpreted to ensure wide support. Throughout her reign she adhered to a small group of advisers, such as Burghley and Walsingham; and despite constant demands on all sides that she should marry, she remained single. She led the country in its opposition to the threat of Spanish invasion in 1588. By a close identification between herself and the people, nurtured by regular journeys throughout the country, she won enormous prestige and loyalty that enabled her to withstand growing opposition in Parliament.

Elizabeth II (1926–), Queen of the United Kingdom and head of the Commonwealth of Nations (r. 1952–). She is the daughter of George VI, and married Philip Mountbatten, Duke of Edinburgh, in 1947. She served as a mechanic and lorry driver during WWII. She was crowned in 1953.

Encyclopedists, French philosophers who presented their rationalist, humanitarian and deist views that epitomize enlightenment thought through the Encyclopédie in the

---

AD 1265–1280

A **Mongol** rule inspired Marco Polo to visit China (1271–95).
Hapsburg dynasty was founded (1273) by Rudolf's election as King of Germany.
England's common law was re-
A formed by Edward I by the Statute of Westminster (1275). London's wool trade was also encouraged. Roger Bacon (c. 1214–92), a Franciscan philosopher, championed empiricism.

French king Louis IX(1226–70) died in Tunis on the last Crusade. *Roman de la Rose* (1280), a 22,000-line poem, included an elaborate allegory on the psychology of love.
Europe saw the peak of commercial fishing through the
A Hanseatic League and the invention of the spinning wheel.
Indian thinker Madhava (1197–1276) was influential.

---

latter half of the 18th century. Encountering severe opposition from the religious and political establishment, the main editor, Denis Diderot, and such prominent thinkers as Voltaire, Rousseau and D'Alembert helped to prepare the philosophical basis of the French Revolution.

Engelbrektsson, Engelbrekt (1390– 1436), Swedish national hero. He led a revolt against Eric of Pomerania, King of Denmark, Sweden and Norway. Engelbrektsson was a mine owner, but in 1434 he became leader of a peasants' and miners' uprising against the king. Engelbrektsson seized castles throughout eastern and southern Sweden until the diet of 1435 accepted his demands and made him regent.

Engels, Friedrich (1820–95), German political writer. He was a disciple of Karl Marx, with whom he formulated the theory of dialectical materialism. As agent in England of his father's textile business (1842–44) he wrote *The Condition of the Working Classes in England* (1845). He had met Marx in Europe during the early 1840s, and together they wrote the *Communist Manifesto* (1848). From 1870 to Marx's death in 1883, Engels supported Marx's research financially and continued to help him with his writings. Engel's materialist reorientation of Hegel's dialectics is most evident in his *Socialism, Utopian and Scientific* (1882) and *Anti-Dühring* (1878).

English Civil Wars (1642–46; 1648), conflicts between Charles I and his opposition in Parliament. The wars were originally fought between companies organized by individual commanders on each side, until Jan. 1645 when the Parliamentarian army was reorganized into the centralized New Model Army. The first war comprised a number of separate campaigns marked by many battles and skirmishes. The king was based in Oxford, and drew his main support from the north and west, and the Parliamentarians had their centre in London, and much of their support came from the home counties. The first main battle, at Edgehill in Oct. 1642, was indecisive, and little

---

AD 1280–1295

Mongol invasions of Japan were repelled (1274 & 1281). Western Mongols rejected the authority of the Khan (1295).
Danish Magna Carta (1282) united royal power.
Mamelukes took Tripoli and Acre (1289–91).
China's Yuan dynasty (1264– 1368) restored canals, built roads and encouraged opera.
A **Ottoman Empire** founded (c. 1293)

A by Osman I proclaiming his in-
A dependence of the Seljuk Turks.
England conquered Wales (1284), campaigned unsuccessfully in Scotland and expelled Jews.
Duns Scotus (c. 1265–1308), a Franciscan realist philosopher, rejected predestination and championed Pelagianism.
Catalan literature flourished with the varied works of Raymon Lully (1232–1315).

---

was achieved in the following year. In 1644 a Scottish army entered England on the Parliamentarian side, and Charles's army, led by his nephew Prince Rupert, was beaten at Marston Moor near York in July. The self-denying ordinance of 1645 made Sir Thomas Fairfax head of the Parliamentarian army in the place of the Earl of Essex; its demand that all the Parliamentarian officers should give up their commands was necessary for the reorganization of the army. Charles met a serious defeat at the hands of Oliver Cromwell at Naseby (June 1645), and eventually surrendered to the Scots in May 1646. The second civil war broke out in Feb. 1648 after Charles escaped from custody and concluded an alliance with the Scots to support Presbyterianism. The uprising was crushed by Cromwell at Preston in Aug. 1648.

Enlightenment, The, word used to describe the intellectual temper of Western Europe in the 18th century. It developed from the spirit of rational enquiry of the scientific revolution and from political theorists of the late 17th century Age of Reason such as Locke. Its centre was France, intellectually dominated by Diderot, Voltaire and Rousseau; but it had its representatives in Britain (Hume, Adam Smith), Germany (Kant) and America (Franklin, Jefferson). Enlightenment thought supposed the susceptibility of nature to rational human investigation, opposed obscurantism and superstition, and therefore tended to Deism in religion. Its belief in the perfectibility of man gave it its note of optimism. It found some political expression in enlightened despotism but it also had a profound influence on the attitudes which produced the French and American revolutions.

Enosis, Greek Cypriot demand, originating in 1878, for political union with Greece, which after WWII included a campaign of violence. In the late 1950s the Turks, alarmed at the prospect of enosis, put forward a counter demand for partition of the island, which they achieved by invasion in 1974. The movement found its greatest leader in

---

AD 1295–1310

French king Philip IV (1285–1314) summoned the Estates General (1302) as a result of a conflict over papal authority. He called for national support.
Venice was governed by an oligarchy of merchants who crushed popular revolts (1300 & 1310).
African Empire of Mali flourished.
A **England** saw Edward summon the
A **Model Parliament.**
Italy produced Giotto's (1266–

1337) solid naturalistic frescoes and the madrigal.
Europe saw the introduction of linen clothes, gunpowder, watermarks in papermaking and stanches or navigation weirs.
Religion saw the papacy moved to Avignon under Clement V to escape military anarchy in Italy (1309). French influence over the papacy then made its temporal power decline.

Archbishop Makarios III; it remains a vital political issue.

Enver Pasha (1881–1922), Turkish military and political leader. Involved in the Young Turk revolution (1908), he became virtual dictator through a coup in 1913. He was instrumental in bringing Turkey into WWI as an ally of Germany. When Turkey signed an armistice (1918), Enver fled to Berlin. He was killed leading an anti-Soviet expedition in Bukhara.

Erasmus, Desiderius (c. 1466–1536), Dutch scholar, considered the greatest of the Renaissance humanists. He was ordained as a Catholic priest in 1492. His *Enchiridion militis* (*Manual of the Christian Knight*) (1503) emphasized simple piety as an ideal of Christianity and called for reform of the Church. *Praise of Folly* (1509) is a satire of late medieval society. His works had an early influence on Luther and other Protestant reformers, but he himself sought change from within the Catholic Church and found the course of the Reformation at least as upsetting as the faults of the Catholic Church that he had criticized. In *On Free Will* (1524) he openly clashed with Luther.

Ericsson, Leif (*fl.* 1000), Norse explorer, son of Eric the Red. He is said to have discovered and wintered in Vinland on the North American continent (c. 1000) when, on a voyage from Norway to bring Christianity to Greenland, he was blown off course. The probable site of his landing is in Nova Scotia.

Essad Pasha (c. 1863–1920), Albanian political leader who aided the Young Turks in their agitation of 1908 for reform of the Ottoman Empire. He represented Albania in the new legislature but later turned against the Turks in search of Albanian independence. When this was achieved in 1913, he had a chequered career in the new state, finally being exiled when the Austrians invaded in 1916. He was assassinated in France.

Ethelred II (968–1016), King of England (978–1013; 1014–16), called the Unready (from the Old English "evil *rede* or counsel"). He suffered continually from Danish

---

AD 1310–1325

India saw a Turkish Tughluk dynasty founded (1320).

A **Aztecs** began to colonize central America (1325), having founded the Mexican capital Tenochtitlan.

Mongol prosperity reached its height when Uzbeg (1312–41) converted the Golden Horde to Islam.

A **England's** Edward II was de-
A feated by Robert Bruce at Bannockburn (1314). Scottish in-

dependence was assured.

A **Italy** produced Dante's *Divine Comedy*, begun c. 1307.

China saw the first Christian missions when Khaistan Kuluk (1307–11) was baptized.

Europe's population growth was slowed by bad harvests (1315). Drainage mills were invented.

Religion saw Marsiglio of Padua championing lay power in the Church.

attacks, and in 994 he began to pay off the raiders with money raised by the Danegeld. The Danes returned nevertheless in 997 and a massacre of Danes in 1002 brought retaliation from the Danish King Sweyn who conquered England in 1013. Ethelred was made king again on Sweyn's death, but was succeeded by Sweyn's son Canute.

Etruscans, ancient inhabitants of Etruria, who developed a sophisticated society and empire by 500 BC. Their racial origins are obscure. They first developed a religious confederation of independent city-states based on Volsinii, and attained cultural unity by the 7th century BC. Much of their naturalistic art and skilled metalwork, like their language, derives from traditions quite unlike those of the rest of the Mediterranean world. By 500 BC their influence was spread throughout the major islands of the w Mediterranean and coastal Spain, and they controlled Umbria and central Italy. They came into conflict with the Greeks, and despite early successes, their authority began to wane in the late 5th century. At the same time Celtic invasions halted their northward expansion and the Samnites forced them from Campagna. The Romans adopted many features of Etruscan civilization before they overtook the Etruscan strongholds, such as Veii in 396 BC. Etruscan independence ended entirely in 88 BC during the struggle between Sulla and Marius.

Euclid (*fl. c.* 300 BC), ancient Greek mathematician about whom little is known except that he taught at Alexandria during the reign of Ptolemy. He is remembered for his text books on geometry, especially *The Elements*, which was first printed in 1482 in a Latin translation from the Arabic. His other works include *Data* (on geometry) and *Phaenomena* (on astronomy). Several books have been lost.

Eugène of Savoy (1663–1736), French prince and general in the service of the Holy Roman Empire. He entered Austrian service in 1683 and fought the Turks at Vienna (1683) and Zenta (1697). In the War of the Spanish

---

AD 1325–1340

A Ottoman Empire expanded into Thrace (1326–61) and threatened Constantinople.

Spanish vulnerability from Africa was ended by Alfonso XI's (1312–50) victory at Rio Salado (1340).

A Hanseatic League grew politically powerful (c. 1340).

A England, having seen Edward II deposed and killed by the nobility (1327), went to war with France (1337) to defend the wool trade and to claim

A the French throne for Edward III.

Italy produced the passionate

A sonnets of Petrarch.

Persian poet Hafiz (1320–88) used complex lyrical imagery in ghazal form.

Religion saw the profound and influential philosophy of William of Ockham (c. 1300–c. 47) develop sophisticated logic.

Euripides

Succession (1702–13), his victories over the French
included Blenheim (1704), Oudenarde (1708) and
Malplaquet (1709), all won with the Duke of Marlborough.
His greatest victory was over the Turks at Belgrade in 1718.

Euripides (c. 480–450 BC), Greek playwright. With
Aeschylus and Sophocles, he is considered to be one of the
three great writers of Greek tragic poetry. He was married
and lived in Athens, but otherwise little is known of his
personal life. The plots of his plays are complicated and his
ideas were sometimes controversial and held to be
offensive. His language is simple. His heroes, whether gods
or mortals, are portrayed with sceptical candour. Only 18
(or perhaps 19) of his 92 plays have survived. His first play
was produced in 455. He won the competition for tragedy at
the annual festival of Dionysus only four times, but his
reputation grew after his death. Among the extant plays are
Alcestis (438), *Iphigenia in Tauris* (c.411) and *Phoenician
Women* (c.408).

Faraday, Michael (1791–1867), British physicist and
chemist. He acquired his scientific education through
reading and from lectures given by Sir Humphrey Davy at
the Royal Institution in London, where in 1825 he became
director of the laboratories. He liquefied chlorine,
discovered benzene and two "chlorides" of carbon and
enunciated the laws of electrolysis (Faraday's Laws).
Moving from chemistry to electricity, he discovered
electromagnetic induction, made the first dynamo, built a
primitive electric motor, and studied non-conducting
materials (dielectrics). The unit of capacitance (the farad) is
named after him.

Fawkes, Guy (1570–1606), English conspirator in the
Gunpowder Plot, who was discovered with barrels of
gunpowder in the Houses of Parliament on the night of 4-5
Nov. 1605 for which he was tried and executed in 1606. He
was a Roman Catholic who fought in the Spanish
Netherlands from 1593 to 1604.

February Revolution, *See* **Revolutions of 1848** (France).

AD 1340–1355

Italy, despite economic decline
after the English monarchy repudiated its debts, and unrest
as a result of Cola de Rienzo's
attempts to set up a Roman republic independent of the papacy,
produced great art. The nov-
A ella was developed by Boccaccio
in the *Decameron*, a humanistic
psychological work of great
verve. Italian painting followed the Sienese tradition in
the works of Simone Martini
(c. 1284–1344) and Pietro and
Ambrozio Lorenzetti. Double-
entry book-keeping methods
were also current in Genoa.
Europe saw the Black Death
(bubonic plague) kill more than
a third of its population.
A England in the Hundred Years
War profited from pillage,
but the Black Death caused
widespread labour shortages.

Fenian movement (Irish Republican Brotherhood), Irish nationalist organization set up in 1858 by James Stephens. It sought independence from Britain by revolution, and most of its support came from the urban lower classes. After several abortive plots the leaders were arrested in 1867, and the focus of of Fenian activity moved to the USA, where there were many Irish who had left Ireland during the famine of the 1840s. Under the leadership of John Devoy and John O'Neill, the Irish Fenians invaded Canada in 1866. The movement continued underground until WWI, when it was superseded by Sinn Fein.

Foch, Ferdinand (1851–1929), French marshal. In WWI he was a commander in the battles of the Marne (1914), Ypres (1914, 1915) and the Somme (1916). In 1918 he became commander-in-chief of the allied armies, shaping their victory over the Germans.

Ford, Henry (1863–1947), car manufacturer and industrialist. He developed a petrol-engined car in 1892 and founded Ford motors in 1903. He brought out the economical Model T in 1908. He initiated the conveyor-belt assembly line in 1913 and introduced the eight-hour day with a $5 minimum wage. In 1936 he established the Ford Foundation, now worth more than $3,000 million.

Fox, George, *See* **Quakers**.

Francis Joseph I (1830–1916), Emperor of Austria (1848–1916), King of Hungary (1867–1916). He succeeded his uncle Ferdinand, who abdicated during the Revolutions of 1848, and quickly brought the revolutions under control, defeating the Hungarians under Kossuth and the Italians under Victor Emmanuel II of Savoy (both in 1849). But he lost Lombardy to Savoy in 1859 and in the Austro-Prussian war (1866) lost Venetia to Italy, and Austria's prestige among the German states declined. In 1867 he was forced to grant Hungary co-equal status with Austria in the Dual Monarchy. He died in the midst of WWI two years before the complete collapse of his empire.

Francis of Assisi (*c.* 1182–1226) founder of the itinerant

AD 1355–1370

A France ruthlessly suppressed the Jacquerie, a peasant revolt (1358) against the war taxes levied for the ransom of John II from England.

A China saw the Ming dynasty created after a popular revolt against the Mongols (1368). Pottery flourished.

A Holy Roman Empire was changed from a monarchy to an aristocratic federation by the pope.

England pillaged France, bringing wealth to all classes. Langland's *Piers Plowman* was a Christian allegory in 11 dream visions. *Gawain and the Green Knight* (*c.* 1370) was a more mysterious and beautiful Arthurian verse romance. Religion saw the spread of the Sufi branch of Islam into India, Malaya and Africa south of the Sahara.

order of the Franciscan Friars, Roman Catholic saint (1228). Born Giovanni de Bernardone, the son of a wealthy merchant, in 1205 he renounced his worldly life for one of poverty and prayer. In 1209 he received permission from Pope Innocent III to begin a monastic order. The Franciscans were vowed to humility, poverty and devotion to aiding mankind. In 1212 he established an order for women, the Poor Clares, and in 1221 a lay fraternity. Like his brother friars he travelled widely, going to Egypt, Spain and to the Holy Land in 1219–20. In 1221 he gave up leadership of his order and later retired to his birthplace, Assisi in Italy. In 1224 he received the Stigmata. He became revered for his love of man and nature, and is often depicted preaching to the birds.

Franco, Francisco (1892–1975), Spanish general and dictator of Spain (1939–75). He joined the 1936 military uprising that led to the Spanish Civil War and assumed leadership of the Falange party. By 1939, with the aid of Nazi Germany and Fascist Italy, he had won the war and became Spain's dictator. He kept Spain neutral in WWII, after which he presided over Spain's accelerating economic development and kept rigid control over its politics. He declared Spain a monarchy in 1947 with himself as regent. In 1969 he designated Juan Carlos as heir to the throne, and he became king upon Franco's death.

Franco-Prussian War (1870–71), conflict in which Bismarck, Chancellor of Prussia, engineered a dispute with France on the Spanish succession as a pretext for invading France, in alliance with the other German states, in Aug. 1870. The French were disastrously defeated at Sedan in Sept. and Napoleon III abdicated. According to the terms of the peace of March 1871 Alsace and Lorraine were ceded to the new German Empire.

Franklin, Benjamin (1706–90), US inventor. He published *Poor Richard's Almanac* (1732–57). He invented the Franklin stove and experimented with electricity. He spent a total of 16 years in England before the American War of

---

AD 1370–1385

Ottoman Empire took Adrianople. Mongols were opposed in Russia Aafter the Tatar defeat at Kulikovo (1380).

Florence suffered a popular revolt (1378), but constitutional reform brought power.

A**England** saw the Peasants' Revolt (1381), which failed in its attempt to end villeinage. Parliament claimed the right to impeach royal ministers.

Japan produced the No play, a formal musical drama without scenery, performed by men.

Religion saw rival popes created in Rome and Avignon (1378) and the rise of the A**Lollards**, a group led by John Wycliffe, proposing a propertyless Church and arguing for direct access to God for individuals.

Germany saw the Meistersingers.

Independence, attempting to reconcile Britain and the colonies. He was a delegate to the Second Continental Congress and helped to draft the Declaration of Independence. He was postmaster general in 1775–76. Sent to France (1776–85), he helped to bring that country into the war on the American colonists' side.

Franks, Germanic people who settled in the region of the River Rhine in the 3rd century. Under Clovis they overthrew the remnants of Roman rule in Gaul in the late 5th century and established the Merovingian empire. The empire was later divided into the kingdoms of Austrasia, Neustria and Burgundy, but was reunited by the Carolingians, notably by Charlemagne. The partition of his empire into the East and West Frankish kingdoms is the origin of Germany and France.

Frederick, name of three Holy Roman emperors. Frederick I (*c.* 1123–90) was a Hohenstaufen, Holy Roman Emperor (1155–90), King of Germany (1152–90) and King of Italy, called "Barbarossa" (Red Beard). He restored order in Germany by appeasing the feuding nobles. He spent 30 years trying to restore imperial power in N Italy and was in conflict with successive popes before the Lombard League defeated him in 1176 and he was reconciled with pope Alexander III. Frederick II (1194–1250), also a Hohenstaufen, Holy Roman Emperor (1220–50), King of Germany (1211–20), King of Sicily (1198–1250) and King of Jerusalem (1229–50), continued the power struggle with the popes and maintained his control of Germany. His rule in Sicily showed him to be a brilliant lawmaker, administrator, warrior, multilingual diplomat and patron of the arts and sciences. Frederick III (1415–93), was Holy Roman Emperor from 1452–93 and German king from 1440–93.

Frederick the Great (1712–86), king of Prussia (1740–86). Adopting an aggressive policy towards Austria, he made Prussia a major European power through his involvement in the War of the Austrian Succession (1740–48), the Seven

---

AD 1385–1400

Mongols under Tamerlane conquered Central Asia, defeated the Golden Horde (1391), destroyed Delhi (1398) and delayed the Ottoman advance on Europe. His grandson Ulugh-Beg (1394–1449) developed astronomical tables, used until the Renaissance.
Portugal defeated Castile (1385).
China developed a naval empire.
Japan based her prosperity on piracy (*c.* 1400).
Islamic world influenced by Ibn Khaldun (1322–1406), the greatest social thinker until modern times.
England, Richard II's absolutist reign (1377–99) ended by Henry IV (1399–1413), produced the first native poetry, Chaucer's *Troilus and Criseyde* (*c.* 1385) and *Canterbury Tales* (*c.* 1395).
Europe had weight-driven clocks.

Years War, which he waged between 1756 and 1763 and the War of the Bavarian Succession (1777–79). He acquired Polish Prussia in the first partition of Poland (1772). Frederick carried out many internal reforms but his government was autocratic and over-centralized. A great patron of the arts, he wrote extensively in French and was a good musician.

Frederick William, name of four kings of Prussia. Frederick William I (1688–1740; r. 1713–40) founded its rigidly organized military and administrative systems. He doubled his standing army to 80,000 men, further centralized the government and seized part of Swedish Pomerania. He was succeeded by Frederick the Great.

Frederick William (1620–88), elector of Brandenburg (1640–88), called the Great Elector. At the Peace of Westphalia (1648), which ended the Thirty Years War, he acquired Eastern Pomerania and, by intervention in the war (1655–60) between Poland and Sweden, won recognition of his sovereignty over Prussia, formerly a Polish fief. He also built up the Prussian army, curtailed the privileges of the nobility and fostered trade.

French Revolution, set of events which took place in France between 1789 and 1799. It began in June 1789 when an Estates General met at Versailles during a political crisis caused by attempts to tax the nobility. Representatives of the Bourgeoisie demanded reform and proclaimed themselves a National Assembly; the government could not resist because the people of town and country rose in revolt. In October 1791 the Legislative Assembly was installed. Faced with growing internal and external pressure, it declared war on Austria in April 1792, and was soon in conflict with most other European states. The war hastened political change: in August 1792 Louis XVI was deposed, and the National Convention met in September to proclaim a republic. After a period of rivalry between Jacobins and Girondins (Nov. 1792–June 1793) strong central government was imposed during the reign of terror and

---

AD 1400–1410

Mongols under Tamerlane de-
A feated the Ottoman Turks
at Angora (1402).
China sent naval expeditions
to India and Africa (1403).
The Emperor Ch'eng Jsu (1403–
24) sponsored the publication
of a large encyclopedia (1403).
France saw civil war between
the Burgundians and the
Armagnacs (1404).
Italy saw Venice seize Vincenza,

Padua and Verona to dominate
the north, and Florence gain
access to the sea by buying
Pisa (1405).
England's Henry IV suffered
Parliamentary demands to super-
vise his expenditure, difficult
to resist since Parliament had
aided his seizure of power.
Religion saw the Council of
Pisa (1409) unsuccessfully try
to resolve the Great Schism.

Louis was executed. This was followed by the confused Thermidorean Reaction (July 1794–Oct. 1795). In 1795 rule by the Directory began, and continued until 1799 when the Consulate brought the decade of revolution to an end.

French Revolutionary Wars (1792–1802), series of wars between France and other European states. France declared war on Austria in April 1792, and defeated an invading army at Valmy in September. In 1793 more states, including Britain, entered the war, forming the first Coalition. Although in desperate straits during 1793, the French government managed to keep its forces intact and gradually moved over to the offensive, winning the battle of Fleurus in June 1794, after which the first Coalition broke up. Austria was forced to make peace at Campo Formio (1797), leaving only Britain in the war against France. In 1798, a second Coalition was formed, including Russia, Austria and Britain. Russia withdrew in 1799, however; the Austrians, defeated at Marengo and Hohenlinden, concluded the Treaty of Lunéville in 1801, and the British signed the Treaty of Amiens in 1802.

Freud, Anna (1895–   ), psychoanalyst, youngest of Sigmund Freud's six children, *b.* Austria. She has spent most of her adult life in Britain. She applied psychoanalysis to the development of children, and was an early user of play therapy.

Freud, Sigmund (1856–1939), Austrian physician and founder of psychoanalysis. With Josef Breuer he developed new methods of treating mental disorders – free association and the interpretation of dreams. These methods derived from his positing the existence of the id, ego and super-ego and therefore emphasizing the unconscious and subconscious as agents of human behaviour. He developed theories of the neurosis involving childhood relationships to one's parents and stressed the importance of sexuality in both normal and abnormal behaviour. He thus established psychology and psychiatry on a pseudo-scientific basis. His works include *The Psychopathology of Everyday Life*

AD 1410–1420

A **Ottoman Empire** was reunited
A under Mehmet I and their Balkan power consolidated.
Portuguese prince Henry the Navigator (1394–1460) explored the African coast and encouraged its study at his court.
A **England** under Henry V captured Normandy (1419) after winning
A the Battle of Agincourt. Parliament was united behind his successful appeal for anti-

French patriotism. Miracle plays were performed and John Lydgate wrote the *Troy Book* and *Siege of Thebes* imitating Chaucer.
Dutch fishing used drift nets to improve the herring catch.
Religion saw the end of the papal schism at the Council of Constance (1414–17) and the burning for heresy of the Bo-
A hemian follower of Wycliffe,
A Jan Hus (1415).

Fronde

(1904), *The Ego and the Id* (1923) and *Civilization and its Discontents* (1930).

Fronde (1648–53), series of civil reactions against the growing power of the French monarchy. The Fronde of the Parliament (1648–49) started when Anne of Austria, acting as Regent for Louis XIV, proposed to reduce the salaries of high court officials. The Fronde of the Princes (1650–53) was a rebellion of the nobility. The Great Condé inspired riots and war against the king but was defeated. The crown's victory established absolute monarchy in France.

Fuller, Richard Buckminster (1895–   ), US architect and engineer. Believing that only technology can solve modern world problems, he invented several revolutionary designs. The best known, and widely used, is the geodesic dome.

Gagarin, Yuri Alekseyevich (1934–68), Russian cosmonaut and national hero, the first man to orbit the earth. His historic flight took place on 12 April 1961, in the five-ton spacecraft *Vostok* ("East"). He attained a height of 300km (188 miles), and made his single orbit in 1 hr. 29 min.; he landed safely in the Soviet Union. Gagarin died seven years later in a plane crash.

Galen (*c.* AD 129–*c.* 199), Greek physician. His work and writings provided much of the foundation for the development of medicine. He tried to synthesize all that was known of medical practice and to develop a theoretical framework for an explanation of the body and its disorders. He made numerous anatomical and physiological discoveries, including ones concerning heart valves, secretions of the kidney, respiration and nervous-system function. He was among the first to study physiology by means of detailed and ingenious animal experimentation. Galen's theories influenced medical practice for centuries.

Galileo Galilei (1564–1642), Italian scientist, lecturer at Pisa, later moving to Florence and then to Padua. He deduced the formula for the period of a pendulum from the

---

AD 1420–1430

A **France** was inspired by Joan of Arc to support Charles VII after recognizing Henry V as heir to the throne (1420). Political unrest led to the attack on courtly love *La Belle Dame Sans Merci* (1424) by Alain Chartier.
Ottoman Empire under Murad II attacked Constantinople (1422).
China had Peking as the Ming capital (1421).

England saw noble factions rise due to Henry VI's weakness.
German writer Nicholas of Cusa held that the Earth revolved daily.
Religion saw the Hussites defeated in imperial crusades (1420–33) and the appearance of Thomas a Kempis' (*c.* 1379–1471) *Imitation of Christ* (1425), said to be the most influential work since the Bible.

oscillation of a hanging lamp in Pisa Cathedral. He later studied falling bodies and disproved Aristotle's view that the rate of fall is proportional to the weight. He also discovered the parabolic flight path of projectiles. He developed the telescope, which enabled him to discover sunspots, lunar craters, Jupiter's satellites and the phases of Venus. In *Sidereus Muncius* (1610) he announced his support for the Copernican view of the universe, with the earth moving around the sun. This was declared a heresy by Cardinal Bellarmine. In *Dialogo Sopra i Due Massimi Sistemi del Mondo* (1632) he defied the pope by making his views even more explicit; as a result he was brought before the Inquisition at the age of 69 and forced to recant.

Gallic Wars, *See* **Gauls**.

Gama, Vasco da (*c.* 1469–1524), Portuguese navigator and discoverer of the sea route to India. In 1497 he led the historic expedition to establish a maritime route to the Indies. He reached South Africa, sailed round the Cape and across the Indian Ocean to Calicut, India. The route is still used by ships today, and opened up the resources of Asia to the Western European powers. In 1524, he went to India as viceroy, becoming head of the first European enclave in Asia. He died there only three months later.

Gandhi, Mohandas Karamchand "Mahatma"
(1869–1948), Indian leader. Known as the Mahatma ("Great soul"), he was regarded as the father of India because of his leadership of the country's nationalist movement from 1919 to 1947, when independence was granted. His method, called *Satyagraha* ("truth-keeping") included all forms of non-violent resistance to British rule, such as strikes, refusal to pay taxes, and refusal to respect courts. His experiences in South Africa, where he spent 21 years trying to end oppression of the Indians, and the massacre of a mob in Amritsar by the British in 1919, led him to believe that freedom could not be gained by force. In 1930 he made a dramatic (388km, 241-mile) protest march to the sea inspiring widespread demonstrations. His

AD 1430–1440

Italy saw Alfonso V of Aragon (1416–58) take Naples (1435) and the controlling of Florence A (1434–94) by the Medicis. The sculptor and musician Leon Battiste Alberti (1404–72) published works on household affairs, ethics and architecture. Donatello (1386–1466) executed his classic bronze *David* (1435). England saw the rise of bastard feudalism, reflecting the short-term interests of the rising knightly class.

A Hapsburg control of the Holy Roman Empire became virtually hereditary with Albert II (1438). Flemish painting was revolutionized by van Eyck (d. 1441). Religion saw John VIII of Byzantium (1425–48) inspiring serious opposition by accepting the primacy of the pope in 1439.

Garibaldi, Giuseppe

methods succeeded, and he came to be considered a moral as well as actual leader. He was assassinated by a Hindu Brahmin who objected to his religious tolerance.

Garibaldi, Giuseppe (1807–82), Italian patriot and guerrilla general who helped to bring about Italian unification. He was influenced by Mazzini. After participating in a naval mutiny in 1834 Garibaldi fled to South America, where he fought in the war between Uruguay and Argentina. Returning in 1848, his defence of the Roman Republic against the French (1849) made him a national hero. In 1860 he successfully led his 1,000 strong guerrilla army against Sicily and Naples, uniting Italy under King Victor Emmanuel II of Sardinia-Piedmont. He failed to capture Rome in 1862 and 1867, and was involved in the Franco-Prussian War (1870–71).

Gauls, Celtic tribes who moved w across the River Rhine in *c.* 1500 BC and had occupied the whole of modern France by 400 BC. They invaded Italy, and sacked Rome in 390 but were confined N of the Alps by 250. Gaul was conquered by the Romans in the 50s BC, and during the next century it was fully Romanized. There was a revival of Gallic civilization during the 3rd century AD, until the Frankish invasions of Gaul in the 5th century.

General Strike, nationwide strike in Britain in May 1926, resulting from the failure of miners and mine owners to reach agreement on terms of employment. Economic difficulties led the mine owners to propose reduced wages and longer hours. The Miners' Federation refused to accept them and the owners ordered a lockout for 1 May, which was answered by the TUC's call for a national strike. It lasted from 3–12 May but was a failure. The miners, who remained on strike throughout the summer, returned to work on the employers' terms.

Genghis Khan (1167–1227), conqueror and Emperor of the Mongol Empire stretching across central Asia from the Caspian Sea to the Sea of Japan. Mongol Emperor from 1206, he united the Mongol tribes and demonstrated his

---

AD 1440–1450

A **Ottoman Turks**, after losing Serbia, defeated a Hungarian crusade (1444).

Italy saw many internal wars, resulting in increased diplomatic activity and the encouragement of the arts for rulers' prestige.

A **French** king Charles VII created a standing army free from feudal obligations.

Japan underwent a period of cultural refinement under Ashikaga rule.

German printer Johann Gutenberg (*c.* 1400–68) produced the first Western book from movable metal type, a process invented in Korea.

England's wool industry moved away from the towns, where economic decline made the guilds increasingly restrictive.

military genius and ruthlessness by capturing Peking (1215), annexing Iran and invading Russia as far as Moscow. He established law codes, tolerated ethnic and religious minorities and fostered contact between the East and West. His empire was divided and expanded by his sons and grandsons.

George I (1660–1727), King of Great Britain and Ireland (1714–27) and Elector of Hanover (1698–1727). Great-grandson of James I and a Protestant, he succeeded Queen Anne and was the first Hanoverian monarch. He favoured the Whigs over the Tories, suspecting the latter of Jacobite sympathies. In 1715 and 1719 he put down Jacobite uprisings. In 1717–18 he formed alliances with Holland, France and Austria that guaranteed Hanoverian succession. He was disliked in England because he did not speak English and spent much of his time in Hanover.

George II (1683–1760), King of Great Britain and Ireland (1727–1760) and Elector of Hanover (1727–1760). Robert Walpole (in office 1727–42) dominated the early part of the reign. George brought Britain into the War of the Austrian Succession (1740–48) to protect Hanover, personally commanding victorious forces at Dettingen (1743). He suppressed the last Jacobite rebellion (1745–46). In the last years of his reign, during the Seven Years War (1756–63), William Pitt the Elder was largely responsible for imperial acquisitions in Canada and India.

George III (1738–1820), King of Great Britain and Ireland (1760–1820); Elector and then King of Hanover (1760–1820); grandson of George II. He initially sought an active role in government during the ministries of Bute, Grenville, Pitt the Elder, Grafton and Lord North (1760–82), influencing the disastrous colonial policy that led to American independence (1776) but effectively suppressing the anti-Catholic Gordon Riots (1780). He consolidated Tory power by calling William Pitt the Younger to office (1783–1801, 1804–06), yet defeating Pitt's plans for Catholic emancipation (1801). Suffering

---

AD 1450–1460

Italy saw an alliance of Florence, Naples and Milan (1450) inspired by Medici diplomacy, ensuring a balance of power between states.

Ottoman ruler Mehmet II took Constantinople (1453), ending 1,000 years of Byzantine rule.

England saw the outbreak of the Wars of the Roses (1455), and the widespread enclosure of common land for sheep.

Bohemian religious wars were ended by the conciliatory policies of George Podiebrad.

French verse was revitalized by François Villon (1420–71).

Indian mystic Kabir (1440–1518) tried to merge Hindu and Sufist Muslim ideas, foreshadowing Sikhism.

Religion saw the production of the first printed Bible at Mainz (1456).

increasingly from bouts of insanity after 1765 (probably caused by the disease porphyria) he became nearly blind in 1805 and completely insane in 1811. Under the Regency Act (1811) his son (later George IV) acted as regent (1811–20).

George V (1865–1936), King of Great Britain and Northern Ireland and Emperor of India (1910–36). He had taken up a naval career but became heir apparent after his elder brother, Albert, Duke of Clarence, died in 1892. He married Princess Mary of Teck in 1893. In 1917 he changed the name of the royal house from the German Saxe-Coburg-Gotha to Windsor. He maintained a strong personal interest in the British Empire throughout his reign and was occasionally active in domestic politics.

George VI (1895–1952), King of Great Britain and Northern Ireland (1936–52) and Emperor of India (1936–47). He was proclaimed king when his brother, Edward VIII, abdicated. In 1923 he married Lady Elizabeth Bowes-Lyon. To boost the morale of his people during WWII he and his family toured bombed areas and inspected mines and munitions factories, and he visited several battle fronts. In 1949 he was recognized as the head of the Commonwealth of Nations.

Geronimo (1829–1908), chief of the Chiricahua Apaches. He led his tribe against white settlers in Arizona for more than 10 years. In 1886 he surrendered his tribe to General Miles and they were taken to Fort Sill, Oklahoma. Geronimo became a prosperous farmer and national celebrity.

Gestapo (Geheime Staatspolizei), state secret police of Nazi Germany. Originally founded in 1933 by Goering in Prussia, it soon became a national organization. It was taken over by Himmler in 1934 and became in effect a unit of the SS (Schutzstaffel). It had virtually unlimited powers and, together with SS, ran the Nazi concentration and extermination camps.

Giap, Vo Nguyen (1912–), Vietnamese general and

AD 1460–1470

Venice fought the Turks for control of the Mediterranean.
France was further unified by Louis XI's ending of urban and provincial privileges.
The kingdom of Songhay reached its zenith in the Middle Niger region under Sonni Ali (1464–92).
Japan entered a century of war over the Ashikaga succession.
A England saw Edward IV, a Yorkist, win the throne from the Lancastrian Henry VI.
Italian writer Leon Battista Alberti (1404–72) crystallized
A Renaissance artistic ideas.
Scottish poetry flourished with Robert Henryson's *Testament of Cresseid* and William Dunbar's *Dance of the Seven Deadly Synnis*.
Europe saw the carrack supplant the trading galleys. A military version followed.

politician. A brilliant guerrilla commander, he led the
Vietminh forces that entered Hanoi in 1945 and that later
defeated the French at Dien Bien Phu (1954). He
commanded North Vietnamese forces in the Vietnam War
(1961–75), and organized the 1968 Tet offensive. He is now
deputy premier of a united Vietnam.

Gladstone, William Ewart (1809–98), British politician. He
entered Parliament as a Tory in 1832 and served as
president of the Board of Trade in Sir Robert Peel's cabinet
(1843–45). He then held several cabinet posts including
chancellor of the Exchequer. He joined the Liberal Party in
1859, became its leader in 1867, and was prime minister
four times (1868–74, 1880–85, 1886, 1892–94). A social
reformer and Christian moralist, his achievements included
Disestablishment of the Church of Ireland (1869), the Irish
Land Act (1870), the Elementary Education Act (1870),
introduction of the secret ballot, the reorganization of the
judiciary and a third Reform Act (1884). His attempts to
establish Irish Home Rule led to his government's defeat in
1886 and 1894 and shattered the Liberal Party.

Glorious Revolution (1688–89), the abdication of James II
of England, and his replacement with William III and Mary
II. After James had aroused the hostility of much of the
political nation with his pro-Catholic policies, the birth of a
male heir to the throne prompted seven leading statesmen
to invite the Dutch William, Prince of Orange, to take the
throne. He invaded England with an army in Nov. 1688, and
James's army, led by John Churchill, later Duke of
Marlborough, defected to William's side. James fled to
France in Dec. 1688, and William and Mary were made
joint rulers the following year. The principles of the
revolution, which won its name from the fact that no blood
had been shed in achieving it, were enshrined in the Bill of
Rights and the Declaration of Rights (1689). These upheld
the rule of law and the principle of toleration. The
revolution was the central point of the movement towards
the establishment of a constitutional monarchy.

AD 1470–1480

Muscovite rule subjected Novgo-
rod (1478) under Ivan the Great.
Burgundy reunited with France.
Florence under Lorenzo de Med-
ici was made bankrupt by his
flamboyant foreign policy.
Painter Sandro Botticelli
(1445–1510) produced *Spring*.
Spain saw the unification of
Aragon and Castile with the
marriage of Ferdinand and
Isabella, who set up the

A **Spanish Inquisition** (1478),
prosecuting Jews, Muslims and
Catholic intellectuals.
A **England's** Edward IV ruled par-
simoniously, asserting royal
independence of the nobility
and Parliament. Sir Thomas
Malory (d. 1471) unified Arthurian legend in the epic prose
romance *Morte d'Arthur*, published (1485) by Caxton.
Europe saw the first rifles.

Goebbels, Joseph

Goebbels, Joseph (1897–1945), German Nazi leader. He joined the Nazi party in 1924 and worked with Gregor Strasser, leader of the left wing of the party. Changing loyalty to Hitler in 1926, Goebbels founded the newspaper *Der Angriff* and became the leading Nazi propagandist. He was elected to the Reichstag in 1928, and when the Nazis came to power in 1933 became Minister of Propaganda. As such he ruled much of Germany's cultural life. He was a brilliant orator and a masterful propagandist. He committed suicide with his entire family in April 1945.

Goering, Hermann, *See* **Gestapo**.

Goethe, Johann Wolfgang von (1749–1832), German poet. One of the greatest German writers and thinkers, his range was vast; from simple love poems to profound philosophical poems or scientific theories. In his long life he was a lawyer, botanist, politician and civil servant, physicist, zoologist, painter and theatre manager. Johann Gottfried von Herder taught him to appreciate Shakespeare, and this influenced his *Götz von Berlichingen* (1771–73). His major works include *The Sorrows of Young Werther* (1774), a novel *Italian Journey* (1816–29), the classical drama *Iphigenie auf Tauris* (1787), *Torquato Tasso* (1789), *Egmont* (1787), *Wilhelm Meisters Lehrjahre* (1795–96), *Elective Affinities* (1808) and his most famous work, *Faust* (1808, 1832).

Gogh, Vincent van (1853–90), Dutch painter, a leading Post-Impressionist and a formative influence on modern art, especially on Munch and the Expressionists. During his brief and turbulent life he sold only one painting. He began to paint in 1880 and was virtually self-taught, with only occasional tuition. His early works were often sombre pictures of peasants, eg *The Potato Eaters*. In 1886 he left Holland for Paris, where he met Gauguin, Seurat and other leading painters. His work underwent a transformation: he adopted the light, colourful Impressionist palette and painted flowers, portraits and Parisian views. Two years later he went to Arles, in Provence, where most of the paintings for which he is remembered were painted, in a

---

AD 1480–1490

A **Muscovite** rule of Ivan the Great ended the Tatar threat (1480).
Spain's Church and Inquisition came under royal control after a concordat with the pope.
Portuguese navigators, including Diaz (who rounded the Cape of
A Good Hope in 1478), da Gama
A and Magellan, with the Italian
A Columbus, encouraged the founding of navigation schools in Portugal and Spain. These pro-

duced trained nautical technicians, greatly influencing European scientific standards.
England saw the establishment of royal independence from baronial support with the emergence from the Wars of the
A Roses of Henry VII (1485).
Religion saw the Church condemn witchcraft (1484), and the appearance of the humanistic philosophy of Agricola.

frenzy of prolific activity interspersed with bouts of mental illness and depression which ended in suicide.

Gordon, Charles George "Chinese" (1833–85), English soldier and administrator. In 1860 he took part in the expedition that captured Peking and was personally responsible for the burning of the Summer Palace. From 1877–80 he was governor of the Sudan, where he attempted to suppress the slave trade. In 1884 he returned to the Sudan and attempted to put down the Mahdi Rebellion. He was killed at Khartoum in 1885 after he and his troops had been besieged for 10 months by insurgents.

Gordon Riots (1780), reply of Protestant zealots in London to the Roman Catholic Relief Act of 1778. Lord George Gordon formed a Protestant Association to agitate for the repeal of the Act and on 2 June 1780 led a deputation to Parliament. That night rioting began: houses, churches and breweries were sacked and prisons opened. Order was restored by martial law. About 450 persons were killed or injured. Gordon was acquitted, but 21 rioters were executed.

Goths, Germanic people who settled on the lower Vistula in the 1st century AD. They began to make inroads on the Roman Empire after 238, but were halted by Gallienus and Claudius. The Visigoths (West Goths) occupied Dacia until resettled by the Emperor Theodosius (382). Under Alaric they ravaged Greece and sacked Rome (410). The Ostrogoths (East Goths) ruled in the Ukraine until conquered by the Huns (*c.* 370). They entered Italy under Theodoric the Great (489). The Franks forced them into Spain where they survived until defeated by the Moors in 711.

Grant, Ulysses Simpson (1822–85), US soldier and politician. He served in the Mexican War (1846–48) and at the start of the Civil War was colonel of the 21st Illinois Volunteers. After capturing Fort Henry and Fort Donelson in 1862, he was made a major-general. In 1864, as a lieutenant-general, he was given command of the Union

AD 1490–1500

Spain captured Grenada from the Moors and expelled 200,000 Jews (1492). Spanish support enabled
A Columbus to discover Cuba (1492).
A Italy, having expelled Charles VIII of France (1495), saw Savonarola establish democratic rule in Florence. Leo-
A nardo da Vinci and Michelangelo emerged as the two giants of
A the Italian Renaissance: the former producing scientific drawings, conceiving helicopters and canal cutters, and painting many masterpieces; and the latter the St Peter's *Pieta*.
A England's Henry VII ensured military control and asserted royal authority in the new Star Chamber court.
Germany produced a music printing process (1498) and Sebastian Brant's satire *Ship of Fools* (1494).

forces. In 1866 he was made a general. Chosen as the Republican candidate for president in 1868, he was elected and served two terms in the White House (1869–77).

Great Trek (1835–40), migration of Boer farmers from the Cape Colony in South Africa northwards into the interior. They were called *voortrekkers*, men of Dutch origin who wished to escape from the British government's attempt to preserve native lands for the Bantu people and to protect the rights of non-European people on the eastern frontier. About 12,000–14,000 farmers and about the same number of slaves and servants made the journey. They founded Natal, the Transvaal and the Orange Free State.

Greece, ancient, civilization of the NE Mediterranean that arose in the 3rd millennium BC in Crete, and reached its greatest achievements on the Greek mainland 500–300 BC. Although politically divided into diverse city-states, Greece and its colonies maintained a universal culture that formed the basis of Roman and European art, philosophy and science until modern times.

Gregory, name of 16 popes. Gregory I (*r.* 590–604) reformed the administration of the papal patrimony, insisted that the Apostolic see was the head of all churches, codified church music and initiated the conversion of Anglo-Saxons. He was canonized and became known as Gregory the Great. Gregory VII (family name Hildebrand; *r.* 1073–85) twice excommunicated the Roman Emperor Henry IV over a conflict on lay investiture. He considered a crusade against the Seljuk Turks and increased the papacy's temporal power.

Grivas, George (1898–1974), Greek Cypriot general who led the Greeks in Cyprus in rebellion against Britain from 1955 until 1959. He formed the guerrilla force Eoka (National Organization for the Cyprus Struggle) to fight for Enosis (union with Greece) but clashed with Archbishop Makarios and retired. He returned in 1964 to head Greek forces in Cyprus, was forced to leave again in 1967, but re-entered the country secretly in 1971.

AD 1500–1510

Italy, scene of the conflict A between the Hapsburgs and the Valois, declined economically but produced commedia dell'-arte from earlier peasant traditions. These boisterous farces influenced later dramatists like Molière. The Renaissance reached its height A with Leonardo's *Mona Lisa* A (1503–6) and Michelangelo's *David* (1504). Paduan medical schools practised systematic human dissection.

Portugal claimed Brazil and traded with India (1500).

Spain introduced African slaves into the West Indies (1501).

A **England** saw Henry VII's thrift make him free of Parliament.

A **Swiss** scholar Paracelsus significantly advanced chemistry.

A **Religion** saw Erasmus' *In Praise of Folly,* satirizing corruption.

Grotius, or De Groot, Hugo (1583–1645), Dutch jurist and statesman. He held the office of chief magistrate of Rotterdam from 1613 until 1618 when he was ousted by his political opponents. He was sentenced to life imprisonment but escaped in 1621 and lived in Paris. His most famous work was *De Jure Belli ac Pacis* (On the Law of War and Peace, 1625), and he is considered the founder of international law.

Guevara, Ernesto "Che" (1928–67), revolutionary leader and political theorist; a key figure in Castro's Cuba. A physician born in Argentina, Guevara became associated with Castro in Mexico, and returned with him to Cuba in 1956 to conduct guerrilla activities against the regime of Fulgenico Batista. When Castro came to power, Guevara was placed in charge of economic planning. He disappeared from public view in 1965. Two years later he was captured and killed while trying to establish a Communist guerrilla base in Bolivia.

Gustavus, name of six Swedish kings. Gustavus II (Gustavus Adolphus) (*r.* 1611–32), the "Lion of the North", spearheaded the Protestant cause in the Thirty Years War. Invading Germany in 1630, he won a series of battles against the imperial commanders Tilly and Wallenstein but was killed at Lutzen. His reign saw economic and administrative reform within Sweden, largely due to his chancellor, Oxenstjerna.

Hadrian, Publius Aelius (AD 76–138), Roman emperor (117–138). He crushed a Jewish revolt and destroyed the Temple of Jerusalem in 135 but promoted major building programmes, including the Pantheon in Rome, his villa at Tivoli and Hadrian's Wall in Britain. He enlarged and reformed the civil service.

Haile Selassie (1892–1975), Emperor of Ethiopia (1930–74), original name Lij Tafari Makonnen. When Italy invaded Ethiopia in 1935, he was forced into exile (1936), despite his appeal to the League of Nations for help. He drove out the Italians with British aid in 1941. Subsequently

---

AD 1510–1520

A **Hapsburg Empire** was created by
A Charles V inheriting the Spanish throne (1516) and being proclaimed Holy Roman Emperor (1519).
A **Spain's** Hernan Cortes conquered the Aztecs.
Portugal controlled the East Indian spice trade (*c.* 1520).
Russia took Smolensk (1514).
A **England's** Henry VIII engaged in costly dynastic French wars,

debasing the coinage to do so.
A Thomas More wrote *Utopia*.
Italy produced Michelangelo's Sistine Chapel frescoes and
A Raphael's Stanza frescoes. Machiavelli wrote *The Prince* (1513).
A **Religion** saw Martin Luther affix his *95 Theses* to a church door in Wittenberg (1517) and the foundation of Sikhism (*c.* 1519) by Nanak (1469–1533), combining Islam and Hinduism.

---

he became a leader among independent African nations, helping to found the Organisation of African Unity (OAU) in 1963. Unrest at lack of reforms led to his being deposed by a military coup in 1974.

Han dynasty (206 BC – AD 220), Chinese dynasty. It was founded by Liu Pang and was ruled by his family for more than four centuries. It is considered by the Chinese to be one of their greatest periods of rule. Han rulers laid the administrative and ideological basis for the subsequent greatness of the Chinese Empire. Under the Han the Confucian state cult was formalized through the examination system; art and literary traditions were established and imperial expansion began to spread Chinese influence throughout E Asia.

Hannibal (247–183 BC), Carthaginian general, one of the foremost military commanders in history. Commander of the Carthaginian forces in Spain (221 BC), he conquered much of the country. With about 40,000 select troops and elephants he crossed the Alps into Italy in 218 and won brilliant victories at Ticino and Trebia. At Cannae in 216 he wiped out at least 48,000 Romans in his greatest victory but, deprived of support from Carthage, was gradually forced south. In 203 he was ordered to return to Carthage; after 16 years of battle in Roman territory he was finally defeated at Zama in N Africa by Scipio Africanus. Political enemies forced him to flee to Syria, then probably to Bithynia where he poisoned himself rather than fall into Roman hands.

Hanseatic League, commercial union of German, Dutch and Flemish towns established in the 13th century, which grew from smaller local unions, or Hanse. The League functioned as protector of the merchants of its member towns by controlling the trade routes from the Baltic region to the Atlantic seaboard. The League began to decline in the late 15th century with the opening up of the New World and aggressive trading by the British and Dutch. The League's diet met for the last time in 1669.

Hapsburg (Hapsburg), name of a royal Austrian

AD 1520–1530

A **Mogul Empire** was founded in India by Babur (1526).

A **Italy** saw the Medici driven from Florence (1527). Court life was portrayed by Castiglione's *Libro del Cortegiano*. Titian produced the altarpiece at Pesaro.

A **England's** Henry VIII failed to gain papal or imperial support for his plan to divorce Catherine of Aragon. Cast iron was produced and sold in large quantities; coal was a major fuel.

Germany produced Durer's (1471–1528) *Four Apostles* (1526).

A **Religion** saw Luther's excommunication (1520) and his preaching

A start the Reformation. He translated the Bible into the vernacular (c. 1525). Frederick III of Saxony's support and peasant revolts in Swabia followed in consequence.

family, one of the principal houses of Europe from the 15th century onwards. From Werner, the first count of Hapsburg in the 11th century, there was a direct male line until 1740, when the Pragmatic Sanction allowed a daughter, Maria Theresa, to succeed. Frederick III, the Hapsburg King of Germany, was crowned Holy Roman Emperor in 1452, and the title remained in the family until the empire was dissolved in 1806. His descendants gained, by marriage and war, vast territories, including the Netherlands, Spain, Naples, Sicily and Sardinia. But the empire's size proved too unwieldy and the family split into two branches in 1558: the Spanish and the Austrian Hapsburgs. The Spanish line died out in 1700; the last ruling Austrian Hapsburg, Charles I, abdicated in 1918.

Hardie, James Keir (1856–1915), British socialist and a founder of the Labour Party. He organized the Ayrshire miners' union, founded the newspaper *Labour Leader* and was chairman of the Independent Labour Party (1893–1900; 1913–14). He was the first Labour Member of Parliament and for three years (1892–95) was the sole representative of that party in parliament.

Hastings, Battle of (1066), battle fought near Hastings, Sussex, between King Harold of England and a claimant to his throne, William, Duke of Normandy (William I "The Conqueror"). Harold's defeat and death in battle led to the establishment of the Norman dynasty by William.

Haydn, Franz Joseph (1732–1809). Austrian composer. One of the greatest composers of the Classical period, he served from 1761 to 1790 as musical director for the wealthy Esterházy family and composed many of his best works during these years. Later he twice visited England, composing the last 12 of his 104 symphonies for concerts there. Haydn brought the sonata form to masterful fruition in these symphonies, which included the *Military*, the *Clock* and the *London*. One of the most prolific of all composers, he also wrote many songs, string quartets, masses, chamber works, concertos and choral works, the most famous of

---

AD 1530–1540

A Ottoman power reached its peak
A under Suleiman the Magnificent.
Mogul Emperor Humayan was expelled from Afghanistan.
A **Spain's** Pizarro took Peru.
Italy produced Ariosto's *Orlando Furiosio* (1532), a romantic epic, and Telesio's system of physics, arguing that heat and cold were the motive powers of the universe.
England saw Hans Holbein settle
and paint court portraits.
Religion was revolutionized by the rapid spread of Protest-
A antism in Europe. Henry VIII dissolved England's monasteries, remarried in defiance of the Pope (1533) and assumed full authority over the English Church. Anabaptist and Memonite sects sprang up. Ignatius of Loyola (1491–1556) formed the
A Catholic Jesuit order (1540).

Heath, Edward Richard George

the latter being the oratorios *The Creation* (1798) and *The Seasons* (1801). He influenced and was in turn influenced by his friend Mozart.

Heath, Edward Richard George (1916–   ), British politician. He entered parliament as a Conservative in 1950 and subsequently held several offices, including government chief whip (1955–59), minister of labour in 1965 and prime minister on winning the general election of 1970. Heath successfully concluded negotiations for Britain's entry into the EEC in 1973 but was defeated by Labour under Harold Wilson in 1974. Margaret Thatcher succeeded him as party leader in 1975.

Hegel, Georg Wilhelm Friedrich (1770–1831), German philosopher. He was professor of philosophy at Heidelberg, and subsequently at Berlin, where he became famous for a romantic, metaphysical system that traced the self-realization of spirit by so-called dialectical "movements" towards perfection. First in the *Phenomenology of Mind* (1807) and then in *Science of Logic* (1812–16) Hegel claimed to express the course of universal reason with his Metaphysical Dynamism.

Henry II (1133–89), King of England, son of Geoffrey Plantagenet and Matilda, daughter of Henry I. He inherited the Angevin lands, obtained Aquitaine by marrying Eleanor in 1152, and succeeded to the throne in 1154. He reformed the judicial, monetary and military systems, and set up a system of peripatetic royal justices. His attempt in 1164 to bring church courts under secular control through the Constitutions of Clarendon failed. By the Treaty of Montmirail (1169) Henry secured France's sanction for his sons' succession to his territories and Prince Henry was crowned heir in 1170. After the murder of Thomas à Becket in 1170, Henry's life was beset by trouble with the Church, revolts in Ireland and Normandy, and a continual struggle with his own sons.

Henry V (1387–1422), King of England, eldest son of Henry IV. After fighting on his father's behalf at

---

AD 1540–1550

France absorbed Brittany (1547). La Pleiade, including the poet Pierre de Ronsard, established the Alexandrine metre and dealt with classical themes. Art copied Italian models at the palace of Fontainebleau. Biologists Gesner, Belon and Rondelet published major works.

A **Polish** astronomer Copernicus founded heliocentric cosmology
Italian Mannerist painters such

as Parmigianino searched for the unusual and untried. The lute was popular.

A **Religion** saw Calvin establish a Puritan theocracy at Geneva (1541). He believed in predesti-

A nation. The Counter-Reformation was instituted by the Council of Trent's decrees (1545),

A inspiring Charles V's war with

A the Protestant princes. Jesuits evangelized Japan.

Shrewsbury in 1403, in Wales and in Scotland, he succeeded him in 1413 and immediately demanded the restoration of territories formerly ceded to France. Invading France, he captured Harfleur and won the decisive victory at Agincourt in 1415. Further military and diplomatic success led to his adoption as the French king's heir by the Treaty of Troyes in 1420.

Henry VII (1457–1509), King of England, founder of the Tudor dynasty. Having come to the throne by killing Richard III at Bosworth in 1485, Henry united the warring factions by marrying the Yorkist heiress, Elizabeth. His financial acumen restored England's fortunes after the devastation of civil war and gave the monarchy considerable independence of action. He concluded various advantageous foreign treaties, such as the Treaty of Etaples in 1492, and took effective action against pretenders to his throne, thereby securing the future of his dynasty.

Henry VIII (1491–1547), King of England who succeeded his father, Henry VII, in 1509. In 1513 victories over the French (at Tomnai) and the Scots (at Flodden) re-established England as a European power, a position maintained by the diplomacy of Cardinal Wolsey. He, however, was dismissed in 1529 after Henry's decision to divorce Catherine of Aragon (who had not borne a male heir) in favour of Anne Boleyn led to conflict and his eventual excommunication. With the help of Thomas Cranmer, Archbishop of Canterbury from 1533, Henry compelled the clergy to acknowledge him as supreme head of the Church, and executed those, such as Sir Thomas More, who protested. Under Thomas Cromwell's direction he initiated other anti-ecclesiastical legislation in the 1530s, including transferring church revenues to the Crown, and appropriating monastic property. From his six marriages (Catherine of Aragon, Anne Boleyn, Jane Seymour, Anne of Cleves, Catherine Howard and Catherine Parr), he had one son and two daughters.

Henry, French *Henri*, name of four kings of France.

AD 1550–1560

Spain experienced inflation because of the influx of American silver.

France produced the comic prose work *Gargantua and Pantagruel* (1552) by François Rabelais.

German doctor Georg Bauer (Agricola) published *De Re Metallica* (1556), still the major source on the state of technology in the Middle Ages.

Religion saw the Peace of Augsburg (1555) allow German princes to decide the religion of their subjects. Philip II of Spain took over the Catholic offensive, although Mary I briefly restored Catholicism to England, burning heretics, until Elizabeth I's accession. Scotland adopted Protestantism (1560) due to the unifying work of the Calvinist John Knox in the Scottish Parliament.

Heraclius

Henry IV, or Henry or Navarre (1553–1610), King of Navarre (as Henry III, 1572–1610) was the first Bourbon King of France (1589–1610). Raised as a Huguenot, he nevertheless married Margaret of Valois, the Roman Catholic sister of the French king Charles IX in 1572. He escaped the Massacre of Saint Bartholomew's Day (1572) by agreeing to renounce his Protestantism, and was kept as a virtual prisoner at the French court until he escaped in 1576, to join the Huguenot forces. He became heir to the French throne in 1584 on the death of the younger brother of Henry III. Henry III was persuaded by Henry de Guise, leader of the Catholic League, to deny Henry of Navarre the succession. The War of the Three Henrys resulted. Henry of Navarre defeated the king's forces in 1587 and was reconciled with him after the Catholic League expelled the king from Paris (1588). Henry III was assassinated in 1589, but Henry of Navarre did not gain Paris until after he renounced his Protestantism in 1594. During his reign he reconciled the Huguenots by the Edict of Nantes and laid the foundations of French Absolutism, before his assassination by a religious fanatic.

Heraclius (*c.* 575–641), Byzantine emperor (*r.* 610–41). One of Byzantium's greatest rulers, he came to power at a time of economic, political and military crisis. Byzantium's enemies had overrun vast territories, but, under Heraclius, far-reaching reforms in the army and administration led to an improvement in the internal situation and to Byzantium's defeat of the Persians (622–628).

Hereward the Wake (*fl.* 11th century), leader of Anglo-Saxon resistance to the Norman Conquest of William I. With the aid of a Danish fleet he sacked Peterborough in 1070 and consolidated his forces on the Isle of Ely. William captured Ely in 1071.

Herod Antipas (21 BC–AD 39), tetrarch of Galilee and Petraea (4 BC–AD 39), son of Herod the Great. He had John the Baptist beheaded at the instigation of his wife Herodias and his step-daughter Salome. He refused to intervene in

---

AD 1560–1570

France was torn by religious wars between Catholics and Huguenots. Vieta pioneered letter symbols for algebra.

A **Netherlands** began a war of independence from Spain (1568). **Mogul Empire** under Akbar (1556–1605) expanded and became tolerant and cosmopolitan. **Flemish** painting produced the great landscapes and satire of Bruegel the Elder. Mercator's

map appeared (1568). **England** produced the poetry of Thomas Wyatt (1503–42). **Religion** saw England's adoption of the 39 Articles (1563), combining Protestant doctrine with Catholic church organization. Dissenting groups included Puritans, Separatists, Presbyterians and Brownists. All but Catholics and Brownists were tolerated.

---

the trial of Christ, leaving His fate to the Roman procurator Pontius Pilate. The Emperor Caligula banished him to Gaul in AD 39.

Herzl, Theodor (1860–1904), Jewish leader and the founder of political Zionism, *b*. Austria-Hungary. A lawyer and a journalist, in 1897 he became president of the World Zionist Organization, which worked throughout Europe to establish a Jewish national home in Palestine. Herzl wrote of himself as the founder of the Jewish state, and in 1949 his body was reburied in Israel.

Himmler, Heinrich, *See* **Gestapo**.

Hindenburg, Paul Ludwig Hans von Beneckendorf und von (1847–1934), German general and president (1925–34). Commanding the army on the eastern front in WWI, he defeated the Russians in the Battle of Tannenberg (Aug. 1914). In 1916 he became supreme commander and, with his chief-of-staff, Erich Ludendorff, directed the entire war effort (civilian as well as military) until the end of the war. Elected president in 1925, he held office during the collapse of the Weimar Republic.

Hippocrates (*c*. 460–377 BC), Greek physician, often called "the father of medicine". Although little is known about him, and the writings known as the *Hippocratic Collection* probably represent the works of several people, he exerted a tremendous influence. He freed medicine from superstition, emphasizing clinical observation and providing guidelines for surgery and for the treatment of fevers. Most important, he is credited with providing the Hippocratic Oath, a code of professional conduct still followed by doctors today.

Hirohito (1901–   ), emperor of Japan (1926–   ). His visit to Europe in 1921 made him the first Japanese crowned prince to travel abroad. Although he exercised little political power, he persuaded the Japanese government to surrender to the Allies in 1945, announcing that surrender himself on the radio. Under the constitution drawn-up by the occupation forces he lost almost all his remaining power.

Hitler, Adolf (1889–1945), German dictator, *b*. Austria.

AD 1570–1580

A Ottoman fleet was defeated by a European alliance at Lepanto.
Portugal settled Angola (1574).
France saw Jean Bodin's influential *Six Books of the Commonwealth* (1576), analysing sovereignty. Michel de Montaigne's *Essays* appeared in 1580.
England produced Lyly's *Euphues*, a prose work on manners. Sir Thomas Gresham established a scientific institute which

later housed the Royal Society.
A Sir Francis Drake circumnavigated the world. Trade was upset by the Dutch wars.
China saw the publication of the erotic realistic prose work *The Golden Lotus* (*c*. 1575) and Li Shih-Chen's *Great Pharmacopoeia* (1578).
Italy produced Tarquato Tasso's pastoral romance *Aminta* (1573).

Hittites

He served in the ranks of the German army during WWI and was decorated for bravery. After the war he returned to Munich and in 1921 became the leader of the small National Socialist Workers' (or Nazi) Party. In 1923 a Nazi Putsch failed to overthrow the Bavarian government and Hitler was imprisoned. While serving his sentence he set out his extreme racist and nationalist views in *Mein Kampf*. After his release, Hitler worked to revive the Nazi Party and finally, partly in consequence of economic depression and ineffectual democratic government, became Chancellor in a coalition on 30 Jan. 1933. Within a month the Reichstag Fire gave him the excuse to establish a one-party state, and the following year he launched a purge in which all possible rivals were liquidated. In the following years Hitler rearmed Germany and occupied large areas of central Europe. Germany's attack on Poland (Sept. 1939) precipitated WWII, a conflict of global proportions, during which the Jewish people were systematically exterminated by the Germans in all parts of occupied Europe. Hostilities ceased in 1945 with Germany's total defeat and Hitler's suicide (30 April).

Hittites, ancient people who built a powerful empire in Asia Minor and N Syria (*c.* 2000–*c.* 1200 BC). Primarily of Indo-European stock, they invaded Babylonia (*c.* 1590 BC), seized Cappadocia and conquered Syria and Palestine. Rameses II of Egypt checked them near Kadesh on the River Orontes (*c.* 1284), which led to a treaty. Boğazköy and Carchemish were their great cities. After 1260 BC the Thracians, Phrygians and Assyrians invaded the Hittite lands, and their loose empire broke up. The Hittites moved southwards, but their culture survived in city states established by refugees in N Syria. By the 8th century BC these last remnants of the Hittites had been entirely absorbed into the Assyrian empire.

Hobbes, Thomas (1588–1679), English philosopher. In *De Corpore* (Concerning the Body), *De Homine* (Concerning Man) and *De Cive* (Concerning the Citizen) he presented

---

AD 1580–1590

England, having assisted the Revolt of the Netherlands (1585) and executed Mary Queen of Scots (1587), defeated the Spanish Armada (1588). Drama flourished with Marlowe's *Dr Faustus* (*c.* 1588) and Kyd's *Spanish Tragedy* (*c.* 1589). Sir Philip Sydney produced *Arcadia*. **Spain** united with Portugal on Philip I's death (1580). **European** art continued its Mannerist phase with the work of El Greco, the German Spranger and the second French Fontainebleau school. The Dutchman Simon Stevin introduced decimals (1585) and the Danish astronomer Brahe and his assistant Johannes Kepler extended Copernican theory. **Religion** saw Akbar, the Mogul Emperor, try to establish Din Illahl as a universal creed.

his view that matter and its motion comprise the only valid subject matter of philosophy. His greatest work, *Leviathan* (1651), argued that man is not naturally a social being but most obey moral rules in order to maintain civilized society.

Ho Chi Minh (1890–1969), Vietnamese political figure, *b.* Nguyen That Thanh. In 1911 he left Vietnam and lived successively in the USA, Britain and France. In 1920 he joined the French Communist Party. He returned to Vietnam and presided over the founding of the Vietnamese Communist party in 1930 but, threatened with arrest, fled to Moscow and later China. In 1941 he returned to Vietnam and founded the Viet Minh to fight the Japanese. With the Japanese driven out, he declared Vietnam an independent nation (1945) and was himself appointed president. The French returned and contested Ho's authority until their defeat in 1954. The 1954 Geneva Conference recognized Ho as president of the Democatic Republic of Vietnam (North Vietnam). When the government of the South, backed by the USA, refused to hold reunification elections, Ho helped the National Liberation Front (Viet Cong) in its attempt to gain control of the South. He did not live to see the unification of an independent Vietnam at the end of the Vietnam War.

Holy Roman Empire, European empire founded in 962, when the German king, Otto I, was crowned in Rome, and surviving until 1806. Some historians date it from Charlemagne's coronation in 800. The emperor claimed to be the temporal sovereign of Christendom, ruling in co-operation with the spiritual sovereign, the pope. However, the empire never encompassed all of western Christendom and its relations with the papacy were stormy. The imperial authority was based on the German monarchy. Once elected by the German princes, the German king sought papal election as emperor. He did not always receive it; and from Maximilian I (*r.* 1493–1519) the title Emperor was assumed without papal coronation. By that time,

---

AD 1590–1600

France ended the wars of religion by Henry IV granting Huguenots and Catholics equal rights by the Edict of Nantes.
Japan invaded Korea (1593), but was expelled by the Chinese.
Spanish power slowly declined.
England suffered economic depression; Elizabeth I became increasingly dependent on Parliament to pay for her

Spanish wars. William Shakespeare's plays showed consummate mastery of the English language and profound psychological insight.
Italy's baroque painters Carracci and Caravaggio radically opposed each other in artistic theory. Galileo championed the Copernican system (1597).
Religion saw the rise of tolerant Arminianism.

---

although the office remained elective in theory, the empire had become hereditary in the house of Hapsburg, which held the office from 1438. Earlier dynasties included the Salians and Hohenstaufens, under whom (11th–13th century) the empire was at the height of its power. Under the Hapsburgs it became an increasingly nominal entity, its rulers concentrating on their dynastic interests in Austria while the other German princes pursued their own ends. Pressure from Napoleon caused Francis II to resign the imperial title in 1806.

Homer (c. 8th century BC), Greek epic poet. He is traditionally considered to be the author of the great epics of the Trojan Wars, the *Iliad* and the *Odyssey*. Traditionally, too, he is represented as blind, but this may have been because of the false attribution to him of the *Hymn to Apollo*, in which he portrays himself as blind. No definite facts are known about Homer and even his very existence has been the cause of controversy among scholars, many considering that his epic poems are the work of many poets in collaboration with each other. However, the works attributed to him are the beginning of Greek, and therefore European, literature.

Hoover, John Edgar (1895–1972), US director of the FBI (Federal Bureau of Investigation) (1924–72). He reorganized the bureau, compiling a vast file of fingerprints and building a crime laboratory and training academy. During the 1930s he fought organized crime; after WWII he concentrated on what he saw as the threat of Communist subversion in the USA.

Hoxha, Enver (1908–   ), Albanian Communist leader. He came to prominence in WWII, when he was active in the National Liberation Movement, and in 1941 he established the Albanian Communist Party. In 1944 he became Premier. Following the USSR rift with Communist China in 1960, Hoxha joined Peking in its ideological struggle with Moscow.

Huguenots, French Protestants of the 16th–18th centuries.

AD 1600–1606

Japan's power struggles ended with the Tokugawa (Edo) period. Education advanced.
Sweden's Charles IX (1604–11), a Protestant, succeeded to the throne after his Catholic predecessor's deposition.
Russia underwent a period of anarchy resulting from boyar rivalry. Boris Godunov was opposed by a pretender, Dmitry.
AEngland saw Guy Fawkes' Gun-

Apowder Plot (1605) and James I ending war with Spain (1604). William Gilbert produced a study of electricity (1600).
Altaly's Galileo, the father of experimental science, studied falling bodies.
Spain produced Cervantes' *Don Quixote*, an influential work.
Religion saw the rise of Polish Unitarianism, which denied the Holy Trinity.

The name probably comes originally from the German Eidgenossen ("confederates"), but is possibly also influenced by the name of the gate, Roi-Hugen, where the Protestants of Tours assembled at night. In 1559, in the face of persecution, a national Protestant synod adopted a confession of faith and an ecclesiastical structure, influenced by Calvin more than by Luther. During the Wars of Religion the Huguenots continued to be persecuted. The Protestant Henry IV came to the throne in 1589, and, despite adopting the Roman faith in 1593, he promulgated the Edict of Nantes (1598). This recognized Catholicism as the official religion, but gave the Huguenots certain rights. It was revoked by Louis XIV in 1685 and thousands of Huguenots fled France. In 1789 their civil rights were restored and by the Code Napoléon (1804) they were guaranteed religious equality.

Hundred Years War, war between France and England pursued sporadically between the French seizure of English-held Guyenne in 1337 and the English defeat at Castillon in 1453. The refusal of Edward III of England to do homage for his French possessions began the war. Early English successes at Crécy and Calais and the capture of the French king, John II, in 1356 brought England territorial gains in the Peace of Brétigny (1360). The French gradually won their lands back and although Henry V won the Battle of Agincourt, subsequent English failures at the siege of Orléans (1428–29) and the Battle of Patay (1429) ensured their ultimate expulsion from most of France.

Huns, nomadic Mongol people, probably of Turkish, Tataric or Ugrian stock who spread from the Caspian steppes (present-day USSR) to wage a series of wars on the Roman Empire. Lacking the cultural development attributed to more sedentary peoples, they were very skilled in the arts of war, particularly military horsemanship. By the first half of the 4th century they had conquered the Ostrogoths and the Visigoths, reaching west as far as the River Danube. By about 432 the Huns were collecting an

---

AD 1606–1612

Japan introduced Confucianism (1608) and traded with the Dutch (1609).
France's religious stability
A was threatened by Henry IV's murder (1610).
A **England's** James I encouraged colonial development in North America and tried to get a regular financial grant from Parliament. Drama flourished with Jonson's *Volpone* and *The Al-*

chemist, Webster's *White Devil* and the works of Middleton, Dekker, Beaumont and Fletcher.
A **Mogul** art and architecture reached its zenith with Jahangir's reign (1605–27).
Italy produced Europe's earliest opera, *La Favola d'Orfeo* (1607), by Monteverdi.
Dutch spectacle-maker Hans Lippershey invented the telescope (1608).

annual tribute from Rome. Their leader Attila (*r.* 434–453) invaded the Eastern Empire and then moved still farther westward to Italy and Gaul, but after his death in 453 the power of the Huns was broken. Many took service in the Roman armies; the rest settled on the lower Danube.

Hus, Jan, or Huss, John (*c.* 1369–1415), Bohemian (Czech) religious reformer. A teacher and priest at Prague, he was influenced by the beliefs of the English reformer John Wycliffe, became leader of a reform movement, quarreled with the pope and other church authorities and was excommunicated. In 1415 he was burned as a heretic.

Hussein I (1935–), King of Jordan (1953–). He was educated in England and his pro-Western views were attacked by other Arab leaders, especially President Nasser of Egypt. To stress his non-alignment he dismissed (1956) Gen. John Bagot Glubb (Glubb Pasha), British commander of the Arab Legion (Jordanian Army). In 1967 he led his country into the Arab–Israeli War and lost all of Jordan w of the River Jordan to Israel. At the 1974 Arab summit meeting he was forced to relinquish his country's claim to west-bank Jordan to the Palestinian Liberation Organization (PLO).

Ibn Saud (*c.* 1880–1953), founder and first King of Saudi Arabia (*r.* 1932–53). Although in exile, his family were considered the leaders of the orthodox Wahhabi movement. The Wahhabia city, Riyadh was recaptured in 1902 and by 1912 Ibn Saud ruled all of Nejd (central Arabia). He defeated his rival, Hussein Ibn Ali, in 1924–25 and constituted his kingdom in 1932.

Ibrahim Pasha (1789–1848), Egyptian general. The son of Mohammed Ali, governor of Egypt under the Ottoman Empire, he campaigned against the Wahhabis of Arabia in 1816–18 and later fought the Greek insurgents with great brutality, sending many into slavery in Egypt. When his father defied Ottoman supremacy, Ibrahim conquered Syria (1832–33) and became its governor. In 1841 Turkey, supported by Britain and Austria, forced him to withdraw to

---

AD 1612–1618

England extended her trading influence to India, ousting the Portuguese as rivals to the

A Dutch. Walter Raleigh was executed to placate Spain (1618).

A Shakespeare, having produced his great tragedies in the previous decade, wrote his last play, *The Tempest* (*c.* 1612). Henry Briggs prepared tables to facilitate the use of Napier's logarithms.

Russian royal authority was established by Mikhail Romanov's (1613–45) ending local autonomy and strengthening serfdom.
Japan persecuted Christians.
China saw the rise to power of the Tungus tribes under Nurachi (1615–16) in Manchuria.

A Flemish painter Rubens was influenced by Caravaggio.
Religion saw the Synod of Dort (1618) reject Arminianism.

Egypt. He was named regent of Egypt in 1848.

Ignatius of Loyola, Saint, *See* **Counter Reformation** *and* **Jesuits**.

Inca Empire, empire established by a South American Indian group that migrated from the Peruvian highlands into the Cuzco area in about AD 1250. The Incas expanded and consolidated their empire slowly and steadily until the reigns of Pachacuti (*r.c.* 1438–71) and his son Topa (*r.c.* 1471–93), when Inca influence dramatically increased to include the area between Ecuador in the N and Chile, Bolivia and Argentina in the S. The Inca Empire was bureaucratic and militaristic: local leaders were moved to other regions and co-opted into Inca society. Good roads facilitated communication and tax collection. All products were the property of the state. Although the Incas never developed a system of writing, their standards in architecture, pottery, weaving, jewellery-making and other crafts were high. Religious rites included sun worship and the mummification of their dead. When Pizarro, the Spanish Conquistador, arrived in 1532, he took advantage of civil war between two Inca claimants to the throne to complete the downfall of an already weakened empire.

Independents, or Separatists, English Puritan sect which evolved from Brownism and sought organizational and intellectual independence as separate congregations from the established Church of England. Separatists established a base in The Netherlands in 1608, and as the Pilgrim Fathers settled in Plymouth, Massachusetts. The first truly Independent church was founded in Southwark, London, in 1616 by Henry Jacob but the most famous Independent was undoubtedly Oliver Cromwell. Independents formed the backbone of his army and his support guaranteed their strength during the English Civil War although it was to be eroded after the Restoration by the Act of Uniformity. The name "Independent" was first used during the 1640s and although it continued to be used until the 19th century, the term "Congregationalist" was more common by that time.

AD 1618–1624

A **Bohemia** saw the Defenestration of Prague begin the Thirty Years War (1618) after a nationalist and Protestant revolt there. Ferdinand (1619–37) had restored Catholicism by 1619.

Spain invaded the Protestant Palatinate to ensure a route to the Netherlands.

North America saw the Pilgrim Fathers land (1620).

England saw Edward Coke (1552– 1634) support common law against the monarchy. Francis

A **Bacon's** *Novum Organum* (1620) argued for the usefulness of science. John Donne (1572–1631) and George Herbert (1593–1633) established Metaphysical poetry.

A **Italian** sculptor Bernini's work epitomized the baroque style.

A **German** scientist Kepler tried to relate music and astronomy.

Indian mutiny

Indian mutiny (1857–58), also called the Sepoy mutiny, uprising begun by the Indian troops (sepoys) in the Bengal army in India. The revolt occurred when Governor-General Canning continued policies that disregarded the traditions of Hindus and Muslims. The army had cartridges (lubricated with the fat of cows and pigs) which had to be bitten open before use, and the outraged sepoys rebelled against their introduction. They gained a stronghold by taking Delhi, and the Mogul Emperor Bahadur Shah II reluctantly took their side. The revolt was eventually suppressed with the aid of Sir Hugh Rose and Sir Colin Campbell.

Inquisition, court set up by the Roman Catholic Church in the Middle Ages to seek out and punish heresy. The inquisitor was authorized by the pope to take testimony, question witnesses and those accused of heresy, and pass judgment. The accused were sometimes questioned under torture. Punishments for the guilty ranged from penances and fines to banishment, imprisonment, and death by fire. Kings and nobles supported what amounted to organized persecution of Jews, Protestants and others considered enemies of Church and state, including those charged with witchcraft. The medieval Inquisition was active in much of Europe from the 12th to the 15th century. A later tribunal, the Spanish Inquisition, was instituted in 1483 at the request of the rulers in Spain and was not finally and formally abolished until 1834.

IRA (Irish Republican Army), semi-military, primarily Roman Catholic organization dedicated to establishing a united Irish republic. Formed in 1919, the IRA waged guerrilla warfare against British rule. Some members ("Irregulars") rejected the Anglo-Irish settlement of 1921, fighting a civil war until 1923. Periodically active since that time, the "provisional" wing ("Provos"), committed to armed struggle, split in 1969 from the "official" IRA, which emphasized political activities and a Marxist rather than religious approach. Thereafter, the Provos became

---

AD 1624–1630

A **Hapsburgs** were opposed (1625) by an alliance of England, the United Provinces, Denmark and France.

A **France's** Richelieu rebuilt royal power and attacked the

A Huguenots (1628). French settlements in the West Indies began, as did emigration to Canada. Classicism in painting produced Poussin (1594–1665). **Korea** was overrun by the

A Tungus Manchus (1627).

A **England** saw Charles I marry the Catholic Henrietta Maria and lead an abortive expedition to assist the Huguenots (1627).

A William Harvey discovered the circulation of the blood (1628),

A complementing Galileo's mechanistic view of the universe.

A **Dutch** jurist Hugo Grotius developed international law in *On law* (1625).

---

prominent in the violence among Catholics, Protestants and British troops in Northern Ireland.

Ireland, Partition of, division of Ireland in 1920 into two parts after the breakdown of British government after 1918. By an agreement signed in Dec. 1921 and taking effect in 1922 the six predominantly Protestant counties of Ulster remained part of the UK and the 26 predominantly Catholic southern counties became the Republic of Ireland.

Islam, *See* **Mohammed**.

Ismail Pasha (1830–95), ruler of Egypt (1863–79). In 1867 he received the title khedive. The high price received for Egyptian cotton at the time enabled him to build extensively. Much money was wasted, however, and in 1875 Egypt was forced to sell to Britain its interest in one of the largest constructions, the Suez Canal. Egypt's finances were put in the control of a Franco-British debt commission. The Ottoman sultan replaced Ismail Pasha with his son Tawfiq Pasha in 1879.

Ivan, name of two grand princes of Moscow and three tsars of Russia. Ivan III (1440–1505) was Grand Prince of Moscow from 1462 until his death. He laid the foundations of a centralized monarchy and began the conquest of the Ukraine from Lithuania and Poland. Ivan IV (1530–84), known as Ivan the Terrible, was the first Tsar of Russia (1547–84). He created a centrally administered Russian state and began the expansion of Russia into non-Slavic lands. He gave Russia its first national assembly (1549). He earned the nickname by the oppression of political opponents in his last years, more than 3,000 of whom died.

Jackson, Andrew (1767–1845), 7th US President (1829–37), general and Indian fighter. At the age of 13 he was captured by the British in the American War of Independence but later as a general in the Battle of New Orleans (1815) he defeated them and became a national hero. A frontiersman, intolerant of formal education, he soon emerged as the symbol of a new egalitarian society. During his presidency the balance of power shifted from the

---

AD 1630–1636

A **Europe**, dislocated by the Thirty Years War, saw Gustavus Adolphus of Sweden's entry to protect the Protestant cause. Tilly, a Catholic general, sacked Magdeburg (1631). **Dutch** trade flourished with the seizure of part of Brazil.

A **England** saw Charles I rule without Parliament (1629–40), and A Strafford suppress Ireland. Trade and industry prospered, especially coal production, iron mining and metallurgy. Van Dyck (1599–1641) painted court portraits.

A **Italian** scientist Galileo began modern science, uniting physics and mathematics. He was forced A by the Inquisition (1633) to retract his heliocentric view of the universe. Pietro da Cortona's painting epitomized Roman high baroque.

urban East to the farmers and small businessmen of the West.

Jackson, Thomas J. ("Stonewall") (1824–63), US Civil War Confederate general. His stand against overwhelming odds at the first Battle of Bull Run (1861) gained him the nickname "Stonewall". He drove his troops so hard that they were known as "Jackson's Foot Cavalry". He was considered Gen. Robert E. Lee's best general. Jackson was accidentally shot by one of his own men at Chancellorsville, where he had just defeated the Unionists.

Jacobins, *See* **French Revolution** *and* **Robespierre**.

Jacobites, supporters of James II and his Stuart descendants, who attempted to regain the English throne after the Glorious Revolution of 1688. With unofficial French encouragement, Jacobites were found among Scots (the homeland of the Stuarts), Irish (James II was Catholic) and disgruntled Tories (Whigs dominated the government).

Jacquerie, insurrection of peasants against the nobility in NE France in 1358. Enraged by the increased taxes to finance the Hundred Years War and pillaging by English invaders and the French nobility, the peasants and some townsmen revolted. They destroyed several castles. The revolt was defeated by the nobles, who executed the leader Guillaume Carle and massacred thousands of peasants.

James I (1566–1625), King of England, son of Mary, Queen of Scots. Crowned James VI of Scotland on his mother's abdication (1567), James passed his minority mainly under the control of the Presbyterians, who determined to shield him from Roman Catholic influence. Forced to decide between France and England as an ally for Scotland, James chose Protestant England in 1586. On Elizabeth I's death in 1603 he became King of England. He supported the Anglicans and sponsored a translation of the Bible in 1611 that is known as the King James Version, but his failure to conciliate either the Puritans or the Roman Catholics caused discontent. His reliance upon favourites and his troubled relationship with the House of Commons

---

AD 1636–1642

Japan cut foreign trade after Christian peasants revolted (1637).

A **France** entered the Thirty Years War (1639). Literature became regulated by classical forms with Corneille and de Malherbe.

A **René Descartes** established the deductive method and invented co-ordinate geometry.

Spain was weakened by Portuguese independence and a Catalan nationalist revolt (1640).

England was close to civil war (1641) because of constitutional opposition to royal absolutism.

A **Charles I** recalled Parliament (1640) to finance a military expedition to end Scottish religious revolt.

A **Dutch** art produced Rembrandt, Vermeer and Hals.

Religion saw Jansen, supported by Pascal, attack the Jesuits over predestination.

---

weakened his effectiveness as a ruler.

James II (1633–1701), King of England, second son of Charles I and younger brother of Charles II. After the Restoration (1660), James, then Duke of York, played a prominent part in naval affairs and as Lord High Admiral in 1672 defeated the Dutch fleet at Southwold Bay. As a Roman Catholic, however, he was forced to resign all his offices in consequence of the Test Act (1673). Despite the rival claim of the Duke of Monmouth, an illegitimate but Protestant son of Charles II, James succeeded his brother (1685). His adherence to Roman Catholicism, however, alienated his subjects, and James was forced to abdicate. Whig lords invited William III and his wife Mary, James's Protestant daughter, to assume the English throne; he landed at Brixham in 1688. In an unsuccessful campaign (1689–90), James failed to hold Ireland against William. The Stuart cause was carried on hopelessly by his son and grandson, the Old and Young Pretenders culminating in the defeat at Culloden in 1746.

Janissaries, élite corps of soldiers of the Ottoman Empire. The practice of recruiting Christian youths and other war captives who were converted to Islam was begun in the 14th century by the sultan Orkhan. Later membership became hereditary and the corps wielded supreme power within the empire until 1826 when by order of Sultan Mahmud II the corps was massacred.

Jarrow March (1936), progress of unemployed workers from Jarrow, in county Durham, to London. Jarrow, a small ship-building town, relied upon one firm, which closed down in 1933. By the end of 1935, nearly three-quarters of the town's insured workers were out of work and 200 of them marched (5–31 October) to draw national attention to their plight.

Jefferson, Thomas (1743–1826), third President of the USA (1801–09) and one of the authors of the American Declaration of Independence. A scholar and philosopher, he believed in agrarian democracy. In 1769 he was

---

AD 1642–1648

A **China** saw the Ming dynasty replaced by the Manchu Ch'ing dynasty (1644). Art developed.

A **English** Civil War resulted in victory for Parliament and

A the Puritans (1646) under Oliver Cromwell. Burton's *Anatomy of Melancholy*, Browne's *Religio Medici* and Walton's *The Compleat Angler* marked a new eloquence in prose writing.

France defeated Spain at Rocroi (1647). René Descartes founded modern philosophy, relying on mathematical logic and espousing a total dualism between mind and matter. Pascal invented an adding machine (1642). Claude Lorrain developed landscape painting.

Italian scientist Torricelli invented the barometer (1643).

America saw the foundation of the New England Confederacy.

Jesuits

elected to the Virginia House of Burgesses and, six years later, represented the state of the Second Continental Congress. After independence he served as governor of Virginia, represented the USA in Europe, and became the first US secretary of state in 1789. The main achievements of his presidency were the Louisiana Purchase, the avoidance of US involvement in the Napoleonic Wars and the abolition of the slave trade.

Jesuits, officially the Society of Jesus, a Roman Catholic religious order, founded by St Ignatius of Loyola in 1540. They played a significant role in the Counter-Reformation. The Jesuits were often the first Christian missionaries in the New World, and in parts of Asia and Africa. They antagonized many European rulers because they gave allegiance only to their general in Rome and to the pope. In 1773 Pope Clement XIV abolished the order, under pressure from the kings of France, Spain and Portugal, but it continued to exist in Russia. The order was reestablished in 1814. Jesuits have distinguished themselves in education, scholarship and missionary work and they remain a potent force within Roman Catholicism today. Famous Jesuits include the martyr Saint Edmund Campion and Pierre Teilhard de Chardin.

Jesus Christ (*c.* 4 BC–*c.* AD 30), the inspiration for Christianity and to Christians the Son of God. "Jesus" is a Greek form of the Hebrew name *Joshua*; "Christ" comes from the Greek translation of the Hebrew *messiah*, the "anointed" whose coming had long been prophesied as the deliverance of the people of Israel. Present knowledge of Jesus's life is based mostly on the biblical gospels of Matthew, Mark and Luke, of which Mark is the earliest and Luke the most detailed. Although BC (before Christ) and AD (*anno domini*, in the year of the Lord) dates are timed from the birth of Christ, Jesus was probably born in 4 BC – the calendar error was made by Christians of the 6th century. It was near the end of the reign of Herod the Great and was just at the time that the Romans had ordered a census of all

AD 1648–1654

Europe saw the end of the Thirty Years War (1648). **France** crushed the Fronde, a noble and peasant uprising. **England's** Charles I was executed (1649) and the Commonwealth set up under Oliver Cromwell. The Navigation Act (1651), which made the colonies economically dependent on the mother country, led to war with the Dutch. Utopian ideas flourished. George Fox founded the Quakers, and the Diggers and the Levellers both sprang up. Poetry divided into Cavalier (Suckling, Herrick and Lovelace) and Puritan (Marvell). **Italy** perfected the violin. **German** scientist Otto von Guericke (1602–86) developed the air pump and worked with vacuums, demonstrating the power of air pressure.

their Empire's inhabitants at their places of birth. For the census Jesus's mother Mary had to travel with her husband Joseph from Nazareth in Galilee to his place of birth, Bethlehem in Judaea, where Jesus was also born, in a stable. He probably grew up in Galilee.

In about AD 26 or 27, John the Baptist began preaching his message of repentance and baptism in the area. Jesus was one of many baptized in the River Jordan by John, who may have been a relation. Thereafter Jesus began His own ministry, preaching to large numbers and gathering many followers as He wandered throughout the country. He also taught – through spiritual insights, parables and even miracles – a special group of 12 of His closest disciples who were later to be sent out as the nucleus of the spread of the gospel, and to be called Apostles. His teaching was to "love God and love one's neighbour" (comprising all fellow men), and that salvation depended on doing what was patently God's will rather than necessarily adhering to the letter and the contemporary intepretation of the Jewish Law. This tenet did not find approval with the hierarchy of the Jewish religion, particularly those of the Temple in Jerusalem who themselves were the butt of some of Jesus's ridicule.

In about AD 29 or 30 Jesus and His disciples went up to Jerusalem to celebrate the Jewish feast of the Passover. It was a dangerous place for Him, for although the common people loved Him, the chief priests and elders of the Jewish faith were by now trying to devise means of silencing Him in an exemplary manner. A few days later Jesus gathered His disciples for a Last Supper, at which He instituted the Eucharist. The next morning, after a night of prayer, He was arrested by agents of the priests and denounced before the Roman governor, Pontius Pilate, on a charge of sedition: that He had claimed to be a King of the Jews. Roman soldiers crucified Jesus on a hill outside the city wall. After His death His body was buried in a sealed rock tomb. Two days later He rose from the dead and appeared several times to His disciples and to other people. Forty days after His

AD 1654–1660

Russia rose in military strength with Brandenburg, bringing conflict in the Baltic and Poland (1655–60).
Venetians drove the Turks from the Dardanelles (1656).
England fell into anarchy on
A Cromwell's death and the monarchy was restored (1660).
A Thomas Hobbes suggested a form of atomism already occurring in his political tract *Leviathan*

in *De Corpore* (1655).
A **Italian** architect Bernini produced the Piazza of St Peter's.
Spanish painter Velazquez' work was characterized by realism and superb handling of colour.
Dutch poet Joost van den Vondel produced the religious drama *Lucifer* (1654). His countryman Christiaan Huygens invented the pendulum clock (1656).

resurrection He ascended into heaven, leaving His disciples the promise that His spirit would give them the courage and strength to go on proclaiming His message to the world.

Christians believe that Christ is at the same time truly man and truly God, and that He came into the world to reconcile sinful man to God by His sacrificial death.

Jinnah, Muhammad Ali (1876–1948), founder of Pakistan. He obtained a law degree in England and returned to practise in India. In 1906 he joined the Indian National Congress and became a keen advocate of Hindu-Muslim unity, but his views changed over the years and by 1940 he had come to believe that when independence was achieved there must be a separate Muslim state to prevent the Hindu majority from dominating the entire subcontinent.

Joan of Arc (*c.* 1412–31), national heroine of France, canonized by the Roman Catholic Church; also known as Joan of Lorraine and the Maid of Orléans. A deeply religious peasant girl, she claimed to hear heavenly voices and see visions of saints urging her to save France, which was then in the midst of the Hundred Years War. In early 1429, wearing men's clothes, Joan and some French troops broke the long English siege of Orléans. She then drove the English from the Loire towns and defeated them at Patay. After this victory she persuaded the indecisive dauphin to proceed to Reims and be crowned. She attempted to liberate Paris but was unsuccessful. In early 1430 she was captured by the Burgundians, handed over to the English and burnt at the stake for witchcraft and heresy (1431). She was declared a saint in 1920.

John XXIII (1881–1963), Catholic churchman who became pope in 1958. Before his election he had served as director of the Society for Propagation of the Faith, had been papal nuncio in France and from 1953 patriarch of Venice. John's place in church history rests on his courage and foresight in calling the Second Vatican Council, which met in 1962 to provide an *aggiornamento* (renewal or updating) of a large proportion of Roman Catholic

---

AD 1660–1666

A **French** king Louis XIV suppressed noble authority and created bureaucracy for local government.

A **Colbert**, with other Mercantilists held that a nation's economic power depended on its store of bullion.

Chinese cultural splendour was introduced by K'ang Hsi.

England took Bombay (1661) and New Amsterdam (1664).

A **Charles II** restored peace and promoted trade. Public musical concerts were instituted. The Royal Society was founded (1660)

A and physicist **Robert Boyle** formulated Boyle's law.

Spanish painting flourished with Murillo, who founded the Seville Academy (1660).

German literature produced Gryphius' comedies and their first novel, Grimmelshausen's *Simplicissimus*.

religious life and doctrine. His reign was also notable for the emphasis he put on questions of peace and justice.

John (*c.* 1167–1216), King of England, youngest son of Henry II. During Richard I's absence on a Crusade John tried to seize control in 1193 and, on the king's return, had to forfeit all his lands. But Richard soon relented and on his death in 1199 was succeeded by John. His probable murder of his nephew Arthur in 1203, the loss of vast territories in France (1204–05) and heavy taxation to finance abortive attempts to regain them made him extremely unpopular. He was forced to submit to the pope after he had been excommunicated. At Runnymede in 1215 he was compelled to accede to the demands of his barons and affix his seal to the draft of Magna Carta. Civil war ensued, during which John died, possibly poisoned.

John of Austria, also called Don John (1547–78), Spanish prince and military leader, illegitimate son of Emperor Charles V and half-brother of Philip II of Spain. In 1571, as head of the naval forces of the Holy League formed by Pope Pius V, Spain and Venice, he defeated the Turks in the naval Battle of Lepanto. He took Tunis from the Turks in 1573.

John of Gaunt (1340–99), fourth son of Edward III of England and Duke of Lancaster. His name comes from the Middle English *Gaunt* for Ghent, his birthplace. He led the English army against the French from 1372 to 1374. He was the greatest of medieval "overmighty" subjects and for a brief period in the middle 1370s was the most powerful man in the kingdom. The Tudor line was descended from him and Catherine Swynford, his third wife.

Johnson, Lyndon Baines (1908–73), 36th President of the USA (1963–69). In the House of Representatives (1937–48) and the Senate (1948–60), he acquired a reputation as a liberal and a skilled representative. As vice-president under John F. Kennedy he took charge of the space programme, and after Kennedy's assassination embarked on the most ambitious legislative programme since the New Deal. He sought to built a "Great Society" through free medical care

---

AD 1666–1672

France invaded the Spanish Netherlands, but was opposed by the United Provinces. A secret alliance with Charles II was concluded. Racine and Molière revitalized drama; the palace at Versailles took shape. **England** fought an indecisive war with the Dutch and founded the Hudson Bay Company. The Great Fire of London (1666) meant much rebuilding. Isaac Newton conceived of gravity and discovered the spectrum. **Russia** defeated Poland for the Ukraine (1667). Old Believers broke with the Russian Church, disliking Greek influence. **Mogul** emperor Aurungzebe revoked Hindu toleration (1669). **Italian** naturalist Redi refuted spontaneous generation. **Dutch** landscape painting flourished with Hobbema (1638–1709).

---

for the aged, strong civil rights acts, and anti-poverty and urban renewal projects. His domestic success was over-shadowed by his Vietnam war policy. He increased US commitment to more than 500,000 troops and in 1965 authorized the bombing of North Vietnam. Costs burgeoned and the war became widely unpopular in the USA. In March 1968 Johnson declared that he would not seek re-election and announced a partial halt to the bombing, opening the way to the start of peace talks.

Johnson, Dr Samuel (1709–84), British lexicographer, poet and critic. He settled in London in 1737 and began writing pieces for *Gentleman's Magazine*. He was a prolific writer and witty conversationalist, and his works include the satire *The Vanity of Human Wishes* (1749), *Rasselas* (1759), the 10-volume *Lives of the Poets* (1779–81), the periodical *The Rambler* (1750–52), the *Dictionary of the English Language* (1755) – which established his reputation – and an edition of Shakespeare's plays (1765), and the essays comprising *The Idler* (1758–61). He was a founder (1764) of *The Club*, later known as *The Literary Club* whose members included David Garrick, James Boswell, Edmund Burke and Oliver Goldsmith. Boswell wrote a noted biography of Johnson.

Juan Carlos I, *See* **Franco, Francisco.**

Jung, Carl Gustav (1875–1961), Swiss psychiatrist. After working with Sigmund Freud from 1906 to 1914, Jung broke with him to found his school of analytical psychology. His investigations into personality, especially its spiritual and unconscious aspects, led him to his concept of a collective unconscious. He believed introversion and extraversion to be basic personality types, and stressed the importance of personal transformations and self-discovery for the development of a healthy personality. Among his noted works are *Wandlungen und Symbole der Libido* (1912, tr. *Psychology of the Unconscious*; 1952 rev. ed., tr. *Symbols of Transformation*) and *Modern Man in Search of a Soul* (1933).

Justinian, name of two Byzantine Emperors. Justinian I,

AD 1672–1678

France attacked the Dutch. They were opposed by Spain
A and the Holy Roman Empire. England evolved the two-party system, passing the Test Act (1673), banning Catholics from
A office. John Milton produced *Paradise Lost* (1674). Chris-
A topher Wren began St Paul's Cathedral (1675). In science,
A Isaac Newton developed calculus and the Greenwich Observatory

was founded (1675). Danish scientist Roemer showed light's speed as finite (1675). Dutch biologist Van Leeuwenhoek discovered protozoa and bacteria. Portuguese philosopher Spinoza tried to find a rational ex-planation of the universe. In *Ethics* (1675), he supported
A democracy, refuted Descartes' dualism and held that free will was illusory.

"the Great" (*c.* 482–565; *r.* 527–565), the son of an Illyrian peasant, became one of the most cultured men of his time and one of the greatest rulers of the Byzantine Empire. During his reign large parts of the old Roman Empire in North Africa, Italy and Spain were reconquered for Byzantium, and his vast building programmes included the erection of the Church of St Sophia in Constantinople. His most lasting legislative achievement was his revision of Roman law. Justinian II (*c.* 669–711; *r.* 685–95 and 705–11) was surnamed Rhinotmetus ("with a cut-off nose"). A tyrannical ruler, he was deposed in 695, mutilated (hence the surname) and exiled. Ten years later, with the help of the Bulgarians, he regained the throne but was killed in 711.

Kant, Immanuel (1724–1804), German philosopher. From 1740–46 he studied at Königsberg University, then worked as a private tutor. In 1755 he returned to the university and was made a professor in 1770. The order, regularity and modesty of his life was undisturbed by the notoriety caused by the publication of his "critical philosophy", particularly *Critique of Pure Reason* (1781), *Critique of Practical Reason* (1788) and *Critique of Judgment* (1790). In addition to his technical treatises, Kant produced several topical essays in support of religious liberalism and enlightenment.

Karamanlis, Konstantinos (1907–   ), Greek politician. After practising law in Athens he was elected to Parliament in 1935. He became Prime Minister in 1955 and formed his own party, the National Radical Union, a year later. He reached agreement with Britain and Turkey over Cyprus in 1960 in an attempt to ease strained relations with those countries, but was forced to resign in 1963. During 11 years of self-imposed exile he was an opponent of the Greek military junta, and when it fell in 1974 he returned as Prime Minister.

Kaunda, Kenneth (1924–   ), President of Zambia from 1964 when the country gained its independence from Britain. He became leader of the United National

---

AD 1678–1684

China took Formosa (1683). **Turks** besieged Vienna (1683) but were defeated at Mohacs. **French** explorer Robert de la Salle travelled the Mississippi. Bossuet upheld Louis XIV's absolute monarchy against Protestantism. Mme. de la Fayette wrote a psychological novel, *La Princesse de Cleves*. Denis Papin invented the pressure cooker (1679).

A England tried to exclude James II after the Popish Plot. Ralph Cudworth, a Christian humanist, published his *True Intellectual System* (1678). John Bunyan produced *Pilgrim's Progress* (1678). John Ray prepared the ground for plant classification. **Italian** composer Alessandro Scarlatti (1660–1725) wrote many cantatas.

Independence Party in 1960, nationalized the copper mines and, in 1973, imposed single party rule.

Kennedy, John Fitzgerald (1917–63), 35th President of the USA; he held the office from 1961–63. He was the son of Joseph P. Kennedy and the brother of Robert F. Kennedy and Edward M. Kennedy. After distinguished service in the navy in WWII, he was elected to the House of Representatives as a Democrat in 1946. He served there until he entered the Senate in 1953. He made an unsuccessful bid to become vice-presidential candidate in 1956 and immediately began preparations for the presidential nomination of 1960, selecting Lyndon B. Johnson as proposed Vice-President. He defeated Richard M. Nixon by a small margin, and at 43 became the second-youngest President. He called for increased federal involvement in civil rights, education and health services. It was foreign affairs, however, that occupied most of his attention. His most spectacular success occurred in Oct. 1962 when, during the Cuban missile crisis, he forced the USSR to remove its missiles from Cuba. In Nov. 1963, Kennedy embarked on a political tour of Texas and was assassinated in Dallas. The Warren commission later found that the sniper, Lee Harvey Oswald, had no connection with any conspiracy.

Kennedy, Robert Francis (1925–68), US lawyer and political leader. In 1960 he managed the successful presidential campaign of his brother John F. Kennedy and became US attorney general from 1961 to 1964, a post in which he vigorously enforced civil rights laws and investigated corruption in organized labour. After his brother's assassination, he left the cabinet and was elected senator for New York in 1964. While a candidate for the Democratic presidential nomination, he was assassinated after a speech in Los Angeles in June 1968.

Kenyatta, Jomo (*c.* 1893–1978), President of Kenya. He entered politics to defend his own tribe, the Kikuyu, and black African rights. He was imprisoned in 1953 for Mau

---

AD 1684–1690

A France revoked the Edict of Nantes (1685). Many Huguenots fled. Poet La Fontaine produced his verse *Fables*. Charles Lebrun was director of the Academy and produced the Hall of Mirrors at Versailles. **Russia** clashed with China. **Japan** saw the rise of a merchant culture. Matsuo Basho perfected the haiku verse form.

A **England** expelled James II for trying to restore Catholicism. The Bill of Rights (1689) confirmed a constitutional monarchy. Isaac Newton published the *Principia* (1687), a revolutionary work dealing with moving bodies, gravitation, fluids and the heavenly bodies. This work was fundamental to the development of mechanistic and optimistic 18th century philosophy.

Mau terrorism, exiled and then elected president of the Kenya African National Union (1960). He helped to gain Kenya's independence from Britain in 1963 and became president in 1964, suppressing opposition and outlawing opposing political parties.

Kepler, Johannes (1571–1630), German astronomer who in 1609 put forward the theory that the planets travel round the Sun in elliptical orbits. He was assistant to the Danish astronomer Tycho Brahe and, on Brahe's death, used his teacher's observations of the positions of the stars and the movements of the planets to formalize three fundamental laws of planetary motion, on which Isaac Newton later based his theory of gravitational force, and on which modern astronomy is based. Kepler also revolutionized optics with his ray theory of light to explain vision.

Kett, Robert (*d.* 1549), English peasant leader. He was a tanner of an old Norfolk family and led about 12,000 men who gathered at Norwich in 1549 to protest against enclosure. Although their demands were moderate, the rebels were attacked and routed in August by a mercenary army under the Earl of Warwick. Kett was executed as a traitor.

Keynes, John Maynard (1883–1946), British economist who came to prominence with his book *Economic Consequences of the Peace* (1919), which criticized the economic provisions of the Treaty of Versailles. *The General Theory of Employment, Interest, and Money* (1935) was profoundly influenced by the Depression. In it Keynes established the foundation of modern macro-economics. He advocated governmental economic planning and the active intervention of government in the economy to stimulate employment and prosperity. His views had great influence on the Bretton Woods conference of 1944.

Khrushchev, Nikita Sergeyevich (1894–1971), Soviet politician who was First Secretary of the Communist Party from 1953 to 1964 and premier of the USSR from 1958 to 1964. He joined the party in 1918 and was elected to the

---

AD 1690–1696

A **Russia's** Peter the Great visited Western Europe and continued expansionist policies.

A **England**, ruled by William III and James II's daughter Mary, joined the war against France. Trade in India grew, and the Bank of England was founded

A (1694). John Locke produced the empiricist study *An Essay concerning Human Understanding* (1690), denying the existence

of innate knowledge. He just-
A ified the Glorious Revolution in his *Two Treatises on Government* (1690). Drama flourished with Congreve, Dryden and Wycherley.

Spanish architect Churriguera influenced the baroque style.

Italian composer Corelli developed the concerto.

Dutch physicist Huygens suggested a wave theory of light.

central committee in 1934. Noted for economic success and ruthless suppression of opposition in the Ukraine, where he was a party secretary, he was elected to the Politburo in 1939. After Stalin died he made a speech denouncing him to the Twentieth Party Congress (1956), and expelled his staunchest backers from the central committee. Favouring détente with the West, he yielded to US President John F. Kennedy in the Cuban missile crisis in 1962. This development, economic setbacks and trouble with China led to his downfall in favour of Leonid Brezhnev and Alexei Kosygin in 1964.

Kim Il-sung, Marshal (1912–), chief of state of the Democratic People's Republic of Korea (North Korea) and chairman of the Korean Workers' Party from 1948; b. Kim Sung Chu. He joined the Korean Communist Party in 1931 and led guerrilla fighting against the occupying Japanese in the 1930s and a Korean unit in the Soviet army during WWII. In 1950 he led a North Korean invasion of South Korea that precipitated the Korean war (1950–53).

King, Martin Luther, Jr (1929–68), US clergyman and civil-rights leader. Pastor of a Baptist church in Montgomery, Alabama, he led the Black boycott of Montgomery's segregated transport system in 1956, and subsequently attracted national attention for the passive-resistance protests he advocated. Thereafter he founded and worked through the Southern Christian Leadership Conference to further the cause of national desegregation. He organized the march on Washington in 1963, opposed the Vietnam war and had begun a national campaign against poverty when he was assassinated in Memphis, Tennessee, on 4 April 1968. In 1964 he was awarded the Nobel Peace Prize.

Kissinger, Henry Alfred (1923–), US political leader, b. Germany. While a professor at Harvard University, he wrote several books on political science and served as advisor to various government agencies. He became President Richard Nixon's assistant for National Security in 1969 and became the chief advisor on foreign policy.

AD 1696–1702

Spanish king Charles II's death A led to the War of Spanish Succession (1702–13).
Turks lost Hungary to Austrian control (1699).
Prussia emerged under Frederick II, Elector of Brandenburg.
England saw the foundation of the Stock Exchange (1698). Dryden ended his career with *Fables Ancient and Modern* (1699). Baroque architecture

was developed by John Vanbrugh and Nicholas Hawksmoor. Savery invented the steam engine (1696). Newcomen developed the atmospheric steam engine. Jethro Tull invented a drill for sowing seeds in rows (1701).
Religion saw Govin Rai encourage A armed resistance to Mogul persecution of Sikhs, who came to dominate the Punjab.

President Nixon named him Secretary of State in 1973 and he continued in that post under President Gerald Ford. In 1973 he shared the Nobel Peace Prize with Le Duc Tho for his part in negotiating a ceasefire in the Vietnam war, even though fighting continued until 1975. He worked for détente between East and West during the Nixon presidency and acted as mediator in the Middle East crisis of 1973–74.

Kitchener, Horatio Herbert, Earl (1850–1916), British soldier involved in the defeat of the Mahdi in the Sudan. As a major in the Egyptian Cavalry, he took part in the relief of Khartoum (1883–85). In 1892 he became a major-general in the Egyptian army and achieved the pacification of the Sudan in 1898 with the victories at Atbara and Omdurman. After service in the South African War, and then in India and Egypt, he was appointed Secretary of State for War in 1914. He was later lost at sea when the cruiser in which he was travelling to Russia sank after hitting a mine.

Knox, John (c.1514–72), leader of the Protestant Reformation in Scotland. Ordained a Catholic priest, he nevertheless took up the cause of the Reformation. Having being imprisoned in France (1547), he lived in exile in England as a Reformed preacher. When the Catholic Mary I came to the throne in 1553 he fled to Switzerland where, in Geneva, he was influenced by Calvin. In 1559 Knox returned to Scotland, where he continued to promote the Protestant cause through preaching and pamphlets advocating rebellion against tyrannical rulers. In 1560, with military help from England and while the young and Catholic Mary, Queen of Scots was away in France, the Scottish Parliament, under Knox's leadership, made Presbyterianism the state religion.

Korean War (1950–53), conflict between Communist (North Korea and People's Republic of China) and non-Communist (South Korea, us and un) forces. On 25 June 1950, North Korea invaded South Korea. The un Security Council demanded a halt, in which it called upon the help of

AD 1702–1708

France won control of the *asiento* contract (1702), allowing transportation of slaves to Spanish colonies. Portugal joined the alliance against them (1703) and they were defeated at Blen-
Δheim by Marlborough (1704).
ΔMogul Empire disintegrated on Aurungzebe's death (1707), as European-assisted local princes asserted their autonomy.
England became united with Scotland (1707). A new journalism arose with Daniel Defoe's *Review* (1704), Richard Steele's *Tatler* (1709)
Δand Joseph Addison's *Spec-*
Δtator (1711). Newton produced *Opticks* (1704), encapsulating his previous work on light. Halley asserted that comets orbit the Sun.
ΔGerman suites by Bach drew on dance forms.

member nations. US President Harry Truman, without recourse to Congress, ordered land, sea and air forces to aid South Korea. Token forces from 16 UN countries supported the South Korean and US armies and Gen. Douglas Macarthur was appointed commander. British and Commonwealth forces acquitted themselves well; four Victoria Crosses were won, two of them in the heavy fighting on the Imjin River (April 1951), where the 1st Bn the Gloustershire Regiment were cut off from the brigade. The war tested the strength of both sides, and marked the appearance of the Soviet MiG-15 fighter. Although the conflict ended inconclusively in a truce (27 July 1953) at the cost of about 4 million casualties, its containment may have prevented worldwide nuclear war.

Kosygin, Aleksei Nikolayevich (1904–), Soviet politician elected to the Communist Party Central Committee in 1939 and the Politburo in 1948. He was removed in 1953 but regained his seat in 1960. After Khrushchev's fall in 1964, he became Chairman of the Council of Ministers, and was regarded as second to Leonid Brezhnev.

Kublai Khan (1215–94), Mongol emperor (1260–94) who was the grandson of Genghis Khan. In 1279 he completed the conquest of China, deposing the Sung dynasty and founding the Yüan dynasty, which ruled until 1368. Marco Polo visited his court at Peking.

Lafayette, Marie Joseph Paul Yves Roch Gilbert du Motier, Marquis de (1757–1834), French general, statesman and hero of the American cause, who arrived in Philadelphia in 1777 and was commissioned a major-general. In 1781 he distinguished himself in the Yorktown campaign that led to Cornwallis's surrender. He returned to France in 1781, where he later became a first member of the States-General then of the National Assembly. After the Fall of the Bastille (1789) he was appointed commander of the National Guard but lost all popular support when in 1791 he ordered his troops to fire on a crowd petitioning for the abolition of the monarchy. He was given military commands in 1792, but

---

AD 1708–1714

France caused war between the native Brazilians and the Portuguese by attacking Rio de Janeiro. The Treaty of Utrecht confirmed that Spain and France should not be united and left Britain in charge of the *asiento* slave trade.

German emigration to America began in 1709.

Britain saw the publication of Bishop Berkeley's *Principles* of *Human Knowledge*. It argued Aagainst Locke, stating that all knowledge comes from perception and affirming religious belief. English Classicism found its wittiest poet in Pope, whose *Rape of the Lock* appeared in 1714. Abraham Darby produced high-quality iron and Hawksee made accurate observations of capillary action in glass tubes.

deserted to the Austrians in August. He lived in retirement under Napoleon, but at the Restoration (1814) became a member of the Chamber of Deputies. He made a triumphant visit to the USA (1824–25) and in France in 1830 he played a major role in the July Revolution, his prestige being largely responsible for the installation of Louis Philippe as king of the French.

Lamarck, Jean-Baptiste Pierre Antoine de Monet, Chevalier de (1744–1829), French biologist. His theories of biological transformation, according to which acquired characteristics are inheritable, influenced evolutionary thought throughout most of the 19th century. He proposed in *Philosophie zoologique* (1809) that new biological needs of an organism promote a change in habits from which develop new physical structures. These are then transmitted to offspring as permanent characteristics.

Lao-tze, or Lao-tzu (*c.* 604–*c.* 531 BC), Chinese philosopher. According to Chinese legend he founded Taoism, a religion which became a mystical reaction to the moral-political concerns of Confucianism. Although there is uncertainty about his identity, he is believed to have been the author of *Tao Te Ching*, the sacred book of Taoism; *tao* is the "way"; *te* is its "virtue". It has greatly influenced Chinese culture.

Latimer, Hugh (*c.*1485–1555), English clergyman and Protestant martyr. He first became prominent by defending Henry VIII's divorce from Catherine of Aragon and in 1535 was made Bishop of Worcester. A man of strong Protestant convictions, he strongly disapproved of the temporary reaction in favour of Catholicism, and resigned his see in 1539. With the accession of Edward VI (1547) he resumed preaching against the abuses of Church and clergy. When the Roman Catholic Mary came to the throne (1553) he was charged with heresy and, refusing to recant, was burned at the stake.

Laud, William (1573–1645), Archbishop of Canterbury (1633–45). Laud considered the Church of England to be a

AD 1714–1720

A **Prussia's** Frederick William I set up a standing army.

A **France** saw Louis XIV die (1715) and the economy exhausted. Alain Le Sage's *Gil Blas* (1715) continued the picaresque novel tradition. Antoine Watteau introduced the *fête galante* genre of painting and the first phase of rococo was exemplified by Oppenordt's work.

A **Manchu** rule was firmly estab-

lished in Tibet (1720).
Britain set up the South Sea Company (1710) to increase trade with South America.

A **George I** suppressed Jacobite risings. Handel composed Italian opera after 1719.

A **German** philosopher Leibniz stated that this was the best of all possible worlds. Farenheit invented the mercury thermometer (1714).

branch of the universal church, claimed apostolic succession for bishops and believed that the Anglican ritual should be followed strictly in all churches. Working closely with Charles I, he sought to remove Puritans from important positions in the Church. Laud was impeached (1640) by the Long Parliament. The House of Lords found him innocent of treason but the Commons condemned him to death under a bill of attainder.

Lavoisier, Antoine Laurent (1743–94), French chemist. His careful experiments enabled him to demolish the Phlogiston theory by demonstrating the function of oxygen in combination. He named both oxygen and hydrogen and showed how they combined to form water. In collaboration with Berthollet and others he published *Methods of Chemical Nomenclature* (1787), which laid down the modern method of naming substances. His *Elementary Treatise on Chemistry* (1789) established the basis of modern chemistry. He was guillotined during the Revolution.

Lawrence, Thomas Edward (1888–1935), British archaeologist, soldier and author known as Lawrence of Arabia. He worked on the excavation of a Hittite settlement in the Euphrates valley from 1911 until 1914, when he became an intelligence officer in Cairo. He joined the Arab revolt against the Turks in 1916, and proved himself an extremely successful guerrilla fighter, leading Arab forces first into Aqaba (1917) and then into Damascus in October 1918. Disillusioned by the repeated failure of his plans for an independent Arab state, and disturbed by his war experiences, he finally sought obscurity in the ranks of the RAF as T.E. Shaw. In 1926 he published his memoirs of the Arab revolt as *The Seven Pillars of Wisdom*. He also translated the *Odyssey* (1932). He died of injuries sustained in a motorcycle accident.

League of Nations, international organization (1920–46), forerunner of the United Nations. Created as part of the Treaty of Versailles ending WWI, it required that members

---

AD 1720–1724

Austria–Hungary's indivisibility was established (1720) by the acceptance of the Pragmatic Sanction. Lukas von Hildebrandt founded Austrian baroque architecture.

North America saw Spain occupy Texas and the Piedmont region colonized by Swiss, Germans and Scots. Smallpox inoculations were administered by Boylston. A **Britain** saw Robert Walpole

become the first Prime Minister (1721) and bring prosperity. Daniel Defoe produced *Robinson Crusoe* and *Moll Flanders*. **France** produced Rameau's *Traite de l'harmonie* (1722), the foundation of harmonic theory for two centuries. **German** philosopher Wolff made rational philosophy popular. **Religion** saw Ba'al Shem Tov found Hasidism in Poland.

respect the territorial independence of all other members and recognize the need for disarmament. The refusal of the USA to participate impaired the League's efficiency although during the first few years of its existence it was instrumental in preventing war in the Balkans and in settling several inner-European disputes. Despite extending financial and administrative aid to poorer countries and furthering co-operation in the field of international relations, the problems of imposing League decisions on the great powers was never solved. The threats to world peace from Germany, Spain and Japan caused the League to collapse in 1939. It was dissolved in 1946.

Le Corbusier, (1887–1963), Swiss-born French architect, real name Charles-Édouard Jeanneret, among the most influential of the 20th century. His early work, mostly housing, exploited the qualities of reinforced concrete with cube-like forms and incorporated principles which are summarized in his famous *Five Points of a New Architecture* (1925). Later Le Corbusier evolved a less strictly rational, more poetic, style, of which the highly sculptural chapel of Notre-Dame-du-Haut at Ronchamp (1955) is the finest example. In the 1950s he also laid out the town of Chandigarh, the new capital of the Punjab, and built its majestic supreme courts and secretariat. He designed Tokyo's Museum of Western Art (1957) and the Cistercian Monastery of La Tourette (1960) in central France, a concrete block of immense force. His last major work was the Visual Arts Center at Harvard (1963).

Le Duan (1907–), politician, theorist and military organizer of North Vietnam. He was a founder of the Indo-Chinese Communist Party in 1930, joined the Viet-Minh in 1945 and helped to organize the NLF (National Liberation Front) of South Vietnam in 1960. He later became First Secretary of the Vietnam Workers' Party, and in the early 1970s was considered one of the most influential men in the country.

Lee, Robert Edward (1807–70), commander of

AD 1724–1728

Russia, her border with China fixed (1727), had industrial growth, centralized administration and a subdued nobility; A results of Peter the Great's policies.

France underwent a peaceful and economically fruitful period during Fleury's ministry.

A **Britain's** George II gave power A to George I's former opposition. Jonathan Swift produced *Gulliver's Travels* (1726), an imaginative political satire, and John Gay's *Beggar's Opera* was first played in 1728. John Harrison developed the chronometer. Stephen Hales' *Vegetable Staticks* (1727) founded plant physiology.

Italian writer Giambattista Vico traced social development in his masterpiece *The New Science* (1725).

Confederate forces in the American Civil War. Although Lee regarded slavery as evil and saw advantages in the Union, his loyalty to his native Virginia was paramount. Declining Lincoln's offer of the field command of Union troops, he became military adviser to Jefferson Davis, the Confederate president, and in 1862 was appointed commander of the Confederate forces. In that year he successfully defended Richmond and won the second battle of Bull Run. He was defeated at Antietam (1862) but inflicted on the Union its worst defeats at Fredericksburg (1862) and Chancellorsville (1863), although in the latter Lee lost his most able lieutenant, Thomas "Stonewall" Jackson. Lee's attempt to penetrate the North ended in his defeat at Gettysburg in July 1863. He surrendered to Ulysses S. Grant at Appomatox Court House on 9 April 1865.

Leibniz, Gottfried Wilhelm (1646–1716), German philosopher and mathematician. He never took an academic position, but served as a courtier and diplomat (in Paris, 1672–76), and corresponded with most of the leading thinkers of his day. He made many practical inventions, including a calculating machine (1671), and published his discovery of differential calculus in 1684. He created a rationalist metaphysic, according to which the universe comprises a multitude of interrelated and organized units, called "monads", within a divine harmony. This belief led him to argue that evil is divinely motivated, and that this is the best of all possible worlds. He wrote voluminously, although few of his works were published during his lifetime. His major works include *New Essays Concerning Human Understanding* (1765) and *Monadology* (1898).

Leicester, Robert Dudley, Earl of (*c.* 1532–88), English nobleman, favourite of Queen Elizabeth I. The mysterious death in 1560 of his wife, Amy Robsart, apparently cleared the way for Leicester to marry Elizabeth. The Queen, however, knew that the match would be politically unwise and instead offered his hand to Mary, Queen of Scots.

AD 1728–1732

Russia saw Anna (1730–40) found the Corps of Cadets to encourage noble support for her.

A **Holy Roman Empire** dissolved Britain's rival, the Ostend East India Company, by order of the Treaty of Vienna (1731).

Britain forced Spain to confirm Britain's possession of Gibraltar (1729). Agricultural enclosures increased food production. James Bradley con-firmed Copernicus' theory by explaining stellar aberration. John Hadley invented the sextant. French writer Voltaire produced his *Lettres Philosophiques*, advocating the empiricism of

A Newton and Locke (1734).

A **German** ideas of the Enlightenment were summed up by the works of Gottsched.

Italian musician Vivaldi advanced instrumental techniques.

Leicester, however, remained influential, despite his feud with William Cecil, Lord Burghley. In 1585 he was placed in command of an expedition to help The Netherlands against the occupying Spanish, but his military efforts were undistinguished.

Lenin, Vladimir Ilyich (1870–1924), Russian politician, originally named Vladimir Ilyich Ulyanov. He was attracted to revolutionary politics while at school, particularly after his brother was executed for his part in an anti-tsarist plot (1887). He studied law at Khazan University (1887–89), and practised as a lawyer (1893–95). He was exiled to Siberia (1897–1900) for his connections with Plekhanov's Marxist group, and in Munich he wrote *What is to be Done?* (1902). At the second congress of the Marxist Social Democratic Party in London (1903), he argued for an active, disciplined party to lead the workers on to revolution. This split the party into the Bolsheviks (led by Lenin) and the Mensheviks. He returned to Russia in Nov. 1905, and refused any alliance with the liberals. He returned to Europe (1907–17), and settled in Switzerland on the outbreak of WWI, analysing the causes of war in *Imperialism: the Last Stage of Capitalism* (1917). He returned to Russia with German assistance in April 1917, and refused to recognize Kerensky's government, supporting the Soviet movement. He justified his policy in *The State and Revolution* (1917), and with Trotsky organized the successful November coup. He became chairman of the Council of People's Commissars, negotiated the Treaty of Brest-Litovsk with Germany, and in 1918 dissolved the freely elected Constituent Assembly. He organized the defence of the Bolshevik Revolution in the civil war (1918–20), declaring the independence of the separate nationalities of Russia, and formed the Communist International (1919) to promote the Russian Revolution abroad. He put forward a programme of economic reconstruction in 1921 (the New Economic Policy), but became ill in 1922 and died in Jan. 1924.

AD 1732–1736

Britain prohibited trade between her American and West Indian colonies by the Molasses Act (1733). Georgia was founded.
A **Walpole** introduced excise duty on wine and tobacco, causing great unrest. Hume's *Treatise on Human Nature* asserted that knowledge was unattainable. John Kay invented the flying shuttle.
France established the Compagnie des Indes (1735). Montesquieu, a thinker and satirist, produced socio-political analysis.
Poland was weakened by a war over the succession.
A **Swedish** botanist Carl Linnaeus published *Systema Naturae*.
Japan declined economically.
Italian art flourished through Canaletto and Servandoni.
German religious music was dev-
A eloped by Bach.

Leonardo da Vinci

Leonardo da Vinci (1452–1519), Florentine painter, sculptor, architect, engineer and scientist. He was apprenticed to Andrea del Verrocchio at whose studio he remained probably until 1476. He was the founder of the Classic style of painting of the High Renaissance and was among the first to use the Chiaroscuro technique. His early works include the unfinished *St Jerome* (*c.* 1480) and a portrait, *Ginevra de' Benci*. In about 1482 he became civil and military engineer to Duke Lodovico Sforza in Milan, where he executed *Madonna of the Rocks, Portrait of a Musician* and numerous other works, including the *Last Supper* (1495–98). While in Milan he made many architectural drawings and designed and directed court festivals; he also began his scientific work and wrote the notes for what was to become his *Treatise on Painting*. In 1500 he returned to Florence where he executed the *Mona Lisa* and began *Virgin and Child with St Anne*. One of his last known paintings is *St John the Baptist* (*c.* 1515). In 1517 he became chief painter, architect and engineer to Francis I at Amboise, France, where he died.

Lepanto, Battle of (1571), naval engagement in the Gulf of Patras off the coast of Lepanto, Greece, between forces of the Ottoman Empire and various Christian powers. When the Ottoman Turks attempted to take Cyprus from Venice in 1571, Greece, Austria, Spain, Venice and the papacy stopped them in this battle.

Lesseps, Ferdinand-Marie, Vicomte de (1805–94), French diplomat who in 1832 conceived the idea of a canal linking the Red Sea with the Mediterranean Sea. Digging was begun, by Egyptian labourers, in 1859 but it was necessary to import mechanical equipment from Europe to complete the work. The Suez Canal, as it became known, was opened by the Empress Eugénie in November 1869.

Levellers (*fl.* 1645–49), Puritan political and religious movement in England. The name alludes derisively to their ideals of equality. Their leader was John Lilburne, and their campaign, which found extensive support in Oliver

---

AD 1736–1740

Russia, clashing with the Turks over their Polish policy, captured Azov, but was prevented by the Treaty of Belgrade (1739) from having a base there.

Britain went to war with Spain over trading rights (1739).

AWalpole's authority was weakened by Queen Caroline's death.

AJohn Wesley founded Methodism. France produced Voltaire's philosophical poem *Le Mondain*

(1736). His scorn for prejudice and distrust of accepted ideas epitomized the ideals of the Enlightenment. François Boucher exemplified rococo art, while Jean Chardin produced realistic genre scenes. Bernoulli related fluid flow to pressure (1738).

German contrapuntal music reached a peak with the work

Aof Bach, including *Mass in B Minor* (1738).

Cromwell's army, demanded complete constitutional reform, with abolition of the monarchy and corporate privilege, and the creation of one supreme representative legislature elected biennially by adult male suffrage, the extent of which was not firmly defined. Cromwell finally crushed the movement.

Lévi-Strauss, Claude (1908–), Belgian-born French anthropologist and founder of structural anthropology. Structuralism, the attempt to find basic patterns for a scientific study of man, contends that history was shaped into a collective, fragmented structure comparable to preliterate mythology. Lévi-Strauss became professor of anthropology at the College of France in 1959 and was elected to the French Academy in 1973. His books include *The Elementary Structures of Kinship* (1949; tr. 1962) and *Structural Anthropology* (1958).

Lilburne, John (*c.* 1614–57), English political figure, leader of the Levellers. After imprisonment (1638–40) for anti-episcopal pamphlets, he fought for the Parliamentarians during the Civil War (1642–45). He resigned from the army, however, because he refused to sign the Solemn League and Covenant required for admission to the New Model army. His pamphleteering against the army leaders led to arrest (1649) for treason, but he was acquitted. In his later years he became a Quaker.

Lincoln, Abraham (1809–65), 16th President of the USA. He was born into a poor frontier family and had little formal education. The family settled in New Salem, Illinois, in 1831, where Lincoln worked in a shop and began reading law. In 1834 he was elected to the Illinois legislature as a Whig and in 1836 was admitted to the bar and began to practise. In 1841 he was elected to the US House of Representatives.

Lincoln, by then a Republican, ran for the Senate in 1858. He was defeated but his oratory won him national fame. As a result, he became a leading candidate for the 1860 Republican nomination, which he won on the third ballot.

AD 1740–1744

A **Prussia's** Frederick the Great (1740–86) introduced religious toleration, agricultural reform and a revitalized army, which occupied Silesia (1740) in the War of the Austrian Succession. **Russia's** Senate gained new authority under Elizabeth (1741–62). **Mahrattas** took Bengal.
A **Britain** saw Walpole fall (1742). Pope produced the *Dunciad*, a work of great

poetic and satirical skill, (1743). Benjamin Huntsman found the crucible method of making steel.
Japan's Kitagawa Utamaro developed colour printing.
Swedish scientist Celsius devised a new temperature scale.
A **German** composer Bach produced the *Well-tempered Klavier*.
Religion saw the puritanical Wahhabi movement in Islam.

Linnaeus, Carl (Carolus)

He defeated the Democratic candidate and was inaugurated as President on 4 March 1861. The Southern states had already seceded and on 12 April Fort Sumter was fired on, the first action in the American Civil War. Lincoln conducted the war with vigour and efficiency: he called up the militia, blockaded southern ports and increased executive powers. With his appointment of Ulysses S. Grant as his commander-in-chief he ensured that the war would be relentlessly pursued.

On 22 Sept. 1863 Lincoln issued the Emancipation Proclamation, freeing the slaves, and on 19 Nov. 1863 delivered one of the noblest public speeches ever made, the Gettysburg Address. Lincoln was re-elected in 1864 and saw the war brought to a successful conclusion, but on 14 Sept. 1865, while attending a performance at Ford's Theatre, New York, he was shot by John Wilkes Booth, a disaffected Southerner. He died the following day.

Linnaeus, Carl (Carolus) (1707–78), Swedish botanist and explorer, also known as Carl von Linné. He was the first scientist to define the differences between species, giving Latin names for the genus and species to each organism, making consistent use of specific names and including all known organisms in a single classification. His *Systema Naturae*, published in 1735, laid the foundation of the modern science of taxonomy.

Little Bighorn, Battle of (25 June 1876), between Indians, under Sioux chiefs Sitting Bull and Crazy Horse and the 7th US Cavalry detachment led by General George Custer. Custer attempted a surprise attack but the 2,500 Indians wiped out his 264 officers and men near the Little Bighorn River in the Dakota Territory.

Little Red Book, popular name in the West for a small volume of the thoughts of the Chairman of the Chinese Communist Party, Mao Tse-Tung. It was first issued during the cultural revolution in 1966 and became the "bible" of the Red Guards.

Livingstone, David (1813–73), British missionary and

AD 1744–1748

Prussia, with France, defeated the Austrians at Fontenoy (1745). **Britain** took Louisburg from the French (1745) and received Madras back from them at the Treaty of Aix-la-Chapelle (1748). A Jacobite resistance was finally crushed at Culloden. William Hogarth satirized social abuses in his engravings. John Roebuck developed a manufacturing process for sulphuric acid (1746).

France produced Montesquieu's *The Spirit of Laws* (1748), examining relationships between a society's law and its other characteristics. D'Alembert wrote *Traité de Dynamique* (1743) on mechanics. **Italian** dramatist Goldoni wrote *The Servant of Two Masters*. **Bohemian** musician Johann Stamitz formed the first real symphony orchestra.

explorer. Coming from a poor background, he first worked in a cotton mill near Glasgow but saved enough to take a medical degree at the age of 27. Sent to Bechuanaland (now Botswana) by the London Missionary Society, he made strenuous efforts to combat disease and slavery. From 1858 to 1864 he explored the eastern Zambezi, and then set off to find the source of the Nile in 1866. He was cut off from all contact with Europe until 1871, when he was found by H.M. Stanley near Lake Tanganyika. Admired by all the peoples with whom he came into contact and a fierce opponent of slavery, Livingstone died at Ilala, in modern Zambia.

Livy (59 BC–AD 17), Roman historian, full name Titus Livius. With Tacitus and Sallust he is regarded as one of the greatest Roman historians. In about 28 BC he began his *History of Rome*, an account of the Romans from the legendary Aeneas' arrival in Italy (753 BC) to 9 BC. Livy used the best sources available at the time. His descriptions are vivid and he frequently draws moral conclusions. Thirty-five of the original 142 books are intact and there are fragments of the rest.

Lloyd George, David (1863–1945), British politician. He was a Liberal MP for Caernarvon Boroughs from 1890 to 1945, when he was created Earl Lloyd-George of Dwyfor. As Chancellor of the Exchequer (1908–15) he greatly increased taxation, above all in the "People's Budget" of 1909, to lay the foundation of the Welfare State. It was he who was chiefly responsible for introducing old-age pensions. In 1915 he was Minister of Munitions and Secretary of State for War. In 1916 he replaced Asquith as Prime Minister and formed a coalition government which lasted until 1922. As Prime Minister he won fame as a forceful war leader and handled the negotiations which led to the founding of the Irish Free State (1921). He remained leader of the Liberal party until 1931, but never again held office.

Locke, John (1632–1704), English Empiricist philosopher whose political theories of social contract, the right to

---

AD 1748–1752

A France's Louis XV was opposed by nobles and clergy when he tried to tax them (1751). The

A Encyclopedist Diderot edited the first volume of the *Encyclopedie* (1751), a monument to

A the philosophes (Lockean materialists). Georges Buffon published *Histoire Naturelle*.

A Britain's Robert Clive established power over southern India. The novel flourished

with Richardson, Fielding and Sterne all producing great works. The rococo style was fashionable. Joshua Reynolds revolutionized art and architecture. Robert Bakewell pioneered selective breeding, and Viscount Townshend improved crop yield. **China** invaded Tibet.

A American Benjamin Franklin established that lightning was electrical.

Lollards

freedom of conscience and the right to property greatly influenced emerging democracies of his day. Suspected of radicalism, he went into exile in Holland (1683–89) and returned to England after the Glorious Revolution, when his *An Essay Concerning Human Understanding* (1690) appeared. In the same year he published *Two Treatises on Civil Government*. He advocated limited sovereignty and held that revolution was not only a right but an obligation if liberty were threatened.

Lollards, followers of the 14th-century English religious reformer John Wycliffe. They challenged many doctrines and practices of the medieval Church, including transubstantiation, indulgences, pilgrimages and clerical celibacy. They rejected the authority of the Pope, and they denounced the wealth of the Church and Church involvement in civil affairs. Lollards went out as "poor preachers", teaching that the Bible was the sole authority in religion. They won support from some nobles as well as many common people and helped to pave the way for the Protestant Reformation.

Long Parliament, English parliament summoned by Charles I in Nov. 1640 to raise taxes to pay for his army. It was the Long Parliament's quarrels with Charles which led to the English Civil War. It executed Charles's minister Strafford and the Archbishop of Canterbury Laud. In 1648 it abolished the House of Lords and the monarchy. After Pride's purge of 1648 it was known as the Rump parliament and consisted only of supporters of Cromwell. It was forcibly ejected in 1653 but continued as the Barebones parliament until 1660, when Charles II was restored to the throne.

Louis XIV (1638–1715), son of Louis XIII and King of France (1643–1715). His personal rule began with the death of the regent, Cardinal Mazarin, in 1661. For the next 50 years Louis was the most powerful monarch in Europe, presiding over a France at the height of its intellectual, economic and military powers. The great figures of French

---

AD 1752–1756

Portugal saw the destruction of Lisbon by an earthquake (1755). Pombal introduced ideas
A of the Enlightenment there.
Russian nobles could go to Moscow University from 1755. Lomonosov published a *Grammar.*
Britain, controlling India by 1754, was ruled by a regular Cabinet.
A **France** produced Rousseau's *Social Contract* (1762), argu-

ing that men were innately equal. The work of Abbé Prévost foreshadowed Romanticism. René Réamur proved that digestion is a chemical process.
A **Austrian** composer Haydn developed the symphony, advancing its instrumentation and the form of its contrasting movements.
German philosopher Immanuel
A Kant published views on the formation of the solar system.

classicism were patronized by him and the palace at Versailles built for him. There the elaborate courtly ritual of the "Sun King", including the famous *levée*, was acted out. In economics Louis was served by Colbert, who, working on foundations laid by his predecessors, made France the most centralized mercantilist state in Europe. Louis destroyed the power of the nobility in the provinces: this was the basis of his absolutism. Abroad, he sought to dominate western Europe. Yet in the War of Devolution (1667–68), the third Dutch war (1672–78), (ended by the Treaty of Nijmegen), the War of the League of Augsburg (1688–97) and the War of the Spanish Succession (1702–13) he depleted the French treasury and was limited to minor gains. The rigidity of the system he imposed upon the country led to France's decline in the 18th century.

Louis XV (1710–74), grandson of Louis XIV; King of France (1715–74). Under his rule, the French monarchy was fatally weakened. He ran an extravagant court, and his personal weakness left him prey to favourites such as Madame de Pompadour. His wars were expensive and ended in defeat in the Seven Years War and the loss of most of the French Empire. He was unable to reform the outdated tax system or prevent national insolvency.

Louis XVI (1754–93), grandson of Louis XV; King of France (1774–92). He attempted to restore the power of the French monarchy, but the aristocracy prevented his ministers Turgot and Necker from implementing their economic reforms. He convened the Assembly of Notables in 1787 and, in desperation, the Estates General in 1789; the French Revolution quickly followed. Although Louis outwardly accepted the Revolution, he was suspected of intriguing with foreign powers, was deposed in 1792 and beheaded on 21 Jan. 1793.

Luddites, textile workers in England who in the early 19th century destroyed power looms and knitting-frames, which they believed to be the cause of unemployment in the cotton and woollen industries. They were named after a mythical

---

AD 1756–1760

A **Prussia** defeated Austria in the A Seven Years War.

Britain emerged with control of Bengal (1757) and most of Canada (1760); new commercial confidence resulted. Joseph Black discovered carbon dioxide (1756) and John Dolland produced the first achromatic lenses (1757).

Mahrattas occupied the Punjab.

A **Portugal** expelled Jesuits (1759).

French physiocrat François

Quesnay produced *Tableau Economique* (1758), the first work to analyse the workings of an entire economy.

Chinese fiction's realism was exemplified by Wu Ching-tse's satirical novel *Unofficial History of Scholars* and *The Dream of a Red Chamber* by Tsao Chan.

Russian Lomonosov observed Venus' atmosphere (1761).

Luther, Martin

"King Ludd", who signed public letters denouncing the new machines. The chief riots, starting in Nottinghamshire and spreading to Cheshire, Lancashire and Yorkshire, took place in 1811–12.

Luther, Martin (1483–1546), leader of the German Reformation. He studied philosophy at Erfurt University and became an Augustinian monk in 1505. Two years later he was ordained and became a teacher of philosophy and theology at Wittenberg University. He was deeply concerned about the problem of salvation, finally deciding that it could not be attained by good works but was a free gift of God's grace. Luther's beliefs made him object to many practices of the medieval Church, particularly the sale of indulgences. In 1517 he affixed his 95 Theses to the door of the Schlosskirche in Wittenberg. This led to a quarrel between Luther and Church leaders, including the pope. Luther decided that the Bible was the true source of authority and renounced obedience to Rome. He maintained his stand in debates with Johann Eck and at the Diet of Worms in 1521. As a result, he was excommunicated, but strong German princes came to his rescue, and he gained followers among churchmen as well as the laity. Luther married a former nun, Katherina von Bora, in 1525.

Luxemburg, Rosa (1871–1919), German socialist leader, *b.* Poland. She became a German citizen through marriage and after 1898 was a leader of the Social Democratic Party. She founded the Spartacist (later Communist) Party during WWI with Karl Liebknecht, and was arrested for her part in the Spartacist uprising in Berlin in Jan. 1919. She was murdered while being taken to prison.

McAdam, John Loudon (1756–1836), Scottish engineer who invented the macadam road surface. He proposed that roads should be raised above the surrounding ground, with a base of large stones covered with smaller stones and bound together with fine gravel. He applied these ideas when he was appointed surveyor general of Bristol's roads in 1815.

AD 1760–1764

Prussia's military power grew after the Seven Years War.

France's trade expanded, despite declining finances. Rousseau's *La Nouvelle Heloise* (1761) advocated simple relationships in a natural setting, deeply influencing Romanticism.

Britain's supremacy in India and Canada was confirmed by the Treaty of Paris (1763).

The Pontiac Conspiracy was suppressed. Overseas trade, doubled since 1720, meant the building of many canals. The School of Common Sense Philosophy was begun by Thomas Reid, rejecting Hume's scepticism. Robert and James Adam revolutionized country house architecture. Joseph Black worked with heat and James Hargreaves invented the spinning jenny (1764).

His views on road-making were adopted after a Parliamentary Inquiry in 1823.

MacArthur, Douglas (1880–1964), us general, who participated in all the important us offensives during WWI. He retired from the army (1937) to work in the Philippines but was recalled to active duty when the USA entered WWII and appointed Commander of the us army forces in the Pacific. From Australia he directed the assault that led to Japanese defeat. MacArthur accepted the Japanese surrender on the USS *Missouri* on 2 Sept. 1945. He was appointed commander of UN troops during the Korean war but, following a policy dispute with President Truman that MacArthur made public, he was relieved of his command.

Macaulay, Thomas Babington (1800–1859), English historian, poet and statesman. After serving as a Liberal in the House of Commons, he was appointed a member of the Supreme Council of India where he lived from 1834–38. He returned to Parliament (1839–1847) and in 1847 began to write *The History of England from the Accession of James the Second* (5 vols, 1849–1861), which enjoyed great success. His poetical work, *Lays of Ancient Rome* (1842), celebrated the events of Roman history.

MacBride, Seán (1904–   ), Irish political figure, the son of the Irish patriots Maud Gonne and John MacBride. He served in the Irish Republican Army (IRA) and founded the Clann na Poblachta (Republican Political Party) in 1946. He was a Member of the Irish Parliament (1947–58), and represented Ireland at the Council of Europe (1954–63). He served as UN commissioner for Namibia (1973–76). Active in the cause of international peace, he was awarded the Nobel Peace Prize in 1974.

McCarthy, Joseph Raymond (1908–57), us senator who gained national attention in 1950 by claiming that the us State Department had been infiltrated by Communists. He was appointed chairman of the Senate's permanent Subcommittee on Investigations in which office he wielded great power.

AD 1764–1768

A **Russia's** Catherine II reformed the law (1767).

Britain encountered local opposition to the Stamp Act and Sugar Act. Bengal and Bihar were British-ruled by 1765. Adam Ferguson's *Essay on the History of Civilized Society* (1766) examined social development. Gothic themes appeared in Horace Walpole's *Castle of Otranto* (1764). Thomas Percy published *Reliques of Ancient English Poetry* (1765). Joshua Reynolds was the Royal Academy's first President.

Egypt gained independence.

Swiss physiologist von Haller established neurology.

Religion saw Moses Mendelssohn establish a synthesis of Judaism and modern philosophical thought, founding Reform Judaism.

MacDonald, James Ramsay

MacDonald, James Ramsay (1866–1937), British politician, illegitimate son of a servant, who became leader of the Independent Labour Party (later the Labour Party). A Member of Parliament (1906–18), his opposition to Britain's role in WWI aroused furious animosity and he was defeated in the 1918 elections. Returned to Parliament in 1922, he became Britain's first Labour Prime Minister in 1924. He was Prime Minister again (1929) but in 1931 was forced to head the National Government, heavily depending on Conservative support. He became increasingly distrusted by the Labour Party and lost power in 1935.

Machel, Samora Moïsès (1933–   ), Mozambique politician. He received a military training in Algeria in 1963, took part in guerrilla activities against the Portuguese in Mozambique as a member of Frelimo, of which he became president in 1970. Following the withdrawal of the Portuguese troops, Machel became president of Mozambique in June 1975.

Machiavelli, Niccolò (1469–1527), Florentine statesman and political theorist, an outstanding figure of the Italian Renaissance. He served from 1498 to 1512 as an official and diplomat of Piero Soderini's republican government of Florence, but lost his post when the Medici family returned to power. He devoted the remainder of his life to writing. His *Discourses on the First Ten Books of Livy* (1513–19) argued that the experience of the past could provide solutions for the present. His most famous work, *The Prince* (1513), propounded a ruler's need to preserve and enhance his own power and that of the state by whatever means necessary.

McKinley, William (1843–1901), 25th President of the US (1897–1901) during whose first administration America became a colonial power. A conservative Republican, he supported high protective tariffs, adopted the monetary Gold Standard and, urged on by such expansionists as publisher William Randolph Hearst and Assistant Secretary

---

AD 1768–1772

American colonists settled Tennessee (1769) and fought with British troops in the Boston Massacre (1770).
France saw intellectual opposition to absolutism and increased Indian trade. Paul d'Holbach, an Encyclopedist, wrote about determinism in *System of Nature* (1770).
Britain's James Cook explored Australasia. Freer elections were established through John Wilkes and political stability through Lord North. Gray's *Elegy* appeared. George Stubbs showed an empirical scientific attitude to art. Arkwright invented the water frame (1768) and Watt the steam engine (1769).
German poet Herder prefigured Romanticism.
Italian Galvani produced electricity.

of the Navy Theodore Roosevelt, declared war on Spain
(1898). At the end of the 113-days war the US annexed
Guam, Puerto Rico, the Philippines, Hawaii and American
Samoa. McKinley was assassinated during his second term
of office by an anarchist, Leon Czolgosz.

Macmillan, Maurice Harold (1894–   ), British
statesman. During the 1930s, Macmillan was one of a small
band of Conservatives prepared to face political death for
attacking their government's foreign policy, in particular
the passive acceptance of Mussolini's invasion of Abyssinia.
In the 1950s he held a number of cabinet posts, including
Minister of Housing and Local Government (1951–54),
Minister of Defence (1954–55), and Chancellor of the
Exchequer (1955–57). He succeeded Anthony Eden (later
Lord Avon) as Prime Minister (1957–63), improving
Anglo-American relations after the Suez crisis and trying
unsuccessfully to obtain Britain's entry into the European
Economic Community. He gave firm support to President
Kennedy over the Cuban Missile Crisis in 1962.

Magellan, Ferdinand (c. 1480–1521), Portuguese explorer
who commanded the first expedition to circumnavigate the
globe; the expedition was completed after his death.
Probably wounded while exploring the East Indies, he took
part in the taking of Malacca which made possible the
exploitation of the vast trade potential in the Spice Islands
(or Moluccas). He fell from the King of Portugal's favour
and moved to Spain, where he organized an expedition to
reach the Spice Islands by sailing west. Leaving with five
ships in 1519, he reached Brazil and sailed south, seeking a
westward passage. In November 1520 he sailed through the
straits which today bears his name and reached the
Philippines in March 1521, where he was killed by natives.
Two of his ships reached the Moluccas, but only one
returned to Spain, thus establishing a new route between
Europe and Asia.

Magna Carta (1215), "the Great Charter" of English
constitutional history. It was issued by King John, under

Magyars

compulsion from his barons, at Runnymede, on 15 June, 1215. John's financial exactions had united clergy and laity in demands for guarantees of their rights and privileges. The 63 clauses into which Magna Carta is traditionally divided protected the rights of the Church, the feudal lords, the lords' subtentants and the merchants, and regulated royal privileges, the administration of justice, and the behaviour of royal officials. For subsequent generations Magna Carta became the basis and epitome of the subject's rights, protecting him and limiting his sovereign's prerogatives.

Magyars, the people associated with the state of Hungary, descendants of Finno-Ugric and Turkic tribes who mingled with Avars and Slavs in the 9th century. They conquered large areas of Germany until defeated by Otto I in 955. Although incorporated into the Austrian Empire from the 16th century, the fiercely independent Magyars demanded special minority rights to preserve their language and culture, achieving first the Dual Monarchy in 1867 and then independence in 1918.

Makarios III (1913–77), Archbishop, *b.* Mikhail Khristodoulou Mouskos. Leader of the Enosis (union of Cyprus with Greece) movement, he was a suspected terrorist but was elected President of Cyprus (1959) when it became independent of Britain. In later years he became less extreme in his views but continued to put pressure on the island's Turkish population. In 1974 the Turks invaded Cyprus and occupied the northern half of the island.

Malthus, Thomas (1766–1834), British economist and minister famous for his *Essay on Population* (1798). According to Malthusian theory, population increases geometrically but the food supply can increase only arithmetically so that population must eventually overtake it, with famine, war and disease as consequences. Malthus objected to any interference in this process, and did not favour family planning.

Mamelukes, ruling dynasty of Egypt (1250–1517). Originally Turkish and Circassian prisoners of Genghis

---

AD 1776–1780

A **American** colonies declared independence (1776), allying with France and Spain.

France blockaded shipping in America and was crippled by

A the war despite Necker's financial reforms. Nicholas Leblanc produced cheap soap.

Britain relaxed anti-Catholic

A laws, causing the Gordon Riots

A (1780). Adam Smith founded modern economics with *Wealth of*

Nations (1776). Goldsmith and Sheridan revived the comedy of manners. Joseph Bramah's many inventions founded the engineering industry. Crompton invented the spinning mule.

Portugal reorganized the administration of Brazil.

Italian patriotism was stirred by Alfieri's verse tragedies.

Russian classicism was led by foreign artists.

Khan, they were sold as slaves to the sultan of Egypt, who trained them as soldiers. They became strong enough to usurp the sultan's political authority and pursued an aggressive foreign policy, although domestic intrigue limited each Mameluke sultan's reign. They were the first to halt the Mongol advance westwards and to defeat the Assassins. The Mamelukes, in turn, were defeated by the Ottoman Sultan Selim I in 1517, but remained a class and kept their lands. As the Ottoman Empire declined in the 18th century, the Mameluke governors of Egypt regained some autonomy; their power was not ended until 1811, when they were defeated by Muhammed Ali.

Manchu dynasty, *See* **Ch'ing dynasty.**

Manley, name of two prime ministers of Jamaica. Norman Washington Manley (1893–1969), a lawyer educated at Oxford, founded the socialist People's National Party (PNP) in 1938, and was Jamaica's first Premier from 1959–62. His son Michael Norman Manley (1923–), was an active trade-unionist before becoming a politician. He, also of the PNP, became Prime Minister of Jamaica in 1972.

Mao Tse-tung (1893–1976), Chinese Communist leader and head of state. He was an early member of the Chinese Communist Party, becoming Chairman of the People's Republic of China in 1949. The most influential person in modern Chinese history, he was a prime mover of events which led to the Communist accession to power in 1949. He joined the revolutionary army briefly in 1911 to fight against the Manchu Dynasty, went to Peking University in 1919, becoming an adherent of Marxism in 1919–20. He organized a Communist group in Hunan in 1920 and in 1923 devoted himself full-time to revolutionary activities, becoming convinced of the revolutionary potential of the peasantry. In 1927 the Communists split with Chiang Kai-Shek's Kuomintang when the latter expelled all Communists from high posts in the organization. The years 1927–49 saw the consolidation of the Communist Party under Mao's increasing control. Mao concentrated his

---

AD 1780–1784

A **American** independence was recognized, after Britain's surrender at Yorktown, at the Treaty of Paris (1783). **Britain** entered the Industrial Revolution with the growth of the cotton industry. Hastings made peace with the Mahrattas A (1784). William Pitt formed his first ministry. Blake and Fuseli's work emphasized the bizarre. William Herschel

discovered Uranus (1781). **Russia** occupied the Crimea. A **German** philosopher Kant's *Critique of Pure Reason* (1781) argued that although knowledge cannot transcend experience, the concepts that organize perception are innate. **French** novelist Laclos produced the decadent *Les Liaisons Dangereuses* (1782). The Montgolfier brothers flew in a balloon.

efforts on the peasantry rather than the urban masses, and after guerrilla activities against the Kuomintang in the late 1920s, became Chairman of the Communist base at Kiangsi in 1931. His dominance in the party was established by 1935 during the Long March from Kiangsi to Shensi in 1934–1936. Mao built his reputation as a Theorist in Yenan from 1936 until the end of WWII, and by the late 1930s his control over the Communist Party was assured with his concept of the "Sinification of Marxism", the adaptation of Marxism to the cultural, historical and economic experiences of the Chinese. In 1949 Mao became Chairman of the People's Republic of China, placing emphasis on rapid collectivization and initially concentrating on the development of heavy industry. In 1956 he propounded the Hundred Flowers policy – the freedom to express diverse ideas – with the aim of incorporating the intelligentsia into the Chinese revolution. The late 1950s saw the Great Leap Forward with emphasis on decentralization and the development of labour-intensive industries leading to the establishment of people's communes. He retired as Chairman of the Republic in 1959 but remained Chairman of the Communist party. Mao's feeling of the growing elitism within Chinese society and leadership struggles with Liu Shao-Ch'i and Teng Hsiao-p'ing led to the Cultural Revolution (1966–69). Mao gradually retired from the day-to-day administration of politics in the early 1970s. A leading Chinese theoretician with a world-wide reputation, his writings cover politics and culture, as well as international affairs and guerrilla warfare tactics. He is an inspirational figure to many left-wing revolutionary movements.

Marconi, Guglielmo (1874–1937), Italian physicist who developed radio. By 1897 Marconi was able to demonstrate radio telegraphy over a distance of 19km (12 miles) and, after forming a wireless telegraph company, established radio communication between France and England in 1899. By 1901 radio transmissions were received

---

AD 1784–1788

US traded with China (1784), but suffered through the post-war loss of contact with the West Indies. The Constitution was signed (1787).
French proposals for financial reform were blocked by aristocratic parliaments (1787). Jacques Charles stated his law governing gas volumes.
Britain saw the *Times* founded (1788). An economic boom was based on cotton and coal. Utilitarianism was proposed by

A Jeremy Bentham's *Principles* (1784). Robert Burns and Cowper dominated poetry. Meikle invented the threshing machine.
Austrian composer Wolfgang

A Amadeus Mozart perfected the Classical style, writing 41 symphonies, much chamber music and several extremely original operas.

across the Atlantic Ocean, and in 1909 Marconi was awarded the Nobel Prize in physics. His later work on short-wave radio transmission formed the basis of nearly all modern long-distance communication.

Maria Theresa (1717–80), Archduchess of Austria, Queen of Bohemia and Hungary (1740–80; co-ruler with her son Joseph II, 1765–80), wife and mother of Holy Roman emperors (1745–65 and 1765–80 respectively). In 1713 her father, the Holy Roman Emperor Charles VI, altered Hapsburg law by the Pragmatic Sanction to allow female succession. But on his death (1740) her succession was disputed by almost all the major European powers. Prussia seized Silesia, precipitating the War of the Austrian Succession (1740–48). In 1756 Austria formed an alliance with France and Russia, thereby antagonizing Prussia and England. In the ensuing Seven Years War (1756–63) Austria lost no territory, but its traditional role as dominant German state passed to Prussia. Although essentially conservative, Maria Theresa devoted her energies after 1748 to a vast programme of reform.

Marie Antoinette (1755–93), Queen of France, daughter of Francis I and Maria Theresa of Austria. In 1770 she married the French dauphin, later Louis XVI, and her life of pleasure and careless extravagance caused deep public resentment. In 1789, during the French Revolution, she was taken with the King from Versailles to Paris. She was seized at Varennes when the royal family attempted to escape and was guillotined in 1793.

Marius, Gaius (*c.* 157–86 BC), Roman politician and general who created a new and highly trained army. Of middle-class birth, Marius was elected consul seven times and became the enemy of the patrician Sulla. When Sulla took command of the Roman forces in the east, Marius jealously sought to deprive him of the command but was defeated in battle and forced to flee. In 87 he raised an army in Etruria and with Cinna captured Rome, where they were elected consuls. Marius ordered the destruction of his numerous

---

AD 1788–1792

France, after the financial crisis could not be solved by Louis XIV, saw the French Revolution erupt (1789). Middle-class radicals, backed by the Paris mob, took over the administration. Church lands were nationalized and religious orders suppressed. Paine became an apologist for the rebels, while Burke was more cautious. Lavoisier founded chemistry.

US had George Washington as the first President (1789). **Britain** established convict settlements in Australia (1788). **Pitt** survived the crisis caused by George III's temporary insanity. Candid biography was originated by Boswell's *Life of Johnson* (1791). James Hutton founded modern geology. **Italian** composer Cimarosa produced *Il Matrimonio Segreto*.

enemies, and it took 4,000 slaves five days and nights to complete the slaughter. Marius died shortly afterwards.

Mark Antony (*c.* 82–30 BC), distinguished Roman soldier and politician, friend of Julius Caesar and Cleopatra's lover. His affair with Cleopatra led to defeat at Actium by Octavius, after which he and Cleopatra fled to Egypt, where they both committed suicide.

Marlborough, John Churchill, 1st Duke of (1650–1722), English general and statesman. One of the greatest commanders in English history, Marlborough led the Allied armies against Louis XIV in the War of the Spanish Succession, destroying French power and amibition at Blenheim (1704), Ramillies (1706), Oudenaarde (1708) and Malplaquet (1709). On the ascendancy of his political enemies, the Whigs, in 1711 he was dismissed from all his offices but in 1714, with the accession of the Hanoverian George I, he was restored to royal favour.

Marx, Karl Heinrich (1818–83), German social philosopher and political theorist, founder (with Friedrich Engels) of world Communism. He studied history, philosophy and law, was influenced by G.W.F. Hegel, Ludwig Feuerbach and Moses Hess and produced his own philosophical approach of Dialectical Materialism. He proclaimed that religion was "the opium of the people" and in *The German Ideology* (1845–46), written with Engels, described inevitable laws of history. In Brussels he joined the Communist League and wrote with Engels the epoch-making Communist Manifesto (1848). Marx took part in the revolutionary movements in France and Germany, then went to London (1849) where he lived until his death. Although Engels helped him financially, these were years of poverty and illness. He toiled at research in the British Museum and produced a stream of writings, including *Das Kapital* (3 vols, 1867, 1885, 1894, the last two edited by Engels), which became the "Bible of the working class". In 1864 he was founder of the International Workingmen's Association (the First International) and became its leading spirit. He denounced

---

AD 1792–1796

A **France** declared a republic (1792) and executed Louis XVI and many aristocrats. Holland was overrun and the Batavian republic established. Slaves were freed in the West Indies. The Cult of the Supreme Being replaced Christianity. The metric system was instituted.

A **Britain's** Pitt suppressed a campaign for electoral reforms. Mary Wollstonecraft demanded equal opportunities for women, and her husband William Godwin was an energetic radical writer. William Blake produced *Songs of Experience*, a visionary poetic work. Coal gas was produced by William Murdoch.

Italian violin virtuoso Paganini made his debut (1793).

US inventor Eli Whitney produced the cotton gin (1793), revitalizing cotton growing.

both the non-revolutionary reformism of British labour leaders and the anarchy of philosopher Mikhail Bakunin, generally favouring legal methods to hasten the collapse of Capitalism. Marx was one of the most important political theorists of modern times. His ideas exerted a powerful influence after his death and helped to change the course of history.

Mary I, or Mary Tudor (1516–58), Queen of England, daughter of Henry VIII and Catherine of Aragon; she is known as "Bloody Mary". On the death of Edward VI she overcame Lady Jane Grey's challenge for the throne and became queen in 1553. Her determination to re-introduce Roman Catholicism in England occasioned the major errors of her reign – her marriage to Philip of Spain in 1554 and persecution of her Protestant subjects.

Mary, Queen of Scots (1542–87), daughter of James V of Scotland. She married Francis II of France in 1558 and after his death in 1560 married Henry, Lord Darnley, in 1565. He died under mysterious circumstances in 1567 after he had had David Rizzio, her favourite, murdered the year before. She was deposed after her marriage to the Earl of Bothwell and sought refuge in England. After Mary was shown to have been involved in the Ridolfi Plot (1572) and the Babington Conspiracy (1586), Elizabeth I agreed reluctantly to her execution.

Mata Hari (1876–1917), Dutch courtesan and double agent, real name Margaretha Geertruida Zelle. She was the wife of a Dutch colonial officer with whom she lived in Java until 1902, when she left him and travelled to Europe, calling herself Mata Hari. From 1905 she was a professional dancer, performing dances she had learnt while in Java. She became well-known in Paris, and was in the pay of both the French and German intelligence services. She was executed by the French as a spy during WWI.

Mau Mau, Kenyan secret terrorist organization in the 1950s, comprising mainly Kikuyu tribesmen, dedicated by oath to expel white settlers from Kenya. In 1952 the Mau

---

AD 1796–1800

France gained Belgium from Austria (1797). Napoleon's plans to invade England were thwarted by his defeat by Nelson at the Battle of the Nile. He established a dictatorship (1799–1804), his regime bolstered by his successful Italian campaign. **Britain** saw the Combination Acts (1799) ban trade union activity. The Evangical Movement emerged within the Church of England. Malthus published *Essay on the Principle of Population* (1798), warning of the possibility of a population explosion. Wordsworth and Coleridge began the Romantic movement. Edward Jenner discovered vaccination (1796). **US** scientist Count Rumford discovered kinetic energy (1798). **Italian** scientist Count Volta invented the battery (1800).

Maya

Mau began a reign of terror against Europeans; the settlers retaliated, British troops were drafted in and casualties multiplied. Although approximately 11,000 Mau Mau were killed in the reprisals, the Kikuyu resistance developed into the Kenyan independent movement. Jomo Kenyatta, who had been jailed as a Mau Mau leader, became Prime Minister of independent Kenya in 1963. He always denied any connection with the organization.

Maya, one of the most important tribes of Central American Indians. They established a remarkable civilization (which reached its peak from the 3rd to the 9th centuries AD) in what is now the whole of Belize, w El Salvador and Honduras, and parts of Mexico, including Yucatán. They were short, stocky and dark, and are believed to have travelled originally from Asia many thousands of years ago.

The Maya are renowned mainly for their knowledge of astronomy and mathematics. Priests prepared tables of dates by means of which they were able to predict solar eclipses. They also accurately traced the orbit of Venus. They wrote their numbers with a system of dots and dashes, and developed a symbol that served roughly the same purpose as the modern zero. Their surviving architecture is represented mainly by high stone pyramids topped by temples. Religion was based on an ordered cosmology, with a god of fire and creation, also a god represented by a feathered serpent. Human sacrifice was common in the classic period. Today more than 1.5 million Maya Indians still inhabit the region.

Mazzini, Giuseppe (1805–72), Italian patriot and political thinker of the Risorgimento (Italian unification movement). A member of the *Carbonari* (the Italian republican underground) from 1830, he founded the "Young Italy" movement in 1831, dedicated to the republican unification of Italy. He fought in the Italian revolutionary movement of 1848 and ruled in Rome in 1849, but was then exiled. Although he was active in revolutionary activities during the 1850s, he played a minor

---

AD 1800–1802

A **France's** Napoleon I established the prefecture as the main instrument of local government. His nationalist military campaigns were successful in Austria, Italy and the Empire. He improved education and compromised with the Church. Jacquard invented punched card automation in silk manufacture.

A **Britain's** Robert Owen set up a co-operative cotton mill

(1800). Britain and Ireland were constitutionally united. Paley's *Natural Theology* asserted the existence of a creator. Industrial architecture included iron frame buildings. Thomas Young restored the wave light theory and studied elasticity.

Polish scientist Johann Ritter discovered ultra-violet light in the Sun's spectrum.

role in 1861 when the unified Italian kingdom was established.

Medes, group of ancient Iranian tribes from around the Elburz Mts. They frequently clashed with the Assyrians during the 9th century, BC, and were conquered by the Scythians in the 7th century. The Median king Cyaxares drove out the Scythians and also helped the Babylonians destroy the Assyrian Empire; this period (*c.* 615–*c.* 585 BC) saw the greatest extent of Median power. Cyrus the Great defeated the last Median king in 550 BC and incorporated Medea into his empire.

Medici, Italian family who ruled Florence and, later, Tuscany, from the 15th to the 18th centuries. Included in the family were three popes, Leo X (*r.* 1513–21); Clement VII (*r.* 1523–34); and Leo XI (*r.* 1605). The family's name was Medici di Cafaggiolo, and its first member of importance was Giambono de' Medici (Chiarissimo I), who became a member of the Florence general council in 1201. Giovanni di Averdo III (Giovanni di Bicci) (1360–1429) became one of the richest bankers in Italy, and was mainly responsible for the family's rising influence after Salvestro di Alamanno's exile. Cosimo the Elder (1389–1464) spent vast sums of money on the arts and humanist scholarship and sponsored the first public library in Florence. Another Medici famous for his interest in the arts was Lorenzo the Magnificent (1449–92), who provided Florence with its most splendid period under the Renaissance. He was also able, through his abilities as a diplomat, to maintain a balance of power among rival Italian states, and it was as a result of this influence that Florentine politics became more closely allied with the papacy than hitherto. The family's history is one of coup and counter-coup between their imperial interests and the Florentine republican cause.

Mehmet, name of six sultans of the Ottoman Empire. Mehmet I (1387–1421) came to the throne in 1413, reunited the empire and consolidated his power in the Balkans. Mehmet II (1431–81) came to power in 1451 and

AD 1802–1805

France was opposed by Britain, Austria and Sweden (1805). She defeated Russia at Austerlitz, but Britain's naval victory at A Trafalgar resulted in a crippling shipping blockade. Law was rationalized under the Code Napoleon. Say's *Traité d'Economie Politique* stated the law of supply and demand. Chateaubriand's *La Genie du Christianisme* introduced a mystical Christianity into literature. Lamarck held that evolution had occurred, coining the term "biology".
Britain's Factory Act tried to limit child labour. Maudslay developed screw-cutting machines, and Trevithick built the first railway locomotive.
German poet Schiller wrote *William Tell* (1804).
Greek architecture was popular.

two years later captured Constantinople, which he largely rebuilt and which became the capital of the Ottoman empire. During his reign the Ottoman state was strengthened sufficiently to dominate the Mediterranean world for the next 200 years.

Meir, Golda (1898–1978), Israeli politician, *b.* Goldie Mabovitch in the Ukraine. In 1906 she emigrated to the USA, and moved to Palestine in 1921 to live on a kibbutz. In 1946–48 she often acted as *de facto* leader of the Jews in Palestine and after independence served as ambassador to the USSR and as Minister of Labour (1949–56). She also served as Foreign Minister (1956–66). In 1969 she became Prime Minister, but resigned in 1974 after criticism over lack of preparedness at the outbreak of the 1973 Arab-Israeli war.

Mendel, Gregor Johann (1822–84), Austrian naturalist. He discovered the laws of heredity and in so doing laid the foundation for the modern science of genetics. Mendel joined the monastery at Brünn (modern Brno) in 1824 and was ordained in 1847; he began plant experiments in 1856 in the monastery gardens. His experimental breeding of the garden pea led him to formulate two laws: the principle of segregation and the principle of the independent assortment of characters. His discoveries, published in *Experiments with Plant Hybrids* (1865), were virtually ignored until 1900, when his work was rediscovered and recognized for its great importance in evolution.

Mendeleyev, or Mendeleev, Dmitr Ivanovich (1834–1907), Russian chemist. He studied at St Petersburg, where he later became professor. After hearing the lectures of Stanislao Cannizzaro, he developed an interest in the relationship between the 63 elements then known. He devised the periodic law and the modern form of the periodic table at about the same time as the German Lothar Meyer. This table enabled him to predict the existence of several elements, including gallium and scandium.

Mensheviks, moderate faction of the Russian Social

AD 1805–1807

France defeated Prussia and, allied with Russia, set up the Continental System to cripple British trade. Art by Ingres and Gros, and Brongniart's Bourse bolstered France's image.

A Holy Roman Empire ended (1806); Francis II renounced the title. Britain abolished the slave trade in the Empire (1807) and blockaded French ports. The Geological Society was founded (1807).

A German philosopher Hegel published *Phenomenology of Mind* (1807), stating that reality is a whole comprising both mind and matter. Beethoven straddled the classical and romantic eras.

US engineer Robert Fulton started a regular steamboat service along the Hudson River (1807).

Democratic Labour party. They broke with the Bolsheviks
at the 1903 Party Congress because of Lenin's insistence on
a centralized party of professional revolutionaries. After the
Bolshevik seizure of power in November 1917, many
Mensheviks capitulated to the Bolsheviks. The Mensheviks
were suppressed in 1922.

Mercator, Gerhardus (1512–94). Flemish geographer and
cartographer who developed the first modern system of map
projection. He worked as a cartographer to the Emperor
Charles V and as cosmographer to the Duke of Cleves after
1559. In 1568 he produced the first nautical chart to use the
so-called Mercator projection (which he did not himself
invent).

Merovingian Empire, *See* **Franks**.

Metternich, Prince Klemens Wenzel Nepomuk Lothar von
(1773–1859), Austrian statesman who came to loathe
revolutionary excesses and who became Foreign Minister in
1809. On taking office he pursued a policy of conciliation
towards Napoleon but in 1813 formed the Quadruple
Alliance with England, Prussia and Russia to defeat him. He
reached the zenith of his influence at the Congress of
Vienna (1814–15), which restored Europe to a group of
anti-democratic states. He was driven from power by the
revolution of 1848.

Mexican War, (1846–1847), armed conflict between the
USA and Mexico, the immediate cause of which was the US
annexation of Texas (1845). Mexico claimed that the
Nueces River should be the SW boundary of Texas, whereas
the Texans insisted that it should be the Rio Grande.
Hostilities commenced when US forces, under Gen. Zachary
Taylor, invaded the disputed area. The Mexicans were
overwhelmed and, by the Treaty of Guadalupe Hidalgo
(1848), were obliged to relinquish all claims to Texas (the
present states of New Mexico, Utah, Nevada, Arizona and
California) in return for $15 million.

Michael (1596–1695), Tsar of Russia (1613–45), founder
of the Romanov dynasty. His election as tsar ended the

AD 1807–1808

France faced a nationalist
revolt in Spain when Joseph
Bonaparte assumed the throne
there. Britain started the
Peninsular War, exploiting
this. France controlled Swedish
foreign affairs. Fourier
began work with sine waves.
Austria reformed her army and
taxation system, as did Prussia,
to improve military capacity,
although Charles of Austria's
appeals to the Germans to oppose
A Napoleon resulted in defeat.
British Parliament was getting
increasingly out of touch with
A industry. Robert Owen advocated social reconstruction.
Davy discovered potassium and
sodium. Dalton proposed the
atomic theory.
A German poet Goethe wrote *Faust,*
A Beethoven the *Pastoral
Symphony.*

Michelangelo Buonarotti

chaotic period known as the Time of Troubles that had existed since the death of Feodor I in 1598. Michael made peace with Sweden in 1617 and Poland in 1618 and, during his reign, some Western influences were introduced but the peasants were further reduced to serfdom.

Michelangelo Buonarotti (1475–1564), Italian sculptor, painter, architect and poet, an outstanding renaissance figure and a creater of mannerism. He trained in Florence, first in the technique of Frescoe, under Ghirlandaio, and then in the Medici School, where he was influenced by the ideas of the humanists. In 1499 he sculptured the *Pietà* for St Peter's, Rome, which established his reputation. Michelangelo spent most of his productive years in Rome or Florence. He considered himself primarily a sculptor and created numerous monumental and heroic figures. Among these are *David* (1501–04), *Moses* (1513–16), *The Slaves* (c. 1513) and the symbolic figures *Day, Night, Dawn* and *Evening* for the Medici Chapel, Florence, which he also designed (from 1520). His masterpiece in painting was his frescoe cycle (1508–12) and *Last Judgement* (completed 1541) for the Sistine Chapel, Rome.

The Laurentian Library, Florence, which Michelangelo started planning in 1524, is among the earliest important examples of Mannerist architecture. In 1539 he began laying out the new Roman Capitol, and from 1546 to 1564 he was chief architect of St Peter's. During these last years he also wrote some of his finest sonnets. Probably no artist has been more influential.

Mill, John Stuart (1806–73), British philosopher who was educated by his father, James Mill – recounted in his *Autobiography* (1873) – and who advocated utilitarianism. His book *On Liberty* (1859) made him famous as a defender of human rights. *System of Logic* (1843) was an attempt to provide an account of inductive reason.

Milton, John (1608–74), English poet and prose writer. He travelled widely in Europe between 1638 and 1639 and served as Latin secretary to the Commonwealth

---

AD 1808–1812

France took Moscow (1812) but had to retreat during winter with serious losses. Napoleon married Marie Louise of Austria. Mme. de Stael wrote *D'Allemagne*. Gay-Lussac's chemical work led to the determination of correct atomic weights.

Spain's imperial authority collapsed with Paraguay's and Venezuela's independence.

Britain saw the anti-mechanization Luddite riots. Jane Austen satirized the middle classes in her novels. Orchestral concerts were popular.

German philosopher Hegel published *Science of Logic*, developing a dialectical science of reasoning aimed at revealing the Absolute.

Italian scientist Amadeo Avogadro studied the volume of gases.

government (1649–60). In 1652 he became blind. His work is characterized by Latinized language and grandeur of imagery. His theology was unconventional, based on the section ideas prevalent in the 1640's. His greatest works are *L'Allegro* and *Il Penseroso* (both 1632), *Comus* (1634), *Lycidas* (1637), *Areopagitica, a Speech* (1644), *Paradise Lost* (1667), *Paradise Regained* (1671) and *Samson Agonistes* (1671).

Ming dynasty (1368–1644), the last of the great Chinese dynasties before the conquest of China by the Manchus. The first Ming emperor, Chu Yüan-Chang (*r.* 1328–98), expelled the Mongol Yüan dynasty and had unified all of China proper by 1382. The Ming brought a period of cultural and philosophical advance during which China influenced many adjacent areas, including Japan. Great seagoing expeditions were launched to the s and w, reaching the E coast of Africa. Peking was laid out in its present form, and the traditional bureaucracy was reinforced. In the later years of the dynasty, however, a growing population, corrupt officials and weak emperors incited revolts among peasants in the border regions, thereby preparing the way for the Manchu conquest of China.

Minoan civilization (flourished *c.* 3000–*c.* 1200 BC), ancient Cretan culture, named after the legendary King Minos. Its capital, Knossos, was twice destroyed by earthquakes and rebuilt. Its palaces were among the finest in the world, particularly those at Knossos, Phaestus, Gournia and Cyclonia. The civilization has been divided into three periods: early (*c.* 3000–2100 BC), middle (*c.* 2100–1550 BC) and late (*c.* 1550–*c.* 1100 BC). The whole period saw the development from the use of neolithic implements to an advanced system of mercantile trade which, at the height of Minoan influence, extended throughout the Mediterranean area. Two scripts were developed, the "A" and the "B", and a distinctive pottery has since been found throughout the island; the Minoans also became skilled in metalworking. The end of the civilization was probably caused by

---

AD 1812–1814

A France suffered Wellington's Allied forces' entry into

A Paris and Napoleon's exile to Elba. Louis XVIII took the throne (1814–24) and Austria and Prussia regained their monarchs through the Congress of Vienna. The conservative tradition found expression in de Maistre and Bonald, who insisted on church supremacy and opposed the philosophes. Cuvier

A improved Linnaeus' classification. Britain controlled the Cape of Good Hope (1814) and saw the expansion of small country banks. Shelley wrote *Queen Mab* and Scott the medieval romance *Waverley* (1814).

Spanish painter Goya chronicled
A the horrors of the Napoleonic Wars.

Swedish scientist Berzelius introduced chemical symbols.

---

an earthquake, followed by an invasion by the Myceneans.

Mintoff, Dominic (1916–), Maltese politician. He helped to reorganize the country's Labour Party in 1944 and was first elected to the legislative assembly in 1947. He became leader of the party in 1949 and was first Prime Minister in 1955–58. He was again elected Prime Minister in 1971.

Mithridates VI Eupator, called the Great, King of Pontus (132–63 BC; r. 120–63 BC), who attempted to extend his rule southwards but was repeatedly defeated by the Romans. He was overwhelmed by the forces of Sulla in the war of 88–85 and lost his kingdom in a second campaign in 83–82. He reconquered it in 74 but was defeated by Pompey in 66 and fled to the Bosporus. He was planning an invasion of Italy, but his troops revolted, and he committed suicide.

Mobutu Sese Seko (1930–), b. Joseph (-Désiré) Mobutu, President of Zaire (formerly the Democratic Republic of the Congo). He worked for Congolese independence with Patrice Lumumba but deposed him in 1960 and assumed control of the army. In 1965 he led a coup against Joseph Kasavubu, becoming Prime Minister in 1966 and establishing a presidential government the following year. He changed the Congo's name to Zaire in 1971. It is Africa's second-largest country.

Model Parliament, English parliament summoned by Edward I in 1295. It was called the "Model" parliament by the 19th-century constitutional historian Bishop Stubbs, because at it the knights of the shire and the burgesses (the representatives of the Commons) for the first time treated of the great affairs of the nation with the king and the magnates. This enlargement of the Commons' function was held to be the model for the future. They had previously merely agreed to what the king and the magnates had already decided. It was a change marked in the very language of the writ summoning the parliament, language which, with minor changes, remained the same for the next six centuries.

AD 1814–1817

A **France** saw Napoleon leave Elba to be finally defeated at Waterloo. Constant's psychological novel *Adolphe* examined a broken love affair. Nicephore Niepce's experiments led to the development of photography. **Italy** saw Ferdinand I (1815–25) regain the throne.

Austria, Prussia and Russia formed the Holy Alliance to crush radicalism.

A **Britain's** Corn Laws protected landowners by excluding foreign corn and keeping prices high. Ricardo's *Principles of Political Economy and Taxation* set out the laws governing the division of the social product among social classes. Davy invented the safety lamp.

A **Germany** produced Schubert's lyrical lieder and Hoffman's grotesque tales.

Mohammed (Muhammad or Mahomet)

Mogul, or Mughal, Empire (1526–1857), Indian empire founded by Babur, a Muslim descendant of both Tamerlane and Genghis Khan, who conquered Delhi and Agra (1526). Under Akbar (*r.* 1556–1605), Babur's grandson, the empire reached its greatest power, extending from Afghanistan to the Bay of Bengal, from Gujarat in the s to northern Deccan. Akbar's grandson, Shah Jahan (*r.* 1629–58), built many splendid buildings, including the twin marvels of the Peacock Throne and the Taj Mahal. Under Aurungzebe (*r.* 1658–1707), a Muslim fanatic, Hindu revolts weakened the empire, which began to disintegrate under Muhammed Shah (*r.* 1719–48). After 1803 the Mogul emperors were merely puppets of the British. In 1857 the last emperor, Bahadur Shah, was forced to abdicate following his part in the Indian Mutiny.

Mohammed (Muhammad or Mahomet) (*c.* 570–632), Arab prophet, leader and the inspiration for Islam. He was born in Mecca; his family belonged to the powerful Hashem clan, led by his uncle into whose care he came when his grandfather died, two years after Mohammed had been orphaned. He married a rich older woman, Khadijah, and became a trader. In about 610, Mohammmed had a vision commanding him to spread the word of God and he began to preach. He gained followers but also enemies, and in 622 he and many of his followers fled to Medina. Muslims, the followers of Islam, later took this Hegira (*hijrah*, "migration") as initiating the first year in their calendar. Thereafter, Mohammed continued preaching, won more followers, and began to war against his enemies. He conquered Mecca in 630, most of the Arab tribes allied with him, and he became the leading figure in Arabia. In Medina following the death of Khadijah he had married the woman who became his favourite wife, Aishah. After his death, his successors began the rapid conquest of a great empire. Mohammed is revered by Muslims as the Prophet of the one God, Allah, and an ideal man, but he never claimed supernatural powers, and he is not held to be divine. The

US border with Canada was fixed (1818).
Italian king Ferdinand I crushed a revolt in Naples and returned with a more liberal constitution. Rossini produced the opera *Barber of Seville* (1816).
Britain founded Singapore as an eastern trade centre, and ruled all India except Nepal, the Sikh and Sind states by 1818. A reform meeting in Man-

A chester ended in the Peterloo Massacre (1819). Lord Byron epitomized the Romantic movement, but produced a political satire in *Don Juan*. Hazlitt wrote astute essays.
German philosopher Schopenhauer emphasized man's will and irrationality.
Danish scientist Oersted discovered electromagnetism and prepared aluminium.

revelations received by him are recorded in the Koran, the sacred book of Islam. Orally transmitted sayings of the Prophet are also important guides to the faith and the daily life of Muslims.

Monck (or Monk), George, 1st Duke of Albemarle (1608–70), English soldier. In the Civil War he fought for Charles I (1643–44) but joined the Parliamentarians two years after his capture by them in 1644. He then served in Ireland and under Cromwell in Scotland. Monck believed in the supremacy of the civil authority over the military and when the protectorate of Richard Cromwell collapsed he became one of the most influential figures in the Restoration of the Stuarts. As Duke of Albemarle, he fought in the Second Anglo-Dutch War (1665–67) and was in charge of London during the great Plague (1665) and the Fire of London (1666).

Monroe, James (1758–1831), fifth President of the United States (1817–25). He served as a member of Congress from 1783–86 and from 1790–94 as a member of the Senate. In 1794 he was made Minister to France, reaching the climax of his diplomatic career when he negotiated the Louisiana Purchase in 1803. A Jeffersonian, Monroe was chosen to succeed Madison as President and won an easy victory in the election of 1816. His administration was marked by improving relations with Britain and Spain, by the acquisition of Florida, and by the first rumblings of the slavery issue, solved by the Missouri Compromise (1820). Monroe is most famous for promulgating the Monroe Doctrine (1823) which was an attempt to prevent European intervention in the affairs of any American country.

Montezuma, name of two Aztec emperors. Montezuma I (*r.* 1440–69) increased the size of the empire through a series of wars. Montezuma II (1466–1520) allowed the Spaniards under Cortés to enter central Mexico unhindered. Montezuma II was imprisoned by the Spaniards and killed by his own subjects when they rose up against the intruders.

AD 1820–1822

Spain, her king captured by liberal rebels, lost Mexico and Peru (1821).
Greece started a nationalist independence war with the A Ottoman Turks (1821).
China traded with India in opium.
Britain's Cato St Conspiracy was crushed (1820). Shelley and Keats were at their peaks and Thomas Erskine, a Scottish theologian, held that Christianity conformed with man's spiritual and ethical needs.
A **France's** Ampère founded electro-dynamics and invented the solenoid. Lamartine produced the anguished *Meditations* (1820).
German Schleiermacher founded modern Protestant theology with *The Christian Faith*, seeing sin as a desire for independence.

Montgomery of Alamein, Bernard Law, Viscount
(1887–1976), British soldier. As commander of the British
Eighth Army in WWII, he defeated Rommel and the Afrika
Korps at El Alamein in Egypt and led the invasion of Sicily
and Italy. He helped to plan the Normandy landings in
1944, leading his troops into Germany and commanding the
British occupation forces there. He was made a Field
Marshal in 1944 and a Viscount in 1946, and was deputy
Supreme Allied Commander, Europe from 1951 to 1958.

Moors, nomadic people of N Africa of Berber and Arabic
stock. The Moors were early converts to Islam and, having
crossed over to Spain and Portugal in 711, they quickly
conquered most of the Iberian Peninsula. Abd ar-Rahman
I, the last survivor of the Umayyad dynasty from Damascus,
established the emirate (later caliphate) of Córdoba in 756.
The Moors were opposed by the Christian rulers of N Spain,
who gradually extended their power s, while dissension
grew within the Moorish ranks. The puritanical Almoravids
crossed from N Africa in 1085 and conquered the more
worldly Spanish Moors. They in turn were replaced by the
even more zealous Almohads. Only Granada remained
Moorish by 1250, although it survived until 1492 when it
fell to Ferdinand and Isabella. Many of the Moors who
remained suffered under the Spanish inquisition after Spain
and Portugal were reconverted to Christianity. Today the
populations of Algeria, Mauretania, Morocco and Tunisia
are of Moorish stock.

More, Sir Thomas (c. 1478–1535), English statesman,
writer and a Roman Catholic saint. A leading Humanist and
friend of Erasmus, his *Utopia* (1516) portrayed an ideal
state founded on reason. He became Henry VIII's adviser
and succeeded Cardinal Wolsey as chancellor, but he
enraged the king by refusing to subscribe to the Act of
Supremacy which made Henry the head of the Church of
England and repudiated papal authority. Henry had him
arrested and imprisoned in the Tower of London in 1534
and he was executed on a charge of treason.

AD 1822–1825

Spain's liberal revolt was
crushed with French help (1823).
US asserted that the American
continent should no longer be
an arena for European colonial
A activity (the Munroe doctrine).
Britain's trade flourished. A
liberal Conservative ministry
repealed the Combination Acts
after a campaign led by Place,
who advocated birth control,
and Hume. De Quincey wrote the
*Confessions of an English Opium
Eater* and Peacock his satirical
novels. Sturgeon made the
electromagnet.
French Romantic art was epitomized by Delacroix. Carnot
began thermodynamics.
German Ranke sought scientific
methods appropriate to the study
A of history. Beethoven extended
the range of artistic expression
available to the symphony.

Mosley, Sir Oswald Ernald (1896–   ), British politician and founder of the British Union of Fascists (1932). He was a Conservative Member of Parliament (1918) but later joined the Labour Party, serving as Chancellor of the Duchy of Lancaster (1924). Dissatisfied with both the democratic left and right, he turned to Fascism coupled with anti-Semitism. He was interned during WWII (1940–43) but after the war founded the Union Movement (1948), a new right-wing party.

Mozart, Wolfgang Amadeus (1756–91), Austrian composer born in Salzburg. A child progidy at the piano, he was taken by his father, Leopold (who was also a musician), on performing tours in Europe (1762–64) and England (1764–65) and by 1770 he had written four operas. In the 1780s he devoted himself to full-time composition. To this period belong some of the most sublime works ever composed, such as the operas *Marriage of Figaro* (1786) and *Don Giovanni* (1787) and the last eight of his 41 full-scale symphonies. In 1787, having almost given up hope of an imperial post, he was appointed court composer by the Austrian emperor. In the last year of his life, wracked by ill health, Mozart wrote the operas *The Magic Flute* and *La Clemenza di Tito*, the clarinet concerto and the *Requiem* (completed by a pupil). He died in poverty and was buried in an unmarked grave. Together with J.S. Bach, Mozart is today rated as one of the greatest of all composers. In his short life he produced more than 600 compositions and exerted a potent influence on musical development. He perfected the Classical style and looked forward to the early Romanticism of Beethoven and later, Brahms, with music that combined elegance of expression with profound emotion.

Muldoon, Robert David (1921–   ), New Zealand politician and Prime Minister (1975–   ). He was Finance Minister (1967–72 and 1975–   ) and became leader of the National Party Opposition in 1974, a year before spearheading a landslide election victory. He became one of the most

---

AD 1825–1828

A **Russia**, after the Decembrist revolt, introduced repressive

A measures under Nicholas I.

A **France's** Charles X restored noble lands. Saint-Simon tried to combine Christianity, science and industrialism to form a religious socialism.

A Comte developed his ideas. **Britain** opened the first public railway (1825), using

A Stephenson's locomotive. Brown,

a botanist, proved the existence of molecules.

US author Fenimore Cooper wrote *The Last of the Mohicans* (1826). Ornithologist John Audubon published *The Birds of America*.

Italian writer Manzoni produced *The Betrothed* (1827).

German physicist Georg Ohm formulated his law, dealing with current, voltage and resistance.

forceful and controversial leaders in New Zealand political history.

Munich Agreement (1938), pact signed by representatives of Britain, France, Germany and Italy. Neville Chamberlain for Great Britain and Edouard Daladier for France acceded to Adolf Hitler's demands for immediate German occupation of the Sudetenland area of Czechoslovakia. The pact also provided for plebiscites, but these were never carried out. The agreement averted war for a year but was to become a symbol of the democracies' policy of appeasement toward Hitler.

Muslim League, political organization of the Indian subcontinent, founded in 1906 by Aga Khan III to protect and promote the political rights of Muslims in India. At first it co-operated with the Indian National Congress but, fearing Hindu domination, it turned to independent action. Under the leadership of Muhammed Ali Jinnah it called (1940) for the establishment of a separate Muslim state. During WWII the League, in contrast with the Congress Party, supported the British war effort. It became the dominant voice of independent Pakistan (1947), but by 1953 it had to contend with several competing parties. During the martial law imposed by Ayub Khan (1958–63) it was officially banned. In 1962 it split into three factions: the Convention Muslim League, the Council Muslim League and the Payyum Muslim League. With Ayub's resignation (1969), the Convention faction ceased to exist. The Council faction fared poorly in 1970 elections and ceased to be a major political force in Pakistan.

Mussolini, Benito (1883–1945), Italian dictator, called Il Duce, founder of Europe's first Fascist party. An active socialist in his youth he abandoned socialism shortly after WWI and embraced ultra-nationalism, organizing the Fascist Party between 1919 and 1921. His Fascist militia's march on Rome in 1922 ensured his appointment as Prime Minister. Parliamentary government was suspended in 1928 and possible conflict between the Roman Catholic

Mycenae

Church and the state was avoided by the Lateran Treaty (1929). The 1930s saw Mussolini's attack on Ethiopia (1935) and even closer ties with Hitler's Germany (the Rome-Berlin Axis). When France was on the verge of collapse (1940) during WWII, Mussolini entered the war as Germany's ally. Military failure caused his fall from power in 1943, but after his arrest he was freed by the Germans and set up in a puppet government in N Italy. With the German defeat (1945) he was captured and executed by Italian partisans.

Mycenae, ancient city in NE Peloponnesos, Greece, now ruined, approx. 11km (6 miles) N of modern Árgos. Dating from the third millenium BC, Mycenae became the centre of the Mycenean civilization (c. 1580–1120 BC). The Myceneans entered Greece from the N, bringing with them advanced techniques, particularly in architecture and metallurgy. The city controlled the route from the Peloponnesos to Corinth, being strategically placed to command the Argive Plain. The Myceneans traded with Crete, which also helped develop their culture, and by 1600 BC they dominated the Aegean. After 1200 BC the city began to decline with the invasions of the Dorians.

Nagy, Imre (1896–1958), Hungarian statesman, Premier 1953–55 and 1956. Expelled from the Communist Party in 1955 for alleged anti-Soviet nationalism, he was recalled to the premiership in 1956 in the wake of the anti-Soviet uprising of late October. He promised free elections, economic reforms and the abolition of the one-party dictatorship. He demanded the withdrawal of Soviet troops and freed Cardinal Mindszenty from prison. Although the USSR promised concessions, demonstrations continued and on 4 November Soviet troops and tanks moved in to suppress the insurgents. Nagy was executed in 1958.

Nantes, Edict of (1598), law granting considerable religious freedom to French Protestants, the Huguenots, promulgated by Henry IV at Nantes. It guaranteed freedom of conscience, social and political equality, and established a

---

AD 1830–1833

A **France** replaced Charles X with Louis-Philippe. Belgium was encouraged to gain independence from the Netherlands. French authority was established in Algiers. Stendhal wrote the novel *Scarlet and Black* and Berlioz his *Symphonie Fantastique*.

A **Britain's** Reform Act introduced industrial constituencies but maintained landowners' supremacy. Back-to-back houses were built. Whitworth standardized screw threads, geologist Lyell wrote *Principles of Geo-*

A logy, and Faraday discovered electromagnetic induction.

Russian Lobachevski developed

A non-Euclidean geometry.

A **Italy's** Mazzini founded the Young Italy movement.

Religion saw the Mormons and the Modern Adventists founded.

special court, composed of both Catholics and Protestants, to hear disputes arising from the edict. Protestant worship was limited, however, to areas they already held (about 100 fortified towns) and was not permitted within five leagues of Paris. Secret agreements promised the crown's financial support of the armies garrisoned in the 100 towns. The last provision gave the Huguenots a virtual state within the state and was incompatible with the centralizing policies of Cardinal Richelieu in the 17th century. Louis XIII, acting on Richelieu's advice, withdrew the political and military provisions of the edict in 1629 and Louis XIV revoked it entirely in 1685.

Napoleon I (1769–1821), general and Emperor of France. He was born Napoleon Bonaparte in Corsica and studied at the military academy in Brienne. He led the French liberation of Toulon from the British in 1793 and was promoted brigadier-general. His future was in doubt during the Thermidorean Reaction, but after saving the National Convention from a right-wing uprising in Oct. 1795 he was given command of the army in Italy in 1796. He won important victories there against Austria, but failed in his attempt to drive the British from Egypt in 1798. In 1798–99 France lost most of Italy and Napoleon returned to France in Oct. 1799 and carried out the coup of 18th Brumaire (9 Nov. 1799) against the Directory. He set up the Consulate, and in Dec. 1799 became First Consul. He defeated the Austrians at Marengo in 1800, and at home centralized local government and the tax collection system. He established the Bank of France, reformed the legal system with the Code Napoleon and made peace with the Roman Catholic Church with the Concordat of 1801.

He conducted the Treaty of Amiens with Britain in 1802, and crowned himself Emperor of the French in 1804, with Pope Pius VII presiding. War broke out again in 1805 and he defeated Russia and Austria at Austerlitz in 1805 and Prussia at Jena in 1806. He reorganized the German states and made members of his family rulers of Spain, Naples and

---

AD 1833–1835

Britain abolished slavery (1833) and increased trade with China. The Tolpuddle Martyrs were transported for union activity and workhouses set up. Keble and Newman began the Oxford Movement. Babbage developed the principles of the mechanical computer and Brunel built the steamship *Great Western*. **France** saw Louis-Philippe introduce strict censorship.

German nationalism focused on their customs union. Gauss, a mathematician, developed a set of units for magnetism. **Spain** saw the Carlist Wars against their liberal regime. **Russian** writer Pushkin introduced realistic language into *The Dead Princess* (1834), and *Eugene Onegin*. **Polish** composer Chopin wrote many dazzling piano pieces.

Napoleon III

Holland. However, he could not defeat the British at sea and led a disastrous expedition to Russia in 1812. He was forced to abdicate in April 1814 and was confined to the island of Elba. He escaped in March 1815, and seemed triumphant for a Hundred Days. He was finally defeated at Waterloo in June 1815, abdicated once more, and was exiled by the British to St Helena, where he died.

In 1796 he married Josephine de Beauharnais. He was divorced from her in 1809 to marry Marie Louis of Austria in 1810. Their son was known as Napoleon II.

Napoleon III (1808–73), Emperor of the French (*r.* 1852–70), also known as Louis Napoleon. He was the nephew of Napoleon I. He twice attempted a coup in France (1836 and 1840) and won some popularity because of his utopian socialist views. He returned to France from exile in Feb. 1848 and was overwhelmingly elected President in Dec. 1848. He supported Pope Pius IX against the Italian republicans in 1849, and in reaction to the ensuing opposition staged a coup in Dec. 1851 and was proclaimed emperor in Nov. 1852. During his reign France experienced both economic growth and political authoritarianism. Napoleon undertook expensive wars in Italy, SE Asia and Mexico, and in response to growing opposition instituted a liberal empire in 1870. He was deposed in September 1870 as a result of early French defeats in the Franco-Prussian war, and retired to England where he later died.

Napoleonic Wars, series of wars during which France, under Napoleon I fought various coalitions of the other European powers. Britain was constantly at war with France from 1803–14, and then again in 1815; after Napoleon's invasion plans had been frustrated at Trafalgar, the main field of conflict between the two opponents was in Spain, during the Peninsular War (1808–14). Austria and Russia joined with Britain in the War of the Third Coalition in 1805, but Austria was defeated at Ulm and Austerlitz and forced to sign the peace of Pressburg. In 1806 Prussia entered the war, only to be defeated at Jena and Auerstadt; and Russia,

---

AD 1835–1837

A Britain saw Victoria ascend the throne. The Boers began the
A Great Trek to evade British rule. Revolt resulted from attempts to unite Upper and Lower Canada. Intervention in Persia to forestall Russian influence proved impossible. A railway-building boom began. Wheatstone invented the electric telegraph and Brown discovered the living cell's nucleus.

Belgian statistician Quetelet applied probability theory to the study of suicide.
US writer Emerson developed transcendentalism in *Nature*. Primitive painting flourished. German poet Heine, a romantic idealist, asserted the political role of literature.
Schumann, the archetypal romantic composer, produced much haunting piano music.

defeated at Friedland in 1807, signed the Treaty of Tilsit with Napoleon. In 1809, at Wagram, Austria was again defeated. Three years later, however, in 1812, Napoleon squandered an army in Russia, and the next year all his opponents united in the Fourth Coalition to defeat him at Leipzig. Forced to abdicate in 1814, Napoleon returned to power in 1815, but was finally defeated at Waterloo. After the wars, Europe was re-organized at the Congress of Vienna.

Nariño, Antonio (1765–1823), Colombian revolutionary. He published a translation of the French Declaration of the Rights of Man, and was deported to Spain in 1795. He returned to s America in 1797 and following the 1810 Revolution became President of Curdinamarca province. In 1821, after some six years in prison in Spain, he became Vice-President of Colombia. As a political leader, he worked towards a strong, centralist government.

Nasser, Gamal Abdel (1918–70), Egyptian political figure, first President of the republic of Egypt (1956–70). He graduated from the Royal Military Academy in 1938, was wounded in action in the 1948 Arab-Israeli War and in 1950 was elected Chairman of the Free Officers movement. In 1952 he led the army coup that ousted King Farouk. As head of the Revolutionary Command Council Nasser controlled Egypt, although Gen. Muhammed Neguib was the nominal premier. Nasser became President in 1956, nationalizing the Suez Canal in the same year. He was the President of the United Arab Republic in 1958–61. After Egypt's defeat in the 1967 Arab-Israeli War he resigned but returned to office amid massive demonstrations in his support. Nasser promoted land reform and economic and social development through a programme called Arab socialism; the completion of the Aswan Dam (1970), built with Soviet assistance after the USA backed out, was the greatest achievement of this programme. Nasser is remembered for his pan-Arab beliefs and enouragement of Third-World unity.

AD 1837–1840

ABritain entered the Opium Wars with China (1839). Economic depression resulted in the AChartists demanding universal Asuffrage. The Anti-Corn Law League was formed and the Penny Post introduced.

France's Auguste Comte coined the terms sociology and positivism. Balzac's *comedie humaine* appeared in over 90 novels (1829–43).

Russian composer Glinka utilized folk themes and heralded the rise of a national school.

US inventor Samuel Morse produced Morse Code and Goodyear discovered vulcanization.

German biologists Schwann and Schleiden described the anatomy of plant and animal cells. Bessel detected stellar parallax, showing that stars are extremely distant.

Nazism, *See* **Hitler, Adolf**.

Nebuchadnezzar (Nebuchadrezzar), (*d.* 562 BC), second king of the Chaldaean or New Babylonian empire (*r.c.* 604–562 BC). He defeated the Pharoah Necho in battle at Carchemish in 605 BC but was himself defeated by Necho in 601 BC. He placed the puppet King Zedekiah on the Judean throne but was forced to destroy Jerusalem after a revolt. He was responsible for many buildings in Babylon; for his Median wife he built the hanging gardens there which became one of the seven Wonders of the World.

Necker, Jacques, *See* **Louis XVI**.

Nehru, Jawaharlal Pandit (1889–1964), Indian leader. He joined the Indian independence movement in 1919, and in 1929 was elected President of the Indian National Congress. He became the first Prime Minister and Foreign Minister of India (1947–64). He led the new nation through its troubled beginning, launching programmes to industrialize and socialize India. In 1948 India became involved in a war over Kashmir with Pakistan, although in foreign policy Nehru advocated neutralism and pacificism.

Nelson, Horatio Nelson, Viscount (1758–1805), British naval commander. He entered the navy in 1771 and from 1793 served in the Mediterranean under Admiral Hood; he lost the sight of his right eye in action in Corsica. He fought with great distinction under Jervis at Cape St Vincent in 1797, and lost his right arm off Tenerife in the same year. He commanded the fleet that won a crushing victory over the French at the Battle of the Nile in 1798 and, promoted to Vice-admiral, he fought in the Battle of Copenhagen in 1801 (which disrupted the Armed Neutrality). Recalled to the Mediterranean in 1803, he blockaded Toulon for two years until the French fleet finally eluded him. He was killed at the ensuing Battle of Trafalgar (1805).

Nero Claudius Caesar (AD 37–68), Roman Emperor (*r.* 54–68), born as Lucius Domitius Ahenobarbus. He was the son of Agrippina II and the stepson of Claudius I, whom he succeeded. He murdered his brother Britannicus (AD 55),

---

AD 1840–1844

Britain annexed Natal. Upper and Lower Canada were united. With the Straits Convention, she closed the Dardanelles and Bosporus to foreign warships. Chinese ports were opened to British trade by the Treaty of Nanking. Brunel's *Great Britain*, an iron-hulled steamer, crossed the Atlantic.

German philosopher Feuerbach advocated humanistic atheism. Danish thinker Kierkegaard's work prefigured Existentialism. Russian writer Lermontov's *A Hero of our Time* was influenced by Lord Byron. Austrian composer Johann Strauss became famous by his waltzes. Swiss naturalist Agassiz studied glaciers. US surgeon Long used anaesthetic.

---

his mother (59) and his wife Octavia (62). He blamed the Christians for a serious fire in Rome in 64 and may have begun the first official persecution of Christians. After discovering a plot against him in 65, he had many distinguished Romans, including Seneca, his former advisor, executed. But he was overthrown in a military revolt and killed himself.

Netherlands, Revolt of the (1568–1648), also called the Eighty Years War, war by which The Netherlands won independence from Spanish Hapsburg rule. By 1576 the United Provinces (Dutch Republic) was formed. In 1579 the Catholic Walloon provinces defected and the rest of the republic had to struggle against Spain until a truce was called in 1609. The fight resumed in 1621 as part of the Thirty Years War. Spain finally recognized Dutch independence in 1648.

Neto, Agostinho (1922–   ), Angolan poet, political leader and doctor. He became a leader of an Angolan cultural and political revival and was often imprisoned for his efforts to achieve Angola's independence. He became President of an independent Angola in 1975.

New Deal, in US history, term for the social and economic programme of the administrations of Franklin D. Roosevelt, between 1933 and 1939. Elected in 1932 during the worst phase of the Great Depression (the severe economic crisis supposed to have been precipitated by the stock market crash of 1929), Roosevelt promised a "new deal" to the American people, hence the name that was given to all the domestic reforms of his administration. These included programmes of agricultural and business regulation, inflation and price stabilization, and extensive public works. The second phase of the New Deal in 1935 introduced social security benefits, which included disability pensions, unemployment benefits, old age pensions, central mortgage finance and industrial relations legislation to strengthen the trade unions.

Ne Win, U (1911–   ), Burmese military and political leader

AD 1844–1846

France involved herself in Indo-China because of Christian persecution there. Utopian socialism was popular. De Tocqueville examined the impact of democracy on non-political institutions. Millet the painter led the Barbizon School.
Britain introduced slum clearance. The Anglo-Sikh War broke out in India. The Bank of England had a monopoly on printing money. Turner's paintings celebrated contemporary technology. Ruskin emphasized truth to nature.
US annexed Texas (1845).
Russian writer Gogol satirized bureaucracy in *Dead Souls*.
Italian chemist Sobrero invented nitroglycerine.
German astronomer Galle discovered Neptune (1846).
Religion saw the Babi sect start.

New Model Army

born Thakin Shu Maung. At the outbreak of WWII he helped the Japanese invade Burma, but in 1945 his Burmese Independence Army also turned against the Japanese. He became commander-in-chief of the army upon Burma's independence from Britain in 1948. In 1958 he deposed U Nu and had himself appointed Prime Minister. U Nu returned to office in 1960, but Ne Win deposed him again in 1962. He became President in 1974.

New Model Army, *See* **English Civil Wars.**

Newton, Sir Isaac (1642–1727), English scientist. He studied at Cambridge and became professor of mathematics there (1669–1701). Many of his discoveries were made in the period 1664–66, but not published until later. His main works were *Philosophiae Naturalis Principia Mathematica* (1687) and *Opticks* (1704). In the former he outlined his laws of motion and proposed the principle of universal gravitation; in the latter he showed that white light is made up of colours of the spectrum and put forward his particle theory of light. He also created the first system of calculus in the 1660s, but did not publish it until Gottfried Leibniz had published his own system in 1684. He built the first reflecting telescope in *c.* 1671, and studied alchemy and biblical chronology. He was president of the Royal Society (1703–27), and master of the mint after 1701. In 1705 he became the first man to be knighted for his scientific work. Newton engaged in violent scientific disputes with Robert Hooke, John Flamsteed and Leibniz.

Nicholas, name of two Russian tsars. Nicholas I (1796–1855), a ruler noted for suppressing all political reform, ascended to the throne in 1825 and immediately crushed the Decembrist revolt led by liberal noblemen who sought constitutional monarchy. He gained strategic territory for Russia in wars against Persia (1826–28) and Turkey (1827–29) and put an end to Polish independence in 1830–31. He expanded the secret police, increased censorship and banned political organizations. He died during the Crimean War.

AD 1846–1848

US invaded Mexico. Irish immigration was accelerated by the potato famine. Hoe invented the rotary printing press.
Prussian liberal hopes rose through the calling of the Landtag for railway funds.
Italian nationalist hopes were

A raised by the liberal Pius IX's accession.

A **Britain** repealed the Corn Laws. The Bronte sisters work was marked by powerful insight.
France produced Proudhon's formulation of anarchy and his

A involvement in the 1848 Revolution. Ingres' paintings were influenced by daguerreotypes.
Hungarian composer Liszt toured Europe as a pianist.
German scientists von Mayer and Helmholtz measured the mechanical equivalent of heat, as did Britain's Joule.

Nietzsche, Friedrich Wilhelm (1844–1900), German philosopher and poet. He studied classical philology at Bonn and taught at Basel in 1869. He met Richard Wagner in 1878 and his treatise *The Birth of Tragedy* (1872) shows Wagner's influence. In 1879 he abandoned philology for philosophy, and celebrated his new notion of the "superman" in *Also sprach Zarathustra* (*Thus Spake Zarathustra*) (1883–91). His aphoristic style was misunderstood but greatly influenced later German thinkers. His later works include *Beyond Good and Evil* (1886), *On the Genealogy of Morals* (1887) and *Ecce Homo* (1888).

Nightingale, Florence *See* **Crimean War**.

Nixon, Richard Milhous (1913–   ), US Republican politician and 37th president. He was elected to the House of Representatives in 1946 and 1948 and to the Senate in 1950. He made a name as an anti-Communist on the House Un-American Activities Committee and was nominated as vice-presidential candidate at the Republican convention of 1952. He was Vice-President during Eisenhower's administrations (1953–60). In 1960 he lost the presidential election to the Democratic candidate John Kennedy. In 1962 he lost the election for the governorship of California and announced his retirement from politics. In 1968, however, he again won the Republican nomination for president and was elected. He was re-elected in 1972. In 1974 he was forced to resign because of the Watergate affair. His administrations were marked by the introduction of prices and incomes controls, the lowering of the voting age to 18 and the ending of military conscription. He was the first US president to pay a state visit to Communist China (1972). In 1973 his administration also ended the US involvement in the Vietnam War.

Nkomo, Joshua Rhodes (1917–   ), Zimbabwe politician. From involvement in black union politics he became President of the African National Congress in 1957, living abroad when it was banned in 1959. Returning to

---

AD 1848–1850

Britain annexed the Punjab. The Public Health Act introduced sewerage. Dickens and Thackeray wrote their greatest novels. The Pre-Raphaelites were founded, rejecting academic art styles. A telegraphic cable connection was laid across the English Channel. France expelled Louis Philippe and established a republic. Austria's Metternich resigned and Hungary declared itself independent until split radically. US saw a Californian gold rush and the foundation of the Christadelphians by Thomas. German thinkers Karl Marx and Engels wrote the *Communist Manifesto*, predicting the revolutionary defeat of capitalism. Hungarian Liszt established the symphonic poem. Physician Semmelweiss demanded asepsis.

Nkrumah, Kwame

Zimbabwe in 1960, he became President of the Zimbabwe African Peoples' Union (ZAPU) the following year. He spent much of the 1960s in prison and he was finally released in 1974 to become an executive member of the African National Congress. He led the ANC delegation at the Geneva Conference on Zimbabwe (1976).

Nkrumah, Kwame (1909–72), African political leader. Educated in Africa and the USA, he returned to the Gold Coast and formed the Convention People's Party in 1949. He advocated self-government and was imprisoned by the British in 1950. He was released in 1951, and became Prime Minister in 1952. Under his leadership the Gold Coast became independent in 1957. British Togoland joined it to form the new nation of Ghana and in 1960 Ghana became a republic with Nkrumah as President. Following a build-up of security forces, he made Ghana a one-party state in 1964, but was ousted by the military in 1966 and took refuge in Guinea.

Nobel, Alfred Bernhard (1833–96), Swedish chemist, engineer and industrialist. He invented dynamite in 1866, patented a more powerful form of blasting gelatine in 1876 and in 1888 produced ballistite, one of the first nitroglycerine smokeless powders. With the immense fortune he made from the manufacture of explosives and from interests in the Baku oil fields of Russia, he founded the Nobel Prizes, first awarded in 1901.

Normans, warrior people of Scandinavian origin who settled in NW France. In 911, Charles the Simple gave Rollo, the leader of bands of Viking pirates, formal control of a coastal area which he and his descendants expanded to form the Duchy of Normandy. The Normans adapted Christianity and feudalism to their needs while still retaining their prowess in war; by 1050, groups of Normans had conquered Sicily, which became an important Mediterranean power under Roger II, and in 1066 Duke William the Conqueror led a Norman army in the conquest of England. Norman knights played an important part in the

---

AD 1850–1853

A **France** was stabilized by Napoleon III. Courbet and Millet were prominent in art. Scientist Claude Bernard advanced physiology and Foucault demonstrated the Earth's rotation. **US** saw California become a free state and a compromise reached on slavery. Hawthorne and Melville established American fiction. Singer developed the sewing machine.

A **China** was torn by the Taiping Rebellion, demanding female equality and communalization. **Britain** subdued Burma. The Great Exhibition symbolized prosperity. Historian Macaulay published his *History of England*. Tennyson wrote *In Memoriam*. **Austria** suppressed national minorities in her empire. **German** Rudolf Clausius conceived of entropy.

1st Crusade, and Anglo-Norman families conquered Wales and Ireland for the English crown. The Normans soon became absorbed into the societies they had conquered; Normandy itself was finally taken by the French in the 15th century.

Numeiry (Nimeiri), Mohammed Jaafur al- (1930–), chief of state in the Sudan. He took control after a military coup in 1969 and was made President in 1971. He was responsible for the end of a 17-year civil war with the southern Sudanese and defeated a Communist revolt in 1971. A Libyan-backed coup in 1976 failed, and led to a strengthening of ties with Egypt.

Nyerere, Julius Kambarage (1922–), first President of Tanzania, formerly Tanganyika. He served as a legislator and Chief Minister in the Tanganyikan territorial government. An African nationalist leader, he became President of an independent Tanganyika in 1962 and in 1964 manoeuvred the union of Tanganyika and Zanzibar into a republic as Tanzania. As a political theorist, Nyerere's socialist views, published as *Freedom and Unity* (1967), and *Freedom and Socialism* (1968) have had considerable influence in Africa. He is strong adherent of Pan Africanism and a leading influence in the Organization of African Unity. He has given strong support, both moral and material, to guerrillas fighting in Zimbabwe and South Africa.

Oates, Titus (1649–1705), English priest who invented the story of the Popish Plot. The son of an Anabaptist preacher, he was ordained into the Church of England but was imprisoned for perjury in 1674. He joined the Roman Catholic Church in 1677, but was later expelled from Spanish and Dutch seminaries. In 1678 he and Israel Tonge invented a story of a Jesuit plot to murder Charles II. Although Oates was convicted of perjury for this in 1685, he was pardoned in 1688. In 1693 he became a Baptist, but that Church expelled him in 1701.

O'Connell, Daniel (1775–1847), Irish nationalist leader,

AD 1853–1855

A **Britain's** Livingstone discovering the Victoria Falls sparked off European exploration of Africa. The Civil Service was
A reformed and Palmerston became Prime Minister. Maurice founded the Christian Socialist Movement. Arnold and Browning were prominent in poetry. Boole founded symbolic logic.
A **Russia's** defeat in the Crimean War checked her ambition.

US saw New York and Chicago linked by rail. Thoreau championed transcendentalism in *Walden*.
French poet Nerval influenced later symbolists.
Italy industrialized Piedmont.
A **German** composer Wagner achieved grandeur through the use of rubato beat. Justus von Liebig gave agriculture a scientific basis.

known as the Liberator. A practising lawyer during the late 1790s, he joined the United Irishmen but refused to take part in the revolt of 1798, preferring peaceful means for the attainment of Catholic emancipation and parliamentary reform. He founded the Catholic Association in 1823 and became an MP at Westminster after the introduction of Catholic emancipation in 1829. He led the small group of Catholic Irish MPs supporting the Whigs in return for reforms which, however, were not forthcoming. O'Connell proceeded to work for the repeal of Anglo-Irish legislative union and founded the Repeal Association in 1839. In 1844 he was imprisoned for three months after a series of mass meetings throughout Ireland. He then played only a minor political role owing to ill-health.

Octavian, *See* **Augustus**.

Orangemen, members of the Orange Society, founded in Ulster in 1795. It was a political and sectarian society named after the Protestant William III, formerly Prince of Orange, who defeated James II at the Battle of the Boyne on 11 July 1690, a victory celebrated now on 12 July, the date of a further Loyalist victory at the Battle of Aughrim in 1691. The Orangemen sought to maintain the Protestant succession and progressively strengthened their position in Northern Ireland, continuing as proponents of Protestant unionist opinion to the present day.

Osman I, or Osman Gazi (1258–*c.* 1326), considered the founder of the Ottoman Empire, who conquered NW Asia Minor and proclaimed his independence from the Seljuk Turks upon the collapse of their empire after 1293.

Ottoman Empire, former state in Asia Minor, founded by Osman I in the 13th century. By the end of the 14th century it had absorbed the Byzantine Empire and conquered Egypt and Syria during the 16th century. During the rule of Suleiman the Magnificent (1520–66) the empire included much of SE Europe, W Asia and N Africa. A series of debilitating wars was fought during the 17th and 18th centuries against Poland, Austria and Russia, bringing

---

AD 1855–1858

Serbia was recognized as independent after the Crimean War, and the Black Sea made neutral. **Britain** suppressed the Indian Mutiny. Chemist Alexander Parkes patented celluloid. Perkin produced mauve, the first artificial dye and Bessemer patented a converter for the cheap production of steel. **AUS's** John Brown pursued the anti-slavery cause. Walt Whitman wrote *Leaves of Grass*. **China** was opened up by the treaties of Tientsin. **French** sociologist Le Play developed a statistical method of collating field data. Taine argued for the scientific study of culture. Baudelaire and Gautier were influential in literature and Flaubert's *Madame Bovary* accurately described provincial life.

---

about a decline which continued until the dissolution of the empire in 1920 with the Treaty of Sèvres. The Turkish nationalists finally overthrew the sultan in 1922.

Owen, Robert (1771–1858), Welsh social reformer. He believed that workers would be more productive if their environment were improved. He founded the New Lanark Mills in Scotland, where he paid high wages, provided better living conditions and, in spite of everything his opponents said, still made a profit. He set out his theories in a three-volume work, *New View of Society* (1813–21).

Paine, Thomas (1737–1809), American political and religious writer, *b.* England. His radical and outspoken views greatly influenced colonial opinion during the American War of Independence. In his pamphlet *Common Sense* (1776) he demanded complete independence from England and the setting up of a strong federal union. A series of 16 papers, *The Crisis* was read aloud to encourage the Revolutionary Army. He returned to England as an ardent supporter of the French Revolution, defending its cause so vehemently in *Rights of Man* (1791–92) that the work was suppressed and he was charged with treason and fled to France. There he made enemies by speaking out against Louis XVI's execution. For more than 10 months he was in prison where he worked on *Age of Reason*, an agnostic argument. He sailed to America in 1802, and died on a farm given to him by New York State in appreciation of his writings.

Palmerston, Henry John Temple, 3rd Viscount (1784–1865), British statesman and Prime Minister, who dominated the early and mid-Victorian political scene. He entered the House of Commons in 1807 and between 1809 and 1828 served as Secretary of War in successive Tory governments. In 1830, associating himself with the Whigs, he became Foreign Secretary in Lord Grey's Reform ministry, a position he held until 1834 and again from 1835 to 1841 and 1846 to 1851. During these periods he supported Liberalism in Europe and was a forceful

AD 1858–1860

Britain built railways as part of investment in India and sent troops to raid Peking. Gladstone signed a trade treaty A with France. Darwin published A his and Wallace's theories of evolution in *The Origin of Species,* arousing much conservative opposition. William Morris and the Arts and Crafts Movement encouraged craftsmanship, opposing mass production.

Italy expelled Austria from Piedmont. Verdi brought romantic opera to a peak. Cannizzaro standardized atomic weights and chemical formulae. A **French** engineer de Lesseps began construction of the Suez Canal. Corot anticipated Impressionism. **German** scientist Kekule von Stradonitz discovered the principles of molecular structure.

Pankhurst, Emmeline Goulden, ("Emily")

protector of British interests in every part of the world. He was Home Secretary from 1852 and after an inquiry into the government's mishandling of the Crimean War, he was Prime Minister from 1855 to 1858. His second administration (1859–65) ended only with his death and is seen in retrospect as a prologue to the Liberal government of 1868–74.

Pankhurst, Emmeline Goulden ("Emily") (1858–1928), British political leader of women's suffrage movement. With her husband Richard Pankhurst she worked to secure married women's property rights. When she set up the Women's Social and Political Union in 1903, the movement for women's suffrage became militant, and she was imprisoned.

Paracelsus (c. 1493–1541), Swiss physician and alchemist, real name Philippus Aureolus Theophrastus Bombast von Hohenheim. He became professor of medicine at Basel, where his lectures discredited past and contemporary medicine and were preceded by the burning of the works of Galen and Avicenna. According to Paracelsus, the body of man is primarily composed of salt, sulphur and mercury, and it is the separation of these elements that causes illness. He introduced mineral baths and made opium, mercury, lead and various minerals part of the pharmacopoeia. According to his enemies, he died in Salzburg after a drunken bout. Others say he was thrown down a hill by hirelings of jealous apothecaries.

Parnell, Charles Stewart (1846–91), Irish nationalist. He entered the British Parliament in 1875, vigorously supporting home rule for Ireland and rapidly taking over leadership of the Irish group in the Commons. To gain concessions, he embarked upon a policy of parliamentary obstruction. He was imprisoned (1881–82), but his power reached its peak in 1886 when Gladstone introduced the Home Rule Bill. After the bill was defeated, there were attempts to show that Parnell had been implicated in the Phoenix Park murders; and although these allegations were

AD 1860–1863

A US elected Lincoln President on his anti-slavery posture,
A later leading to the American Civil War. A telegraphic cable was laid to Newfoundland.
A Italy was united by Garibaldi. Russian serfs were emancipated
A by Alexander II (1861). France occupied Mexico City and set up Maximilian as emperor. The Goncourt brothers developed an impressionist

realist style. Pissarro, Cézanne, Manet and Whistler exhibited in the Salon des Refusés. Doré
A illustrated Dante's *Inferno*. Gounod wrote the opera *Faust*. Britain built an underground railway in London. Graham distinguished colloids and discovered osmosis. German thinker Lasalle urged workers to seek univesal suffrage.

shown to be false in 1889, the proof in 1890 of Parnell's adultery with the wife of one of his supporters led to a rapid decline in his influence.

Pasteur, Louis (1822–95), French chemist and one of the founders of the science of microbiology. He made many important contributions to chemistry, bacteriology and medicine. He discovered that micro-organisms can be destroyed by heat, a technique, now known as pasteurization, used to destroy harmful micro-organisms in food. Pasteur also discovered that he could weaken certain disease-causing micro-organisms – specifically those causing anthrax in animals and rabies in man – and then use the weakened culture to vaccinate individuals against the disease.

Paul, name of six Roman Catholic popes. Paul VI (1897–1978; r. 1963–78) was born Giovanni Battista Montini. He was ordained in 1920 and entered the Vatican diplomatic service in 1923. He was Archbishop of Milan (1954–63). As pope, he reconvened the Second Vatican Council, and in 1965 became the first pope to visit Asia. He tried to foster ecumenism. In 1968, he opposed the use of artificial contraception.

Pavlov, Ivan Petrovich (1849–1936), Russian neurophysiologist. His early work centred on the physiology and neurology of digestion, for which he received the 1904 Nobel Prize in physiology and medicine. However, he is best known for his classical (Pavlovian) conditioning of behaviour in dogs. This work had a permanent effect on Russian psychology and a profound effect on the development of behaviourism in the USA. His major works (in translation) are *Conditioned Reflexes* (1927) and *Lectures on Conditioned Reflexes (1928).*

Pearl Harbor, *See* **World War II.**

Peasants' Revolt, uprisings in England in 1381, especially in the counties of Kent and Essex. The immediate cause of the rebellion was an unpopular poll tax and the uprising took on something of the character of a revolt against the rich. It was

---

AD 1863–1865

US saw the North beat the South in the American Civil War, the abolition of slavery and the assassination of Lincoln. Negro spirituals emerged and mixed with work songs. The Massachusetts Institute of Technology was founded. Rome stayed under papal rule.

Britain, host to Marx's First International, saw demand for electoral reform blocked by Palmerston. J.S. Mill tried to unite the conditions of industrialism with basic freedoms. China was evangelized by Christian missionaries. Russian writers Turgenev and Tolstoy brought the realist novel to its peak. Japan saw allied intervention in her civil war. Her draughtsmanship strongly influenced the Impressionists.

led by Wat Tyler and John Ball. Tyler's men beheaded the Archbishop of Canterbury and for a few days held London, until Richard II met them and promised them a free pardon and the redress of grievances, in particular the abolition of villein status.

Peel, Sir Robert (1788–1850), British politician. He was an MP from 1809 to 1850 and chief Secretary (1822–27); 1828–30) in the Tory governments of Lord Liverpool and the Duke of Wellington. He was twice Prime Minister (1834–35; 1841–46). As leader of the Tory party in the House of Commons he played a major part in the reversal of Tory policy and the passing of Catholic Emancipation in 1829. As the first Conservative Prime Minister he established the Ecclesiastical Commission (1835) and split his party permanently by the repeal of the Corn Laws (1846). Those Conservatives who followed him into free trade became known as the Peelites.

Penn, William *See* **Quakers**.

Pepin III, the Short (*d.* 768), son of Charles Martel, mayor of Neustria, Burgundy and Provence and King of the Franks (*r.* 747–768), the first king of the Carolingian dynasty. He deposed Childeric III in 750, the last Merovingian ruler, and was anointed by Pope Boniface in 751. A firm supporter of the Roman Church, he was again anointed in 754 by Pope Stephen II and defeated the Lombards on the pope's behalf (754, 756). The new papal lands (the exarchate of Ravenna) thus acquired were known as the Donation of Pepin. This event created the Papal States, making the papacy a temporal power for the first time. Pepin was the father of Charlemagne.

Pepys, Samuel (1633–1703), English diarist and naval administrator who became Secretary of the Admiralty (1673–89). His *Diary* (1660–69) frankly describes his private life and English society of his time. It includes a vivid account of the Restoration, the coronation ceremony in 1661, the Plague in 1663 and the Great Fire of London.

Pericles (*c.* 490–429 BC), Athenian statesman who was

AD 1865–1868

Austria, defeated by Prussia (1866), established a dual monarchy of Austria-Hungary, an unpopular compromise.

A Mendel founded genetics with publication of his experiments.
France withdrew from Mexico. Gautier's influence encouraged Verlaine to write disciplined verse. Monet subtly captured light effects in his painting. Offenbach's work raised

light opera to a peak.
Britain established the Dominion
A of Canada. Disraeli introduced household suffrage. The Trades Union Congress was founded. Booth started the Salvation Army, and Lister introduced antiseptic surgery.
A **German** thinker Marx published *Capital*, arguably the most influential work since the Bible.
A **Swede** Nobel invented dynamite.

---

elected to high office every year from 443 to his death. He strengthened Athens' leadership of the Delian League, made a 30-year truce with Sparta in 445, and attempted to make Athens a great cultural centre. He was reponsible for constructing the Parthenon (447–438 BC) and other notable buildings. His character, oratory (which inspired Athens to war against Sparta in 431) and his rebuilding of the Acropolis caused historians to christen his entire period the "Age of Pericles".

Perón, Juan Domingo (1895–1974), President of Argentina (1946–55, 1973–74), one of the most important political figures of Latin America. Through working-class and union support, and the popularity of his first wife Eva, Perón was elected President in 1946 and again in 1951. The Peronist programme of economic nationalism and social justice gave way to monetary inflation and political violence; Perón was ousted by a military coup in 1955. He returned from exile in Spain and was re-elected president in 1973, but died the following year.

Persian Empire, empire founded by Cyrus the Great in 549 BC by uniting the kingdom of Persia with the Median empire to the north. It was also called the Achaemenid empire, after an ancestor of Cyrus. Its expansion was swift. In 546 BC the Lydian empire was annexed, in 538 BC the Chaldean, in 525 BC the Egyptian and over the next 50 years further lands to the N and E. The last of the Persian emperors, Darius III, was defeated by Alexander the Great at the Battle of Arbela in 331 BC. Thereafter the Persian empire was absorbed into the empire of Alexander.

Pétain, Henri Philippe (1856–1951), French soldier and chief of state. In WWI he distinguished himself by holding Verdun against the Germans, was appointed Commander-in-Chief in 1917 and made a marshal in 1918. Between the wars he was the most influential military figure in France and served on the Higher Council of War (1920–30). In 1940, after France had surrendered to Germany at the beginning of WWII, Pétain was recalled from Spain (where

---

AD 1868–1870

France, invaded by Prussia, A saw Napoleon III fall. Pasteur founded bacteriology. The railway system, as in Britain and Belgium, neared completion. **Japan** saw the victory of Mutsuhito lead to a policy of industrialization. **US** introduced negro suffrage. A **Britain's** Gladstone disestablished the Anglican Church in A Ireland. Mill's *The Subjection*

of Women was a classic statement for women's suffrage. Maxwell showed light to be electromagnetic radiation. A **Russian** writer Dostoevsky produced novels of great intellectual power. A **German** composer Wagner's romanticism revolutionized opera. **Religion** saw papal infallibility asserted by the First Vatican * Council.

he was ambassador) and made head of state of the defeated nation; he led the Vichy government which collaborated with the Germans. As a great war hero forced to concede German demands, he symbolized the situation of many Frenchmen during WWII. In 1945 he was condemned to death, a sentence which Charles De Gaulle commuted to life imprisonment.

Peter, name of three tsars of Russia. Peter I (1672–1725), known as Peter the Great, reigned from 1682 to 1725. He ruled jointly with his half-brother Ivan until 1689. He conquered Azov in 1695, travelled in Europe (1696–97) and took back to Russia many western ideas and technicians. He began a series of domestic reforms in 1700: he encouraged industry, reorganized the administration, developed a new civil service class, weakened the Church and introduced western fashions. He built St Petersburg as his new capital, and made Russia a European power for the first time. He fought Sweden in the Northern War (1700–21) and, although losing Azov in 1711, extended Russia towards Siberia.

Peterloo Massacre (1819), dispersal of a radical meeting in St Peter's Fields, Manchester. A crowd of some 60,000 had assembled to demonstrate for the repeal of the Corn Laws and for parliamentary reform. The magistrates ordered the speakers to be arrested by untrained yeomanry who also attacked the crowd. A cavalry charge in aid of the yeomanry resulted in 11 deaths and an estimated 500 injured. The government's endorsement of the magistrates' action caused widespread resentment and intensified the general demand for parliamentary reform.

Petition of Right (1628), statement of civil liberties sent by the English Parliament to Charles I. The petition was based on earlier statutes and charters and asserted four principles: no taxes may be levied without the consent of Parliament; no subject may be imprisoned without cause shown; no soldiers may be quartered upon the citizenry; and martial law may not be employed in time of peace. The king

---

AD 1870–1873

A **France's** revolutionary Commune was suppressed. Symbolist poetry emerged with Rimbaud and Verlaine. Impressionism started with the paintings of Monet, Renoir, Sisley, Degas, Cézanne.
Prussia's seizure of Alsace-Lorraine completed German unity.
Britain's Education Act made primary schooling open to all.
George Eliot wrote *Middlemarch*. The *Challenger* expedition founded oceanography.
US failed to open up Korea. Sholes invented the typewriter.

A **Russian** writer Bakunin stressed the need for violent revolution. His espousal of free revolt led to his expulsion from the

A **Internationale**. Mendeleyev devised a periodic table of the elements.
Dutch scientist van der Waals calculated intermolecular forces.

---

accepted these rights and in return received subsidies from Parliament, although he continued to collect tonnage and poundage duties without Parliament's authorization. The petition is of great importance as a safeguard of civil liberties.

Petrarch, Francesco Petrarca (1304–74), Italian lyric poet and scholar, one of the best known poets of the late Middle Ages. His work influenced Geoffrey Chaucer and was taken as a model by the poets of the English Renaissance, besides exerting an important influence on his Italian successors.

Philip, name of five kings of Spain. Philip II (1527–98) reigned from 1556. He was also King of Portugal from 1580. In 1554 he married Queen Mary I of England. He supported the Inquisition and centralized the absolute Spanish monarchy. The second half of his reign was dominated by the revolt of the Netherlands. The southern part (present-day Belgium) was retained by Spain. He sent the Armada against The Netherlands' ally, England, in 1588. He founded colonies in America and annexed the Philippines, named after him.

Phoenicia, ancient region of w Asia, along the E Mediterranean Sea coast; its great city-states included Tyre, Sidon, Tripoli and Byblos. It was founded c. 1600 BC. The Phoenicians were traders and colonizers controlling the Mediterranean Sea trade, by the 12th century BC. During the 6th century BC Persia began to absorb Phoenicia, completing the process by Roman times, although the Phoenicians fought Alexander the Great to maintain their autonomy. They originated an alphabet that was later developed by the Greeks and they were famous for their purple Tyrian dye.

Picasso, Pablo (1881–1973), Spanish painter and sculptor who lived in France. His first canvases, those of the "blue period" (1901–04), showed scenes from poverty in predominantly sombre blue tints. There followed in the "rose period" (1905–08) lighter paintings, often of circus

---

AD 1873–1875

France set up the conservative Third Republic, and had her power in Indochina confirmed. Jules Laforgue, a symbolist, wrote in free verse.

Britain passed a Public Health Act codifying sanitary law and an Artisans' Dwelling Act to improve slum conditions. Disraeli acquired a quick route to India by buying a decisive share in the Suez Canal. The later Pre-Raphaelites' work was epitomized by Burne-Jones' *Briar Rose* series.

A US President Grant's administration was found to be corrupt.

German Wilhelm Wundt established experimental psychology.

A Brahms carried on Beethoven's tradition, especially in symphonic composition.

Religion saw the rise of the Temperance Movement.

---

life. In 1907 his *Les Demoiselles d'Avignon* appeared, often regarded by critics as analytical cubism; or the manifestation of the first stage of cubism. Thereafter he developed into an artist of great power and variety, producing a steady stream of paintings, sculptures, ceramics, drawings, graphic illustrations and stage designs.

Picts, ancient inhabitants of E and N Scotland, first named ("Pict" means "painted") by the Roman writer Eumenius in AD 297 as northern invaders of Roman Britain. By the 8th century they had a united kingdom extending from Caithness to Fife, and had adopted Celtic Christianity. To the W and S of the Picts, invaders from Ireland had established the kingdom of Dalriada; in 843 its king, Kenneth I, became king also of the Picts, uniting the two kingdoms into what later became the kingdom of Scotland.

Pilgrimage of Grace (1536), uprising of Roman Catholics in N England in protest against enclosures and the dissolution of the monasteries following the abolition of papal supremacy in England. After a small rising in Lincolnshire had failed, Robert Aske and his followers occupied York and then marched to Doncaster with about 30,000 armed men. The Duke of Norfolk, Henry VIII's emissary, promised Aske a pardon from the king and Aske dispersed his men. Further minor outbreaks were suppressed and Aske and more than 200 others were executed in 1537.

Pilsudski, Joseph (1867–1935), Polish general and statesman who established the independence of Poland. As a youth he was exiled to Siberia for five years for an alleged attempt to murder Tsar Alexander III. Thereafter he was dedicated to raising a private army. In WWI he fought against the Russians but was interned by the Germans when he refused to fight further because of their interference. He was Minister of Defence and the de facto ruler of Poland from 1926 until his death.

Pitt, William (the Elder), *See* Chatham.

Pitt, William (1759–1806), British politician, second son of William Pitt, Earl of Chatham. He is known as the younger

---

AD 1875–1878

Britain annexed South Africa and bought more Suez Canal shares. Peaceful picketing was legalized. Victoria became Empress of India. Swinburne's sensual poetry reacted against Victorian confidence; Hopkins' was visionary and deeply religious.

Slav nationalist forces erupted against Turkey in the Balkans, supported by Russia.

Japan's Satsuma rebellion failed to halt reform.

A **French** sculptor Rodin produced *Age of Bronze* (1877).

A **US'** Bell produced the telephone; Edison the phonograph.

German scientist Robert Koch identified bacteria.

Religion saw Ramakhrishna's attempts to reform Hinduism and Helen Blavatsky forming the Theosophical Society.

Pitt. He entered Parliament in 1781, became Chancellor of the Exchequer in 1782 and, at the age of 24, Prime Minister in 1783. He was Prime Minister until 1801, when he resigned in the face of George III's refusal to consider Catholic Emancipation, and then again from 1804 until his death. His reputation rests on his reorganization of the national finances and his resolute prosecution of the war against France and Napoleon. During his administrations were passed the India Act (1784), the Constitutional Act (1791), dividing Canada into French and English provinces, and the Act of Union with Ireland (1800). He considered himself, if anything, a Whig and did not attempt to build a party. Yet he is rightly considered as the founder of the second Tory party and, by implication, of the modern Conservative party.

Pius, name of 12 popes. Pius IX (1792–1878; r. 1846–78) was born as Giovanni Maria Mastai-Ferretti. His pontificate was the longest in history. He was driven from Rome (1848–50), but restored by Napoleon III. The Papal States were seized by the Italian nationalists in 1860, and Rome itself incorporated into the kingdom of Italy, which in 1870 Pius refused to accept. He also defended Catholics in Germany from persecution by Bismarck, and in 1869 called a Vatican Council, proclaiming Papal infallibility. Pius X, Saint (1835–1914; r. 1903–14), was born Giuseppe Melchiorre Sarto. He opposed religious Modernism, placing several modernist books on the index in 1907, condemned the separation of Church and state in France, and recodified Canon Law (published 1917). Pius XI (1857–1939; r. 1922–39) was born Ambrogio Damiano Achille Ratti. He signed the Lateran Treaty with Mussolini in·1929, but later condemned Fascism, and denounced Communism in 1937. He called for unity between the Eastern and Western Churches, and supported scientific research. Pius XII (1876–1958; r. 1939–58) was born Eugenio Pacelli. He tried to remain neutral in WWII, his conduct during which had given rise to controversy. In 1946

AD 1878–1880

Balkan supremacy was debated at the Congress of Berlin after Russia defeated Turkey.
Germany allied with Austria-Hungary. Treikschke began his monumental history of 19th-century Germany.
Britain sought to secure her Indian position against Russia. Parnell mobilized Irish nationalists. Shaw's plays attacked social complacency.

Chile defeated Peru and Bolivia.
Norwegian playwright Ibsen dramatized social issues.
France produced the varied art of Edgar Degas. Pierre Curie discovered piezoelectricity.
US inventor Edison patented his incandescent light bulb.
Religion saw Russell found the Jehovah's Witnesses and Eddy found Christian Science, rejecting medicine for prayer.

he denounced Catholic collaboration with Communists.

Pizarro, name of four Spanish brothers, all adventurers and explorers. Francisco (c. 1471–1541) led the conquest of Peru. Together with his partner and rival, Diego de Almagro, he took control of Peru in 1533 but was later assassinated by Almagro's son. Hernando (c. 1475–1578), Francisco's half-brother, helped his brothers in the conquest of Peru, and in 1538 defeated Almagro and had him executed. For this he served 20 years imprisonment in Spain. Juan (c. 1500–36) served as a lieutenant to his brother Hernando and died in battle during the reconquest of Cuzco. Gonzalo (c. 1506–48), the youngest of the brothers and the most famous after Francisco, was ruthless and tyrannical. After the Peruvian conquest, he explored much of NW South America in search of gold. In defiance of Spain, he set himself up as governor and captain-general of Peru and was eventually beheaded for treason.

Plague, The Great (1665–66), last great visitation of the bubonic plague upon England. It raged in London from April 1665 to the autumn of 1666. The court and parliament moved out of London, but the Lord Mayor remained. It is estimated that between 75,000 and 100,000 poeple died. It was the subject of Daniel Defoe's *Journal of the Plague Year* (1722).

Plantation of Ireland, English policy of permanently settling and subduing Ireland by introducing Protestant settlers to farm areas confiscated from the Irish. The first plantations were set up in Offaly and Leix in 1556 (which were renamed King's and Queen's counties), and plantation continued until the late 17th century. Official plantations were found in most of W and central Ireland; unofficial Scottish plantations were most common in Ulster. Plantations were a major grievance in the Irish rebellion of 1641.

Plato (c. 427–347 BC), Greek philosopher. He studied (407–399 BC) under Socrates, who appears as a central figure in many of his writings. Plato lived in Athens and set

AD 1880–1883

Britain installed occupation forces in Egypt, but was checked by a defeat in the Transvaal. Terrorism began in Ireland. Textile output declined. Tylor developed a theory of social evolution involving the continuity of customs. Gilbert and Sullivan perfected light opera. **Germany** tried to build a solid power structure under Bismarck, allying with Russia, Austria and Italy. Electric trams began running in Berlin. Walter Flemming described cell division. **US** writer Mark Twain produced humorous work; Henry James examined the conflicts arising from New/Old World encounters. Morley and Michelson disproved the existence of the aether. **France's** Cézanne achieved almost abstract qualities with form, colour, planes and light.

up an Academy there in *c.* 387 BC, where he taught. He visited Syracuse three times in about 388, 367 and 361–36 BC in the hope of setting up an ideal political system there. All of the 36 works of Plato survive, many of which form lasting works of literature and deal with aspects of the relationship between the individual and the state. These dialogues include *Gorgias*, the *Republic* (in which Plato outlined his view of the ideal state), *Phaedo* and the *Symposium* (both aesthetic and mystical works). Plato's work has been continually studied, from the time of his pupil Aristotle to the 20th century. Perhaps his most influential concept was that of Ideas or Forms, absolute archetypes more real than earthly phenomena that derive from them.

PLO (Palestine Liberation Organization), agency of guerrilla forces devoted to reclaiming from Israel for Palestine Arabs the w bank of the River Jordan. Founded in 1964, it is officially pledged to the dissolution of Israel. In 1974 the UN recognized the PLO as a government-in-exile.

Podgorny, Nikolai Viktorovitch (1903–   ), Soviet chief of state from 1965 to 1977. A member of the Communist Party from 1930 and of the Central Committee from 1960, he became Soviet President in 1965. His elevation to the presidency marked his removal from effective power in the confusion following the fall of Khrushchev. In 1977 he was replaced by Leonid Brezhnev.

Polo, Marco (1254–1324), first European traveller to cross the length of Asia. As a boy he went with his father, Niccolo, and uncle, Maffeo, on a trading mission (1275) that took them to the court of Kublai Khan, the Mongol ruler of China. Returning to Venice from the Chinese coast in 1295, Marco Polo became involved in a war with Genoa and was taken prisoner, during which time he compiled an account of his travels which remained an important Western source of information on Asia for nearly 600 years.

Pompey, Gnaeus, also called Pompeius Magnus (106–48 BC), Roman general. He fought for Sulla in 83 BC and campaigned in Sicily, Africa and Spain. He was named

AD 1883–1885

European ambition in Africa was circumscribed by the Treaty of Berlin (1884).
Britain, her Afghan and Egyptian positions consolidated, was defeated in the Sudan. Male suffrage led to great party political activity. The Fabians advocated evolution towards socialism. Maxim invented a machine gun and Parsons a steam turbine.

France took Indochina. Emile Zola inaugurated naturalism in literature with the 20 Rougon-Macquart novels. De Maupassant followed him. Seurat developed pointillism.
Serbia, supported by Austria, went to war with Bulgaria and Eastern Rumelia.
Germans Benz and Daimler revolutionized motor transport; the motor car developed.

consul with Crassus in 70, crushed the pirates in the Mediterranean and fought brilliantly against Mithradates VI of Pontus in 66 BC. In Rome in 59 he formed the first triumvirate with Crassus and Caesar, his fierce rival and father-in-law. He was defeated by Caesar at Pharsalus in 48 in the course of a civil war. After fleeing to Egypt he was stabbed to death by one of his soldiers.

Pompidou, Georges Jean Raymond (1911–74), French Premier (1962–68), and President (1969–74). He was a school teacher until 1944, when he served in the postwar government of Charles de Gaulle as an adviser. In 1946 he was appointed to the Council of State but he resigned in 1957 to join the Rothschild banking firm and became its director-general in 1959. When De Gaulle became President, he appointed Pompidou Prime Minister. He dealt with the May riots and strikes which shook France in 1968. Upon De Gaulle's resignation he was elected President and, by reversing government policy, made it possible for Britain to enter the EEC.

Pontiac (c. 1720–69), North American Indian chief who united many tribes south of the Great Lakes against the British. In the early years of the French and Indian War (1754–63) Pontiac kept his confederacy of Ottowa, Potawatomi and Ojibwa neutral, but in 1762 he organized many tribes into a union against the British. From 1763 to 1764 this union, known by the British as Pontiac's Conspiracy, fought a bitter struggle until Pontiac concluded peace.

Poor laws, English legislation designed to alleviate poverty and prevent begging and vagrancy. Introduced in the mid-16th century and consolidated in the Poor Law in 1601, they required individual parishes to provide for the local poor. Because there was everywhere local reluctance to support the poor from other areas, settlement laws were introduced in 1662 to limit migration. From c. 1700 workhouses were established where the poor were expected to support themselves by work. Poor-law amendments of 1834 sought

---

AD 1885–1888

Germany signed a pact guaranteeing peace with Russia in the A Balkans. Nietzsche refuted Christianity in *Beyond Good and Evil*. Tönnies, a sociologist, published *Community and Association*. Hertz produced radio waves.

US Indians were placed on reservations. The Federation of Labor was set up. Hall developed a process for the econom-ical production of aluminium.

Britain agreed with Italy and Austria-Hungary to maintain the Middle East and Mediterranean A status quo. Gladstone's Home Rule Bill met opposition.

Dutch artist Van Gogh produced turbulent portraits.

Russian composer Tchaikovsky A composed lyrical music.

Swedish playwright Strindberg wrote *Miss Julie*.

to provide uniform assistance by placing it under national supervision, but since poverty was assumed to be the consequence of unwillingness to work, relief was maintained at a level lower than that of the poorest labourer. In 1929 the Local Government Act abolished the poor law boards, making relief to the poor the responsibility of local bodies. The Poor Law Act of 1930 placed poor law under the Minister of Health. The poor law was gradually superseded by the introduction of old age pensions (1908) and unemployment and health insurance (1911), which was followed in the 1940s by social security. Workhouses were finally abolished in 1948.

Popish Plot, *See* **Oates, Titus.**

Potemkin, Grigori Aleksandrovich, Prince (1739–91), Russian statesman. Involved in the coup that brought Catherine II to power in 1762, he became her lover for a time and remained until his death the most powerful man in Russia. He played an important part in the annexation of the Crimea in 1783, for which he was created a prince, and was an able administrator of the new province.

Potsdam Conference (1945), meeting of leaders of principal Allies of WWII to clarify and implement agreements reached at the Yalta Conference. The participants included President Truman of the USA, Premier Stalin of the USSR, the Prime Minister, Churchill, of Great Britain and, after the latter's defeat in the British elections, Attlee. The so-called Potsdam agreement established the Council of Foreign Ministers to prepare draft treaties and to make proposals for settling territorial issues. It also transferred the chief authority in Germany to the US, British, French and Soviet commanders in their respective zones of occupation. German industry was decentralized and an ultimatum calling for unconditional surrender was issued to Japan.

Prasad, Rajendra (1884–1963), Indian politician and lawyer who renounced his legal practice in 1920 to follow Ghandi. He was a member of the All-India Congress in

---

AD 1888–1890

Britain, dominating central and southern Africa, developed socialist parties. Irish nationalists were split by Parnell's divorce. Frazer's *Golden Bough* surveyed a vast range of customs and beliefs. Dunlop invented the pneumatic tyre.
Japan's Emperor Meiji granted a Western constitution.
France's Georges Boulanger tried to seize power. Moreau and Redon produced symbolist art. The Eiffel Tower was built.
US produced more steel than Britain. Eastman made photograhic film and paper.
Germany legalized the Social-Democratic Party.
Austrian composers Bruckner and Mahler wrote symphonies.
Italian nationalism was voiced by Carducci's *Odi Barbara*.

1912 and its president four times between 1934 and 1948. Prasad was the first President of the Republic of India from 1950 until 1962. His autobiography, *Atma Katha*, was published in 1958, other works include *India Divided* and *At the Feet of Mahatma Ghandi* (both 1958).

Priestley, Joseph (1733–1804), British chemist. He studied the properties of carbon dioxide (then called "fixed air") and invented carbonated drinks. Although an advocate of the Phlogiston theory, he discovered oxygen (which he called "dephlogisticated air") in 1774 and a number of other gases, including ammonia and the oxides of nitrogen. He emigrated to the USA in 1794, where he renewed a friendship with John Adams. He also wrote about history and political theory.

Princes in the Tower, Edward V and Richard, Duke of York, the sons of Edward IV. On their father's death Edward V, then 12 years old, became king with his uncle, Richard, Duke of Gloucester as Protector of the Realm. The princes were housed in the Tower of London following factional disputes between the Woodville group of nobles, the Queen's party, and the Duke of Gloucester. Gloucester summoned the lords and commons, who proclaimed the children illegitimate and Gloucester king. The princes disappeared; it has been supposed that they were murdered by Gloucester's agents, but the evidence is inconclusive.

Prohibition (1919–33), period in US history in which the manufacture, transport, sale and consumption of alcoholic beverages was illegal, enacted through the 18th Amendment to the Constitution. Enforcement of the ban proved extremely difficult. Smuggling could not be prevented and the illegal manufacture of liquor sprang up with such rapidity that the authorities were unable to suppress it. Illegal drinking of inferior and often dangerous alcoholic beverages became commonplace, while corruption of government officials and local police, paralysis of the courts and the growth of organized crime financed by immense Bootlegging profits all followed. In

---

AD 1890–1894

European alliance blocs formed. Germany, Austria-Hungary and Italy allied. Russia and France allied (1891).

Germany's Kaiser Wilhelm II (1888–1918) dismissed Bismarck.

Brazil adopted a federal republican constitution.

Britain saw the Independent Labour Party founded. The Lords rejected Gladstone's Second Home Rule Bill. Marshall estab-

lished the Neoclassical School of Economics. Hardy wrote many popular pessimistic novels and Wilde's *Picture of Dorian Gray* epitomized the Decadent movement. Beardsley popularized the art nouveau decorative style.

US saw the Populist Party grow out of agrarian protest over currency deflation.

China's K'ang Yu-wei advocated social equality.

1933 the US government had no alternative but to repeal the law under the 21st amendment.

Protectorate (1653–59), in English history, period of absolute rule by Cromwell, his authority resting on the power of the army. Following the execution of Charles I, England was declared a Commonwealth under the rule of the Rump Parliament. In 1653, however, Cromwell replaced the Rump with the nominated Barebone's Parliament, the majority of which was submissive to his will. In December of that year, Cromwell assumed the title of Lord Protector of England, Scotland and Ireland. A virtual dictator, Cromwell divided the country into 11 districts, each under the administration of a major-general. At his death (1658) he was succeeded by his son, Richard Cromwell, who proved inept. After a period of chaos, the Rump Parliament was recalled and in 1660 General George Monck brought about the Restoration of Charles II.

Proust, Marcel (1871–1922), French novelist whose *A la recherche du temps perdu* (*Remembrance of Things Past*; 16 vols, 1913–27) is regarded as one of the great works of literature. Proust was a frequenter of the aristocratic salons of Paris at the turn of the century, and he was actively involved in the Dreyfus Affair (1897–99). He suffered from asthma and his growing ill-health caused him in 1907 to withdraw from society and devote himself to writing. *Remembrance of Things Past* is written in long cascading sentences. It is founded on the effects of involuntary memory, the moments when a chance impression obliterates the present and propels one into a past moment.

Ptolemy, or Claudius Ptolemaeus (*c.* 90–168), Egyptian-born Greek astronomer and geographer. He charted many new stars and his remarkable *Almagest* (*c.* 150) influenced astronomy for the next 1,400 years. His *Geography*, which included Africa and Asia, also had great subsequent influence. He devised new mathematical theorems and proofs and wrote *Optica*, a treatise on optics.

Pugachev, Emelyan Ivanovich (*c.* 1726–75), Russian

AD 1894–1896

Japan defeated China, gaining Formosa and a free hand in Korea. **Russian** finances were reformed by Sergei Witte. Industrialization and eastward expansion were stimulated.

A **France** was split by the Dreyfus Case. Gauguin developed synthetism, rejecting the Impressionists' naturalism. Debussy brought impressionism into music. The Lumière brothers developed cine equipment. Becquerel discovered radioactivity. **Britain's** Joseph Chamberlain began a policy of colonial expansion in southern Africa. Spencer popularized a comprehensive evolutionary theory. Kipling and Wells were well-known literary figures. **German's** Diesel invented the deisel engine and Roentgen discovered X-rays.

Punic Wars

Cossack leader. He led a massive popular revolt against Catherine II and in 1773 proclaimed himself Peter III, promising freedom from serfdom, taxes and military service, and the elimination of landlords and other officials. Defeated in late 1774, he was taken to Moscow for trial and executed.

Punic Wars (265–241, 218–201 and 149–146 BC), three conflicts between Rome and Carthage, during which Rome became the predominant Mediterranean power. The first war arose over a dispute about control of the Straits of Messina. Although the Romans built their first fleet and gained command of the sea, they could not at first take Carthaginian strongholds in Sicily, nor defeat Carthage in N Africa. Eventually a naval victory off the Aegates in 241 led Carthage to sue for peace, and Sicily was surrendered. The second war arose out of Carthage's conquest of Spain (237–219 BC). Hannibal marched into Italy from Spain in 218 via the Alps, but failed to take Rome. Roman victories in Spain and N Africa led to Hannibal's recall, and his defeat at Zama in 202 BC. Carthage surrendered the next year, and became a Roman vassal. The third war arose out of a Roman determination to destroy Carthage and, after a long blockade of the city, the Romans (led by Scipio Africanus Minor) razed Carthage to the ground.

Puritans, English Protestant fundamentalists who were particularly influential during the 16th and 17th centuries. They originated in the reign of Elizabeth I; their chief aim was to make a truly Protestant Church out of the Church of England, which was (and still is) technically not one. Following the ideas of Jean Calvin, their opposition to Anglicanism was initially directed against liturgical vestments, elaborate ritual and other elements of "popish" practice, but they subsequently also demanded the abolition of church government by bishops and the setting up of a policy of Presbyterianism. According to Calvin's concept of Predestination, they thought of mankind as divided into the Elect – those destined inevitably for Heaven – and the

---

AD 1896–1898

Britain faced a Boer crisis after the Jameson Raid. Kitchener conquered the Sudan and met the French at Fashoda. Chamberlain opposed Home Rule. Thomson discovered the electron and Ross traced malaria to the mosquito.

France aimed at consolidation of the Saharan Empire by influencing Morocco. Durkheim linked positivist social ideas with an interest in morality in *Suicide*. The Curies discovered polonium and radium.

US psychologist William James expounded philosophical pragmatism. Sousa wrote marches.

Nicaraguan poet Ruban Dario epitomized "Modernismo".

Austrian artist Klimt promoted art nouveau.

Spanish culture was revived by the Generation of '98.

Reprobate. The Puritans' zenith was reached when Oliver Cromwell, an Independent (Congregationalist), assumed power and disestablished the Church of England; the Church was re-established in 1660, although Presbyterianism became the state Church in Scotland in 1690.

Pym, John (1584–1643), English politician. He was a leader of the opposition to the Duke of Buckingham in the 1620s, and helped to pass the Petition of Right in 1629. He was the leading member of the parliamentary opposition to Charles I in 1640–43, attacking Strafford and Laud. Charles tried but failed to arrest him in Parliament in 1642, and Pym organized the alliance between Parliament and the Scottish Covenanters.

Pythagoras, (*c*. 580–500 BC) Greek philosopher and founder of the Pythagorean school. Little is known of his life except that he was born on Samos and lived in Crotona. The Pythagoreans believed in reincarnation and that numbers constitute the true nature of things. They treated the sexes as equal, were humane to slaves and respected animals; they saw all relations as numerical, made important contributions to geometry, medicine and philosophy, and were probably the first to teach that the Earth is a sphere revolving about the Sun.

Qaddafi, Muammar al- (1942–   ), Libyan political leader and army officer who in 1969 led a coup against the monarchy of Idris I, naming himself Libya's commander-in-chief and Chairman of the Revolutionary Command Council. A militant Arab nationalist, he helped to support the Palestinian guerrillas in their actions against Israel and sought to unite Libya with other Arab nations.

Quakers, nickname for the Society of Friends, a Christian sect which arose in England in the 1650s, founded by George Fox. The name derived from the injunction given by early Quaker leaders that their followers tremble in the sight of the Lord. Quakers rejected the episcopal organization of the Church of England, believing in the

---

AD 1898–1900

US raised its tariff wall and took Puerto Rico and the Philippines. The Chicago School created skyscrapers. Scott Joplin popularized ragtime.
China saw westernization rejected in the Boxer Rebellion.
A**Britain** entered the South African War. The Labour Representation Committee was founded. Rutherford discovered alpha and beta rays in radioactivity.

A**Austrian** Sigmund Freud emphasized the subconscious and founded psychoanalysis.
Russian dramatist Chekhov took realist drama to its peak.
Norwegian painter Munch influenced German Expressionism.
Dutch scientist Beijerinck discovered viruses.
Germany manufactured aspirin.
Greek poet Cavafy described life's ironies.

priesthood of all believers and the direct relationship between a man and the spiritual light of God. Quakers originally worshipped God in silence unless someone was moved by the Holy Spirit to speak or offer up a prayer but have introduced hymns and readings into their meetings since the mid-19th century. The largest Quaker Church is in the USA, where it began with the founding of a settlement by William Penn in 1681.

Quisling, Vidkun (1887–1945), Norwegian Fascist leader whose name became synonymous with "traitor" during WWII. He was Minister of Defence (1931–33), but left the Agrarian Party to found the Fascist National Union Party. In 1940 he collaborated with Germany in the invasion of Norway. He was made Premier of the puppet government in 1942 and stayed in power until Norway's liberation, when he was arrested, convicted of high treason and shot.

Raleigh, Sir Walter (c. 1552–1618), English soldier, explorer, courtier and man of letters. A favourite of Elizabeth I, he organized expeditions to North America and is credited with introducing the potato plant and tobacco to England. After the accession of James I in 1603 he was found guilty of conspiring against the king and imprisoned in the Tower or London, where he wrote his *History of the World* (1614). In 1617 he led an unsuccessful expedition to the Orinoco, Guyana, in search of gold, was arrested on his return and executed under the terms of his original sentence.

Raphael, or Raffaelo Sanzio (1483–1520), Italian painter, one of the finest artists of the High Renaissance. Born in Urbino, he went to Perugia and studied under Perugino. He moved to Florence in 1504, and there learned his draughtsmanship. In Florence he painted many Madonnas, famous for their delicate portraiture based on the example of Leonardo da Vinci. In 1508 he moved to Rome at the request of Pope Julius II, and painted the frescoes of *The School of Athens* and the *Disputa* (1511) in the Stanza della Segnatura in the Vatican.

AD 1900–1903

US Steel Corporation integrated the industry. Canal-building rights were won in Panama. The Pentecostal Movement began. **France** allied with Italy. Villard discovered gamma rays.

A**Britain** won the South African War and allied with Japan, countering Russian presence in Manchuria. Local authorities were made responsible for education and the fingerprint sys-

tem introduced. Yeats, Synge and O'Casey spearheaded the Celtic literary renaissance. Joyce was hostile to it. **Italian** positivist Pareto re-

A futed Marx in *The Socialist*

A *Systems*. Marconi transmitted radio signals.

German composer Strauss

A continued the Wagnerian tradition. Planck's quantum theory was proposed.

Rasputin, Grigori Yefimovich (*c.* 1872–1916), Russian peasant mystic. He exercised great influence at the court of Nicholas II because of his apparent ability to cure the crown prince Alexis' haemophilia. He was influential in Russia during WWI but was assassinated in 1916.

Reformation, The, 16th-century reform of the universal Catholic Church which resulted in the formation of the Anglican and Protestant Churches. More than merely a revolt against the authority, ecclesiastical and doctrinal of the Church, it also represented a protest by many theologians and scholars against the many questionable activities of the contemporary clergy. The influence of Martin Luther from the 1520s was significant, and the effect of the Reformation was felt first in Germany then in Scotland and England, Scandinavia and Switzerland, and finally some of France, but hardly touched Italy or the Iberian peninsula. It took two main forms: Lutheran (emphasizing justification, or salvation, by faith alone) and Calvinist (after John Calvin, who emphasized predestination); Lutheranism predominated, except in Calvinist Scotland and Switzerland, and in Anglican England. All the Reformed Churches established Church organizations independent of the pope.

Reform bills, name given to three British measures that liberalized representation in Parliament in the 19th century. The Reform Bill of 1832, enacted under the Whig administration of Lord Grey, redistributed seats in the interest of larger cities, such as Manchester, that had hitherto been unrepresented; it also extended the franchise in the boroughs to those who occupied premises of an annual value of £10 and simplified registration and voting procedure. Benjamin Disraeli's bill of 1867, by lowering property qualifications, enfranchised the urban working class, thereby almost doubling the electorate. In 1884 William Gladstone's bill added 2,500,000 new voters to the list by enfranchising most agricultural workers. The franchise was not extended to women until the

---

AD 1903–1905

Britain settled her Egyptian dispute with France by the Entente Cordiale. Chamberlain campaigned for protective tariffs, favouring imperial exports. Conrad's novels dealt with man's capacity.
Russia, defeated by Japan in Manchuria, saw a revolution against tsarist autocracy.
France and Germany clashed over Morocco.

German sociologist Weber stressed the causal role of ideas in history. Rilke's work exemplified impressionAism. Einstein published his special theory of relativity.
A Spanish artist Picasso had his Blue Period (1901–4).
AUS aviators the Wrights made the first sustained flight.
Italian opera was perfected by Puccini.

Rembrandt (Harmensz van Rijn)

Representation of the People Act (1918) granted suffrage to women over 30. Universal suffrage was not granted until the Representation of the People (Equal Franchise) Act of 1928.

Rembrandt (Harmensz van Rijn) (1606–69), Dutch painter and graphic artist, prodigious creator of more than 600 paintings, about 300 etchings and nearly 2,000 drawings, many regarded as masterpieces. A miller's son, he was a pupil of Pieter Lastman in Amsterdam in 1624. His early, small, realistic works show the influence of Caravaggio. During his Leiden period (1625–31) he began to paint self-portraits which were to number almost 100. He moved to Amsterdam in 1632, where he spent the rest of his life and became highly regarded as a painter of such group portraits as the *Anatomy Lesson of Dr Tulp* (1632).

Renaissance, The, period of European history lasting roughly from the mid-15th century to the end of the 16th century. The word means rebirth and was used by scholars in late 15th-century Italy to describe the revival of interest in classical learning and classical principles in art and architecture. The Renaissance was immeasurably helped by the fall of Constantinople to the Ottoman Turks in 1453, which resulted in the transport of classical texts to Italy and closed Europe's traditional trading routes to the East; and by the invention, in Germany, of a printing press with moveable type, which greatly assisted the diffusion of the new scholarship. For the Renaissance meant the re-introduction of secular and humanist ideas into a Europe long dominated by the ideology of Christendom united under the Pope and the Holy Roman Emperor. In religion the spirit of questioning led to the Reformation. In politics the Renaissance saw the rise of assertive sovereign states – Spain, Portugal, France and England, and the expansion of Europe beyond its own shores, with the building of trading empires in Africa, the East Indies and America, an expansion led by Portugal and Spain. The growth of a wealthy urban merchant class led to a tremendous flowering

---

AD 1905–1908

France settled the Moroccan question in her favour. Bergson wrote his *Creative Evolution*. Matisse started Fauvism.

Russian tsarist rule was re-imposed. Agreement with Japan over China was reached. Poet Ivanovich led the Symbolists.

Britain agreed with France and Spain to oppose German Mediterranean expansion and convened with Russia about the Middle East. Campbell-Bannerman led a Liberal landslide and reorganized the forces. Wilson perfected the cloud chamber.

German poet Stefan George wrote A the Nietzschean *Seventh Ring*. Fischer worked with proteins and revolutionized molecular biology.

US blues was popular. Mass pro-A duction of Fords began.

A Religion saw Pius X condemn the Modernist movement.

---

of the arts, as city merchants became patrons of artists, jewellers, sculptors and musicians.

Resistance movements, underground organizations which worked against Nazi rule in those countries whose governments had capitulated to German occupation in WWII. They were strongest in Poland, Yugoslavia and France, but they were also helpful to the Allied cause in Belgium, Holland, Denmark and Norway.

Restoration (1660), the return of Charles II to the English throne after the Commonwealth and Protectorate had faltered and a strong reaction had set in against military control. By the Declaration of Breda in 1660, Charles II promised religious toleration, a general pardon to all former enemies of the house of Stuart (except regicides) and payment of arrears in salary to the army. He landed in England in May 1660 to general rejoicing. Anglicanism was restored but certain civil and religious restrictions were placed upon Roman Catholics and some Protestant sects, such as Quakers.

Revolutions of 1848, series of uprisings in western and central European countries, whose object in some places (notably France and Germany) was the establishment of liberal, constitutional regimes; elsewhere (eg, in nations under Austrian rule) national liberation was the aim. Everywhere the ruling authorities – Louis-Philippe in France, Metternich in Austria, Frederick William in Prussia – were forced briefly to give way. But the middle classes, who led the revolutions, were not supported by the peasantry and by the end of 1849 all the revolutions had been crushed.

Rhodes, Cecil John (1853–1902), British financier and statesman. He went to Africa for his health in 1870, where he began mining diamonds and gold. A firm believer in British colonial expansion, he formed the British South Africa Company in 1889 and with it controlled the large areas of SE Africa later called Rhodesia. He was Prime Minister of Cape Colony from 1890 to 1896. Failure to gain

---

AD 1908–1910

Britain, in an arms race with Germany, saw India secure constitutional reforms and the Union of South Africa formed. The Lords rejected the People's Budget.
Austria annexed Bosnia, but avoided war with Serbia.
Spain saw Catalonian unrest.
France's Blériot flew the Channel.
Germany synthesized ammonia for explosives. Expressionist painting developed. Meinecke wrote *Cosmopolitanism and the Nation State.*
US saw jazz popularized and combine harvesters common.
Belgian Baekeland invented Bakelite for electrical plugs.
Japanese fiction saw a naturalist school led by Shimazaki Toson.
Italian Futurists produced their manifesto.

control of the Transvaal by means of a conspiracy (the Jameson Raid, 1895) destroyed his political career. He left his vast fortune to various public works and established scholarships for education.

Richard I (1157–99; *r.* 1189–99), King of England, son of Henry II and Eleanor of Aquitaine, also known as Richard Coeur de Lion or Richard the Lion-Heart. He revolted against his father from 1173 to 1174 and again from 1188 to 1189, succeeding to the throne on his father's death in 1189. In 1190 he set out on the Third Crusade and took Cyprus and Acre in 1191, but failed to gain Jerusalem. On his journey home he was captured and held for ransom in Austria. He eventually returned to England in 1194 in time to suppress a revolt raised against him by his brother John. He then went to France where he spent the rest of his life.

Richard III (1452–85), Kind of England (*r.* 1483–85), brother of Edward IV. When Edward died in 1483 his young son was proclaimed Edward V, but Richard put him and his other young nephew in the Tower of London and assumed the crown himself. His old supporter, the Duke of Buckingham, led an unsuccessful revolt against him shortly after in favour of Henry Tudor. Henry himself landed in Wales in 1485 and killed Richard at the Battle of Bosworth Field. Richard was the last Yorkist king and his death ended the Wars of the Roses.

Richelieu, Armand-Jean du Plessis de (1585–1642), French cardinal and statesman. He became chief of the royal council in 1624, establishing an ever-increasing royal power that lasted until the French Revolution. In foreign affairs, he turned the Swedes and Protestant Germans against the Hapsburgs and advanced the French cause in the Thirty Years War. A wealthy literary patron, he established the Académie Française.

Robespierre, Maximilian-François-Marie-Isidore (1758–94), French politician, one of the most important figures in the French Revolution. He was elected to the National Assembly in 1789, where he became one of the

---

AD 1910–1913

US occupied Vera Cruz.
German ambition resulted in France, Russia and Britain making military pacts. Husserl founded phenomenology. Expressionists such as Heym described visions of social collapse and war. Der Blaue Reiter group included Kandinsky and Klee, using abstract forms to convey spiritual realities.
A **China** saw Sun Yat-sen set up a nationalist republic.
Britain limited the Lords' power and introduced National Insurance. Rutherford announced that the atom had a nucleus and Hopkins held that vitamins are vital to health.
France's Poincaré developed advanced atomic theories, Apollinaire Surrealism.
Russia's Diaghilev produced ballets by Stravinsky.

main spokesmen of radical democrats, and dominated the Jacobins, especially after 1791. The outbreak of war in 1792 gave him even more influence. In June 1793 he became a member of the Committee of Public Safety, the ruling executive, which he soon dominated. In spite of seemingly overwhelming odds he and his colleagues, using authoritarian methods known as the Reign of Terror, defeated the internal and external enemies of the republic. Robespierre was overthrown by the coup of 9th Thermidor in 1794 and executed.

Rodin, Auguste (1840–1917), French sculptor who brought to a climax the age of Romanticism in sculpture. A visit to Italy (1875–77) familiarized him with the work of Michelangelo and Donatello and his first major work *The Age of Bronze* was exhibited in 1878. *The Gates of Hell* (unfinished studies for a bronze door for the Musée des arts décoratifs) was a maze of almost 200 tortured figures inspired by Ghiberti's *Gates of Paradise* (1401–24) and Doré's illustrations (1861) for Dante's *Inferno*. These figures provided him with the subjects for further sculpture which included *Fugit Amor* (1897)

Roman Empire, that part of the world, centred on the Mediterranean, which was ruled from the Italian city state of Rome from the mid-4th century BC to the Barbarian invasions of Italy and the deposition of the last Roman emperor of the West, Romulus Augustulus, in AD 476. Rome itself was, according to Livy, founded in 735 BC by Romulus and Remus and was under Etruscan control until the expulsion of Tarquinius Superbus in *c.* 509 BC. His expulsion marks the beginning of the Roman republic, which was governed by two consuls and a senate; the expansion of Rome began soon after. By 340 BC Rome had defeated the cities of the Latin League and established a political and trading control over Italy south of the Po River.

The next phase of expansion took place against the Carthaginians in the Punic Wars. The defeat of Hannibal and the razing of Carthage in 146 BC left Rome in control of

---

AD 1913–1915

Europe was plunged into World War I after the assassination of Archduke Franz Ferdinand by Serbian nationalists.
Britain was divided by industrial disputes, suffragettes, and the Home Rule question. Russell and Whitehead tried to derive mathematics from logic.
Germany saw the foundation of the left-wing Spartacus group by Rosa Luxemburg. Stainless steel was first produced.
US writer Ezra Pound started the influential *Cantos*. D.W. Griffith made *Birth of a Nation*.
Austrian writer Kafka described spiritual bereavement in works such as *The Trial*.
Russian composer Stravinsky wrote *The Rite of Spring*.
Dane Niels Bohr showed how changes in the electron orbits of atoms produce energy.

---

all of Italy, Sicily, Sardinia, Corsica, the southern coast of Iberia and the northern coast of Africa.

Expansion to the east began in the late 3rd century BC. Philip II of Macedon was defeated in two campaigns (215–205 BC and 200–197 BC) and Antiochus III of Syria was defeated in 190 BC. By 168 BC Macedonia was a Roman province. Greece was never an imperial province, but it became at the same time subject to Roman hegemony. The next great addition of territory was made by Julius Caesar's conquest of Gaul between 58 BC and 51 BC. Britain was added to the empire by Claudius in AD 43. By that time the fact of empire had been recognized by the bestowing of the title emperor upon Octavian, Caesar Augustus, 27 BC.

In AD 167 the first Barbarian invasions from the north crossed the Danube and the Alps into Italy. They, and the spread of Christianity, began to disrupt the stability of Roman society and in 285 the empire was divided by Diocletian into Western and Eastern halves. By the middle of the 5th century the Western empire had disintegrated and its lands were under Barbarian occupation. The eastern, or Byzantine Empire, however, survived and was not finally dismembered until 1453.

Rommel, Erwin (1891–1944), German military commander. He proved his ability as a commander of tanks in France in 1940, and later led the Afrika Korps. Known as "The Desert fox", he was defeated by the British at El Alamein. By 1944, Rommel was disenchanted with Germany's military leadership, and was in communication with plotters who tried to kill Hitler in July; when Rommel's association with the conspirators was discovered, he was forced to commit suicide.

Roosevelt, Franklin Delano (1882–1945), 32nd US president (1933–45), the only one elected for four consecutive terms. He entered politics as Pres. Woodrow Wilson's assistant secretary of the Navy (1913–20). In 1921 he was stricken by polio which left his legs paralysed. Encouraged by his wife Eleanor Roosevelt to resume

---

AD 1915–1918

Germany blockaded British shipping and her submarine's sinking of the *Lusitania* brought
A the US into the war. Einstein's general theory of relativity appeared. Synthetic rubber and cellulose were developed.
Russia's tsar abdicated and
A Lenin's Bolsheviks took over.
Britain saw the Easter Rising
A boost Sinn Fein in Ireland.
Poets Brooke, Owen, Graves and

Sasoon voiced horror of war.
A Austrian psychoanalyst Freud's insistence on the sexual basis of mental disorder led to the defection of Jung and Adler.
France saw Duchamp lead Dada.
US composer Ives wrote the *Concord Sonata*. Charlie Chaplin's films were popular. Tractors were introduced.
China saw a literary revolution, involving use of the vernacular.

political life, he was elected governor of New York (1928). In 1932, during the Depression, he won the presidential election as the Democratic Party candidate. His "New Deal", a set of measures designed to restore the economy through direct government intervention antagonized Republicans and conservatives, but Roosevelt's popularity led to a great electoral victory in 1936, and a narrower success in 1940. Early in his third term, he abandoned the traditional us foreign policy of isolationism and aided Britain against Nazi Germany; after the Japanese attack on Pearl Harbor he led his country into wwii. Re-elected for a fourth time in 1944, he died soon after inauguration.

Roses, Wars of the (1455–85), English civil wars fought for the possession of the crown, taking their name from the badges of the House of Lancaster (red rose) and the House of York (white rose). By 1455 the incompetence of the Lancastrian Henry VI had led to widespread civil disorder. Henry's interests were promoted by his wife, Margaret of Anjou, who was determined to protect the inheritance of their son Edward (*b.* 1453). In 1455 Richard, Duke of York, and a small group of lords attempted to gain control of the government but were at first defeated. York was killed in 1460, but his son claimed the throne, defeated Henry V at Towton Field in 1461 and was crowned as Edward IV. In 1470, Edward's closest ally, the Earl of Warwick, deserted him for the Lancastrians. Briefly deposed, Edward regained his throne and defeated his enemies in 1471. Henry VI and his son were killed. When Edward IV died in 1483, his brother usurped the throne as Richard III and Edward's sons were murdered. Their deaths allowed Henry Tudor to rally the Lancastrian faction and Richard III was overcome at Bosworth in 1485 by Henry who, as Henry VII, married Edward IV's daughter Elizabeth of York in 1486, thus reuniting the two warring factions.

Rousseau, Jean-Jacques (1712-78), French philosopher born in Geneva, considered to be a founder of

---

AD 1918–1920

AEurope saw World War I end with **A**the Versailles Treaty. Woodrow **A**Wilson's League of Nations was set up.

Britain's women over 30 gained the vote. Anthropologist Malinowski developed functionalism. Alcock and Brown flew the Atlantic.

Germany's Spengler published *The Decline of the West.* Hesse wrote *Demian.* The Bauhaus

School was founded by Gropius. **Indian** thinker Mohammed Iqbal voiced growing resentment at Western presence in India. **Dutch** painters Mondrian and van Doesburg founded the de Stijl group, using straight lines and primary colours. **French** writer André Gide became prominent with his *Journals* and dense, consciously artistic novels.

Romanticism. He contributed to the Encyclopédie of Diderot in the 1740s, and won fame for his *Discourses on Science and the Arts* (1750). In *The Social Contract* (1762) he argued that man had been corrupted by civilization; he envisaged a society in which freedom and equality would be achieved by individuals agreeing to contribute to and be subject to a "General Will", and in which executive power was delegated by the people. His ideas on individual liberation from the constraints of society were developed in *Émile* (1762), in which he outlined his theories of education. He described his early, wandering life in a revealing autobiography, *Confessions*, published posthumously in 1782.

Rubens, Peter Paul (1577–1640), Flemish painter and engraver. During two visits to Italy between 1600 and 1608 he painted religious subjects and was greatly influenced in his style by the works of Italian High Renaissance masters. Monumental muscular figures in action are characteristic of his heroic, Mannerist style. When he returned to Antwerp (1608), he established a workshop that became highly successful, producing huge portraits and allegorical series for the wealthy and nobility of western Europe.

Rump Parliament, *See* **Long Parliament.**

Rupert, Prince (1619–82), Bohemian military commander. His uncle Charles I made him general of the horse and as the commander of the cavalry in the English Civil War he was undefeated until Marston Moor (1644). He was dismissed after the Royalist defeat at Naseby (1645) and his surrender to Fairfax at Bristol. He led Privateers against English shipping during the Protectorate and, back in England after the Stuart restoration, served as an admiral in the Dutch wars.

Russell, Bertrand Arthur William, 3rd Earl (1872–1970), British philosopher, mathematician and social reformer. His philosophy was of empiricism and logical atomism, which he applied to mathematics to demonstrate that mathematics could be explained by the rules of formal logic.

AD 1920–1922

Russia saw reactionary forces try unsuccessfully to defeat A the Bolsheviks.

Germany experienced economic chaos, but allied with Russia.

Japan made peace with China.

A **Italy** saw Mussolini rise to power. Pirandello's plays reflected man's spiritual confusion.

A **Britain** partitioned Ireland; Republicans rejected this but met defeat in the civil war.

Austrian thinker Wittgenstein argued that philosophy was analytic, not speculative.

US poet T.S. Eliot's *Waste Land* summed up post-war feelings.

Frank Lloyd Wright was the day's most influential architect.

Radio broadcasting began.

Canada isolated insulin.

France saw Fernand Leger's paintings reflect contemporary interest in machinery.

His most famous work, *Principia Mathematica* (1910–13), was written in collaboration with his teacher, A. N. Whitehead. He was a pacifist except during WWII and was a constant campaigner for educational and moral reforms.

Russell, John, 1st Earl (1792–1878), British statesman; Prime Minister from 1846–52 and 1865–66. He was the third son of the 6th Duke of Bedford and made an important contribution to the development of British politics in the 19th century, especially in the change from an aristocratic Whig Party to a more broadly based liberalism. He was associated with such major reform issues as Roman Catholic emancipation, parliamentary and municipal reform and the repeal of the Corn Laws.

Russian Revolutions (February and October 1917), overthrow of Russian monarchy and Bolshevik accession to power. Incompetent management during WWI, loss of confidence in the regime and riots in the capital occasioned by acute shortage of food forced Nicholas II to abdicate in February 1917. A Provisional Government was formed by liberals in the Duma, with Price Georgy Lvov as Prime Minister, but had to contend with the growing influence of the soviets (local district councils). The Government's decision to continue the war and its failure to introduce land reform caused popular support in the soviets to shift to the Bolsheviks. In July the Bolsheviks attempted to rally popular support to overthrow the Provisional Government with their call of "All Power to the Soviets" but the Provisional Government was able to retain control. Lenin, who had arrived in July after the provisional government restored order in April, fled to Finland. In September, General Kornilov unsuccessfully attempted to overthrow Kerensky who took over as Prime Minister in July from Prince Lvov but was unable to muster support from the army. After the "Kornilov Affair", the Bolsheviks gained a majority in the St Petersburg and Moscow soviets, and increased their popular support with their slogan "Peace, Land and Bread".

AD 1922–1925

Germany saw France occupy the Ruhr and suffered massive inflation despite the Dawes Plan. **Turkey's** modernization was begun by Kemal Ataturk. **US** saw Hubble find external spiral galaxies and Birdseye begin experiments with quick-frozen food. **Britain's** Labour Party became the official opposition under Ramsay MacDonald.

Hungarian Lucaks wrote on revolutionary consciousness. **Italy's** Croce opposed Fascism. A **French** writer Proust evoked the past in a stream-of-consciousness technique. Le Corbusier built with concrete and glass. **Irish** writer Joyce wrote *Ulysses*. **Austrian** musician Schoenberg created serial music. **Russian** director Eisenstein made *The Battleship Potemkin*.

Russo-Japanese War

Russo–Japanese War (1904–05), conflict originating from
rivalry over Manchuria and Korea. In May 1904 Japanese
troops crossed the Yalu River from Korea into Manchuria,
while naval forces seized Port Arthur, which fell in January
1905. In March 1905 the Japanese captured Mukden and in
May destroyed the Russian fleet at Tsushima. The Treaty of
Portsmouth (1905) obliged Russia to recognize Japan's
"paramount interest" in Korea. Japan was also given the
southern half of Sakhalin by the Russians. The war
established Japan as a world power and was a primary cause
of the Russian Revolution of 1905.

Sadat, Mohamed Anwar as- (1918–), Egyptian soldier
and politician. He became president of Egypt on the death
of Nasser in 1970. He was proclaimed military Governor-
General in 1973, and in 1973–74 he also served as Prime
Minister. In 1979, he signed a peace treaty with Israel,
despite much Arab opposition.

Sade, Donatien Alphonse François, Marquis de
(1740–1814), French novelist and playwright. He is one of
the founders of the modern French prose style and the
licentiousness of his works and the moral freedom which he
espoused, especially in sexual relations, have gained him
consideration as a forerunner of Existentialism. During his
27 years in prison for sexual offences, he wrote many novels,
among them *Justine* (1791) and *Juliette* (1797).

Safavid dynasty, Muslim dynasty which ruled Persia from
1501 to 1736. Its name is taken from Sheikh Safī al-Dīn
shāq, the founder of the Muslim order called the Safawiyya.
The first Safavid ruler of Persia was Isma'il I. In 1736 the
dynasty was overthrown by Nādir Shāh.

Saint-Just, Louis-Antoine-Léon de, (1767–94), politician
of the French Revolution, whose stern and ruthless
devotion to the cause of the Republic made him both
admired by some and reviled by others. He became deputy
in the National Convention in 1792, and a member of the
Committee of Public Safety in May 1793; in this latter
capacity he was one of the leaders of France during the

AD 1925–1928

A **China's** Chiang Kai-shek captured Peking, unifying China.

A **Germany** joined the League of

A Nations. Hitler's *Mein Kampf*
drew on Gobineau's ideas of
racial purity. Fritz Lang developed expressionist cinema.

Russia industrialized under
Stalin. Sholokov emerged as
a major writer.

A **Britain** had a General Strike.
The Bloomsbury Group included

Forster and Virginia Woolf.
Pastoral music after Elgar was
produced by Delius and Holst.
US writer J.B. Watson developed
behaviourism. *The Jazz Singer*
was the first sound picture.
Belgium published Lemaitre's
big bang theory.
Austrian Schrödinger founded
wave mechanics.
French expressionist techniques
were used by Chagall.

Reign of Terror. Saint-Just and his close associate Maximilien Robespierre were executed after a coup in July 1794.

Saint-Simon, Claude-Henri de Rouvroy, Comte de (1760–1825), French political reformer and one of the founders of socialism. As a young man he fought in the American War of Independence; he made a fortune by buying nationalized land during the French Revolution. In *Du Système Industriel* (1820–21) and other works, some written with Auguste Comte, Saint-Simon proposed a productive industrialized state directed by scientist-businessmen. His writings were largely ignored during his lifetime, but they influenced later socialists.

Saladin (Salah ad-Din) (1137–93), Sultan of Egypt and Syria. As a lieutenant of Nur-ad-Din, he suppressed the Fatimid dynasty of Egypt, became vizier and then proclaimed himself sultan in 1174. After conquering most of Syria he launched a campaign to drive the Christians from Palestine, gathering around him Muslims of various groups. He won the battle of Hattin and took Jerusalem in 1187. This resulted in the formation of an army for the third Crusade led by Richard I of England and Philip II of France.

Salazar, António de Oliveira (1889–1970), Portuguese politician. He was a professor of economics with right-wing, pro-Roman Catholic beliefs. He became Premier in 1932 and thereafter ruled as virtual dictator until 1968. In the Spanish Civil War he supported the Nationalists but, although sympathetic to the Axis powers kept Portugal neutral in WWII. He presided over Portugal's economic revival after the war but fought an unsuccessful battle to retain the Portuguese colonies in Africa.

Salisbury, Robert Arthur Talbot Gascoyne-Cecil, 3rd Marquess of (1830–1903), British statesman and diplomat. A Conservative, he served in Disraeli's administration (1874–80), first as Secretary for India and then as Foreign Secretary. On Disraeli's death (1881) he became leader of the Conservative Party and served three terms (1885–86,

---

AD 1928–1930

A Russia expelled Trotsky (1929). US saw the Wall Street crash and the Depression. Louis Armstrong and Duke Ellington were prominent in jazz. Hubble related galaxies' direction to their speed of recession.

A India's Gandhi began a campaign of civil disobedience. Britain's second Labour Government failed to cure economic crises. Lawrence, Powys and Lowry were prominent novelists and Auden and Spender were A famous poets. Logie Baird invented television and Fleming discovered the anti-bacterial activity of *Penicillium*.

German thinker Heidegger developed Existentialism. France saw the School of Paris develop Surrealist painting. South Africa's segregation was termed "apartheid".

SALT agreements

1886–92, 1895–1902) as Prime Minister. Notable reforms were introduced at home but his policy abroad of "splendid isolation" left England with few friends during the South African (Boer) War (1889–1902).

SALT agreements, armament control agreements worked out at Strategic Arms Limitations Talks (SALT), from 1969 and signed 26 May, 1972, by the US Pres. Richard Nixon and the Soviet General Secretary Leonid Brezhnev. The SALT agreements limited anti-ballistic missile systems and offensive missile launchers.

San Martín, José de (1778–1850), South American revolutionary, *b*. Argentina. He played a significant part in winning independence for Argentina, Chile and Peru. In 1817 he led an army across the Andes into Chile and in 1821 entered Lima in triumph and became protector of Peru. The following year, however, he resigned in favour of Simon Bolívar and retired to Europe.

Saracens, term applied originally to an Arab tribe in the Sinai Peninsula and then extended to include all Arabs and later all Muslim subjects of the caliph. It was used particularly by medieval christians to denote their Muslim enemies. The Saracens held Sicily from the 9th to the 11th century, leaving a cultural influence that can still be discerned there.

Saxons, ancient Germanic people. Originating in Germany and s Denmark, they extended s and w, and colonized Britain *c*. AD 450, where they amalgamated with the Angles to form the Anglo-Saxon civilization. At the same time the continental Saxons, or Old Saxons, expanded into N Germany, which brought them into conflict with the Franks. They were finally subjugated and converted to Christianity by Charlemagne in the early 9th century.

Schmidt, Helmut (1918–   ), West German political leader. Elected to the Bundestag in 1953, he became chairman of the Social Democratic Party in 1967 and Minister of Defence when the Social Democrat-Free Democrat coalition government was formed in 1969. He replaced

---

AD 1930–1933

Indian nationalist demands were not satisfied by the Round Table Conference.

Germany saw left/right wing fighting due to her slump.

Japan occupied Manchuria.

Spain set up a republic.

Britain had a National Government. Keynes overthrew neoclassical orthodoxy in economics. Chadwick discovered the neutron.

US writers Faulkner and Stein-beck revitalized fiction. Urey discovered deuterium. The cyclotron was developed. Carothers invented nylon. Jansky developed radio astronomy.

A France saw Le Corbusier develop the International style of architecture. Roualt achieved a stained-glass quality in his paintings. Varèse constructed serious music using percussion only in *Ionization*.

Willie Brandt as chancellor of West Germany in 1974.

Schubert, Franz Peter (1797–1828), Austrian composer whose symphonies represent the final extension of the Classical sonata form and whose songs are the height of Romantic lyricism. Among his more popular works are symphonies such as the Eighth ("Unfinished") (1822) and the Ninth in C major (1828). He wrote more than 600 songs to the lyrics of such poets as Heine and Schiller and these include such cycles as *Die Schöne Müllerin* (1823) and *Die Winterreise* (1827). In his tragically short lifetime he also composed much chamber music, and his string quintet (1828) is regarded as a masterpiece.

Schweitzer, Albert (1875–1965), theologian, musician, medical missionary and philosopher. Born in Alsace, he spent most of his life in Gabon (then French Equatorial Africa) where he founded the Lambaréné Hospital in 1913. Honoured as a scientist and humanitarian, as an organist and an expert on Bach, his ethic was "reverence for life" and he was awarded the 1952 Nobel Peace Prize.

Scott, Captain Robert Falcon (1868–1912), British Antarctic explorer and naval commander. He reached the South Pole in Jan. 1912, only to find that Amundsen had been there first. Beset by blizzards, Scott and his party perished during their journey across the ice back from the pole. His diaries were published as *Scott's Last Expedition* (1913).

Scythians, ancient people from central Asia who ruled an empire in s Russia from the 8th–7th centuries BC until they were confined to the Crimea by the Sarmatians in the 2nd century BC. In the 7th century BC they temporarily extended their power into Mesopotamia, the Balkans and Greece. They were a nomadic tribe with an advanced civilization.

Seleucid Empire, Hellenistic kingdom stretching in its heyday from the E Mediterranean to India, set up by the Greek general Seleucus I in 312 BC, and eventually conquered by the Romans in 64 BC. The kingdom, which was centred on Syria, lost most of its Anatolian territory as

---

AD 1933–1935

A Germany's Hitler set up a Nazi dictatorship. Dix, Grosz, Beckmann and Kokoschka opposed this in art.

A US President Roosevelt tried to end the slump. The Lost Generation of writers in Paris included Fitzgerald, Hemingway, Stein and Miller.

A Russia saw Stalin begin a massive

A purge of party officials. Trotsky argued for permanent revolution.

Socialist Realism was officially adopted and the Neoclassic movement was initiated by Stravinsky and Prokofiev.

China's civil war led to the Long March.

Britain's Watson-Watt's work led to radar.

Japan's Yukawa predicted mesons.

France's Joliot-Curie prepared radio-isotopes.

well as Parthia and Sogdiana in the 3rd century. The Bactrians gained their independence in *c.* 250 BC. The kingdom was an important channel for spreading Greek culture through the Middle East.

Seljuk Turks, semi-nomadic tribesman who conquered Khorasan in the first half of the 11th century. They entered Baghdad in 1055 and their leader, Toghrïl, was proclaimed sultan. His successor, Alp Arslan, defeated the Byzantines at Manzikert in 1071, opening the Byzantine Empire to Seljuk invasion. This defeat was one of the causes of the Crusades. In the early 12th century the Seljuk empire began to disintegrate and the Seljuk states were conquered by Mongols in the 13th century.

Sepoy Mutiny, *See* **Indian Mutiny.**

Seven Years War (1756–63), major conflict between Britain and Prussia on the one side and France, Austria, Russia and Sweden on the other. It was fought at sea and on land, in Europe, America, the West Indies and India. It began on 15 May 1756, when Britain declared war on France after France's attack on Minorca. It ended in the signing of the Peace of Paris and the Treaty of Hubertusburg in 1763. The principal results of the war were the supremacy of Britain in India and North America, and the emergence of Prussian power in Europe.

Shaftesbury, Anthony Ashley Cooper, 7th earl (1801–85), British social reformer. A Tory MP (1826–51), he led the factory reform movement in the House of Commons, first proposing the ten-hour factory working day in 1833 (passed in 1847). The Coal Mines Act (1842), which prohibited the employment underground of women and children under 13, and the 1850 Reform Act were also fruits of his work.

Shakespeare, William (1564–1616), English poet and dramatist who is generally regarded as the greatest playwright of all time. Despite this, little is known of his life. By 1592 he was established in London, having already written the three parts of *Henry VI.* By 1594 he was a member of the Lord Chamberlain's Men and in 1599 a

---

AD 1935–1937

A **Germany,** allied with Mussolini's Italy, remilitarized the Rhineland. Thomas Mann developed an idealist style.

Italy invaded Abyssinia.

Spain, after a right-wing coup, A underwent the Spanish Civil War. Lorca studied folk traditions in his drama.

Japan attacked China (1937).

A **Britain's** Edward VIII abdicated. Anglo-Irish relations

weakened. Governmental reforms in India fell short of nationalist demands.

US musical shows reached a peak of sophistication with Gershwin's *Porgy and Bess.* Consumer durable industries grew.

Austria saw the Vienna Circle of philosophers founded, formulating Logical Positivism.

A **Religion** saw Pius XI condemn Communism and Fascism.

---

partner in the Globe Theatre, where many of his plays were presented. He retired to Stratford-upon-Avon in 1614 and died in 1616.

Critics have been tempted into reading personal references in his plays and poetry, especially the 154 *Sonnets*, which were first published in 1609.

The plays are usually divided into four groups: the historical plays, the comedies, the tragedies and the romances. Shakespeare seldom invented the plots of his plays, preferring to take his outlines from earlier works and building characters from hints contained therein and adding others to serve his dramatic intentions.

Shi'ites, *See* **Ali.**

Sihanouk, Norodom (1922–), Cambodian king, head of state and politician. Born into the Cambodian royal family, he succeeded to the throne in 1941 but abdicated in 1955 to become Prime Minister after establishing a socialist government. In 1960 he became head of state and in 1965 broke off diplomatic relations with the USA because of its military involvement in Indo-China. In 1970 he was deposed by Lon Nol in a right-wing military coup but returned from exile when the Khmer Rouge took over in 1975. He resigned in 1976.

Sinn Fein, Irish nationalist party which developed out of the Society of Gaels founded in 1902 by Arthur Griffith. Its aim to achieve total Irish independence was not satisfied with the establishment of the Irish Free State in 1921. It has sometimes been regarded as the political wing of the IRA.

Sitting Bull, *See* **Little Bighorn.**

Six Day War, *See* **Arab-Israeli Wars.**

Smith, Adam (1723–90), Scottish economist who laid the foundation of modern economics. Reflecting the emergence in Britain of the industrial system, he argued that the commercial liberty of a competitive market would stimulate production and act in the interests of the public. He wrote his economic treatise *The Wealth of Nations* (1776) after meeting French Physiocrats.

AD 1937–1940

A Europe was plunged into World War II after Germany annexed
A Austria (Anschluss) and the
A abortive Munich Agreement.
Germany took France. Brecht pioneered epic theatre.
A Spain saw Franco win the Spanish Civil War and become dictator. Many writers had fought against him, including Orwell.
A Picasso's *Guernica* showed this Basque town's destruction.

Japan took eastern China.
A Britain saw Winston Churchill replace Neville Chamberlain as prime minister in the National Government.
A China's Mao Tse-tung adapted
A Marxism to Chinese conditions.
US developed nuclear fission.
A Einstein told the President that the atomic bomb was possible. Hollywood entered its golden age.

Smith, Ian Douglas

Smith, Ian Douglas (1919–), Zimbabwe Prime Minister. He fought in WWII and entered Zimbabwe politics in 1948. He became Prime Minister in 1964 and declared Zimbabwe's independence (UDI) from Great Britain in 1965. Although he rejected African majority rule of his overwhelmingly black country, he made some efforts to negotiate with black leaders during the 1970s.

Smith, Joseph (1805–44), US founder of the Mormon Church of Jesus Christ of the Latter Day Saints (1830). His *Book of Mormon* (1829) was based on sacred writings he claimed to have found on golden tablets. In 1844 he was jailed on a charge of treason with his brother, Hyrum, at Carthage, Illinois. There they were murdered by a mob.

Smuts, Jan Christiaan (1870–1950), South African political leader. A lawyer, he was alarmed by the Jameson Raid of 1895 and entered Boer politics. He was a guerrilla leader during the South African War (1899–1902) but afterwards worked for the establishment of a unified republic, repressing Boer rebellions during WWI. He served in various ministries under Louis Botha and predicted the disastrous consequences of the Treaty of Versailles following WWI. He was Prime Minister from 1919–24 and 1939–48 and helped form the United Nations following WWII. His government was replaced (1948) by the nationalist government of Daniel Malan.

Socrates (*c.* 469–399 BC), Greek philosopher. Information about his life and philosophy is found in the writings of Plato and Xenophon. Believing that the highest meaning of life is attained through self-knowledge, Socrates taught the value of self-analysis. His method of cross-questioning challenged conventional wisdom and his sceptical approach to religion led to his trial for impiety and corrupting the young. Condemned to death, he poisoned himself with hemlock.

Somme, Battle of the (1916), WWI battle, the first major predominantly British offensive on the western front. It was a war of attrition, fought in the trenches, begun on 1 July and ending in the mud on 18 Nov. There were 95 German

---

AD 1940–1943

A **Germany** waged a lightning war in the West, but met stiff opposition from Britain under Churchill. Hitler invaded Russia and started mass extermination of Jews. V2 rockets developed. **Japan** attacked Pearl Harbor, bringing the US into the war. **France's** Merleau-Ponty developed phenomenology and Sartre Existentialism. **US** saw O'Neill, Williams and Miller create serious native drama. Hollywood broke new ground with *Citizen Kane*. The first nuclear reactor was built in Chicago. Glenn Miller's jazz band entertained troops. **Austrian** composers Berg and Webern developed serial music. **Britain's** Frank Whittle developed the jet engine, and the Oxfam charity was founded to combat world poverty.

---

divisions opposed by 55 British and 20 French divisions.
The casualties were: British 420,000, French 190,000 and
German probably 465,000 (although some authorities have
put the German total higher).

South African (Boer) Wars, two wars between the Boer and
British settlers in southern Africa. The first (1880–81) arose
from the British annexation of the Transvaal in 1877. Under
Kruger's leadership the Boers defeated the British at
Laing's Nek and Majuba Hill and won self-government by
the Pretoria Convention (1881). That convention allowed
Britain to retain suzerainty over all of southern Africa. The
second war (1899–1902) was the outcome of the Boers'
desire for entire independence and British desire to take
control of the Transvaal gold mines. It began with the Boers'
besieging Mafeking in Oct. 1899 and ended with the signing
of the treaty of Vereeniging in May 1902.

Spanish Civil War (1936–39), conflict between Loyalists
(often called Republicans) and Nationalists for control of
Spain. Both sides began as loose alliances: the Loyalists, so
called because they were loyal to the government of the
Second Republic, consisted of Republicans, Socialists,
Communists and Basque and Catalonian separatists. The
Nationalists comprised the right-wing professional army,
the more conservative faction of the Roman Catholic
Church, monarchists, Carlists and the great landowners. In
1931 the Spanish Monarchy was abolished and the Second
Republic instituted. Church and state were separated; land
was redistributed and military influence curtailed. All
these measures were anathema to the traditionalist forces of
Spain, especially the Church, the landed interests and the
military. War broke out in July 1936, with an uprising of the
Spanish army in Morocco. The commander in Morocco,
Francisco Franco, soon emerged as the leader of the
Nationalist side. Nazi Germany and Fascist Italy gave aid,
including troops and supplies, to the Nationalist forces.
Franco used this aid unscrupulously and the aerial bombing
of civilians was employed for the first time by the Nationalist

---

AD 1943–1945

A Europe saw Russia stop the Germans, Anglo-American forces take North Africa and invade Italy and Normandy, and Yugoslavian and French Resistance Movements start. Soviet and Western spheres of influence were agreed at Yalta.
Britain saw Karl Popper publish his *The Open Society and its Enemies.* Artists Graham Sutherland and David Piper recorded bomb damage.
Senegal's Senghor initiated the negritude movement.
US saw large diameter pipelines introduced and the swing era of big jazz bands start.
Argentina produced the complex stories of Borges.
Italian poet Quasimodo opposed Fascism.
Chile's Pablo Neruda produced "poetry for simple people".

---

air-force, notably at Guernica in 1937. The democracies, on the other hand, maintained strict neutrality, leaving the USSR to support the Loyalists, which greatly strengthened the Communists within the Loyalist ranks. International Brigades were formed and fought on the side of the Loyalists. The well-organized Nationalists in late 1938 began a major assault on Catalonia. When Barcelona fell in January 1939, the Loyalist cause was doomed. On 28 March 1939 the Nationalists entered Madrid, and the war was over. More than 1,000,000 Spaniards had been killed and more than 250,000 were forced into exile.

Spanish Succession, War of the (1701–14), dynastic struggle for the throne of Spain. When it became apparent that Charles II of Spain would die childless, there were three claimants who had dynastic ties with the Spanish royal family: Louis XIV of France, who claimed the throne for his grandson Maximilian II; Emanuel the elector of Bavaria, who claimed the throne for his son Joseph Ferdinand; and the Holy Roman Emperor Leopold I, who claimed the throne for his son. In his first will, Charles II left all his possessions to Joseph Ferdinand but Joseph's sudden death in 1699 reopened the dispute.

While new negotiations were in progress, the dying Charles II named Philip of Anjou, (grandson of Louis XIV) as his heir. When he ascended the throne as Philip V in 1701, most of Europe was plunged into war. France was supported by Spain, Bavaria and Cologne, and Mantua and Savoy. The Allies comprised the imperial forces, England, Holland, Prussia and other German states, and Portugal. Despite impressive Allied victories at Blenheim, Ramillies, Oudenaarde and Malplaquet, the war lasted for more than a decade. In 1713–14, an exhausted France signed the Treaties of Utrecht and in 1714 those of Rastatt and Baden were concluded. Philip V remained on the Spanish throne but the Allies, and particularly England, gained great territorial and trading concessions.

Sparta (Sparti), town in SE Peloponnesos, S Greece, on the

AD 1945–1947

US dropped two atomic bombs on Japan, ending the Pacific war.

A Truman promised aid to non-Communist countries. Bebop developed under Charlie Parker. The sound barrier was broken.

A Britain, under Attlee's Labour Government, granted Indian independence. Dylan Thomas' poetry was at its peak, as was Henry Moore's sculpture. The first atomic power station appeared.

German sociologists of the Frankfurt School argued for a social revolution and theologian Bonhoeffer that God was dead. Italian novelists Pavese and Moravia described modern estrangement and neo-realist cinema developed.

Swiss sculptor Giacometti was prominent.

Russia produced Pasternak's humanistic *Doctor Zhivago*.

Stalin, Joseph Vissarionovich Dzhugashvili

River Evrotas; capital of Lakonia department. Just s are the ruins of ancient Sparta, a Greek city-state founded by the Dorians *c.* 1000 BC in the province of Lakonia. Spartan society consisted of three classes: the Spartiates (ruling class), perioeci (free inhabitants with no political power) and helots (slaves). After its conquest of Arcadia, Argos and Messinia (*c.* 734–716 BC), Sparta flourished as an economic and cultural centre. After a massive helot revolt in late 7th century BC, it changed into an armed camp with all Spartiates trained as soldiers from an early age. It was originally ruled by two kings and later by the *gerousia*, the assembly (*apella*) and *ephors*. In *c.* 500 BC the Peloponnesian League was formed with Sparta as the most powerful member. After the Persian Wars (500–449 BC), Athenian power began to rival Sparta's, leading to the Peloponnesian War (431–404 BC), which ended in the defeat of Athens. Sparta dominated Greece until 371 BC when it was defeated by Thebes at Leuctra, and Messinia was freed. Prosperity revived under the Romans but Sparta was destroyed by Visigoths in AD 396.

Stalin, Joseph Vissarionovich Dzhugashvili (1879–1953), Soviet Communist leader and head of the USSR. Educated at the Tiflis theological seminary, from which he was expelled in 1899 as a revolutionary, he became a Bolshevik in 1903. From 1913 he began to use the nickname "Stalin" (man of steel) while editor of the party newspaper, *Pravda*. He played an important role in the Civil War, as Commissar for Nationalities (1919–23). Following Lenin's death in 1924, Stalin was able to manoeuvre for supreme power, suppressing his main rival Trotsky and becoming by 1927 virtual dictator. He introduced forced industrialization and Collectivization, and began the purges of the 1930s to consolidate his power over the state; by 1938 more than 10 million people were believed to have been killed and Stalin controlled the party, the government and the police. In 1941 he became premier and personally supervised the Soviet WWII war effort. His personality cult reached its peak in the

---

AD 1947–1950

Europe saw Berlin isolated from the West by the USSR, a socialist coup in Czechoslovakia, and the North Atlantic Treaty Organization.
Israel was set up. It won the support of Martin Buber in *Paths to Utopia*.
Indonesia gained freedom from the Dutch.
A **China's** Mao Tse-tung set up a People's Republic.
Britain curbed the Lords' power

and introduced the Health Service. Hoyle had a steady-state theory of the universe.
US produced the abstract expressionism of painters Jackson Pollock and Theodore Rothko.
France produced Sartre's *Roads to Freedom* trilogy, Camus' formulation of the Absurd in *The Plague* and *The Outsider* and the feminist novels of Simone de Beauvoir.

---

postwar era when purges were revived, and his last years were characterized by increasing fear and suspicion.

Stephenson, George (1781–1848), British engineer and inventor, regarded as the father of the locomotive. He built his first locomotive, the *Blucher*, in 1814 in which flanged wheels were incorporated for the first time. His most famous locomotive, the *Rocket*, was built in 1829 and set a record speed of 47km/h (29mph). It later ran on the Liverpool to Manchester line, which he also built.

Stopes, Marie Charlotte Carmichael, (1880–1958), British pioneer of birth control. After obtaining a doctorate in botany from Munich University in 1904, she began an academic career at Manchester University. She soon became concerned about inadequate contraceptive measures and campaigned for a more rational and open approach to contraception, and established the first birth control clinic in Britain in 1921.

Strafford, Thomas Wentworth, 1st Earl of (1593–1641), English nobleman, leading adviser of Charles I. Wentworth was appointed Lord President of the North in 1628 and a privy councillor in 1629. As Lord Deputy of Ireland (1633–39) he sought to strengthen royal authority, defend Protestantism and stimulate agriculture and trade. He was made an earl in 1640. Strafford's advocacy of sovereign power led to conflict with Parliament and his impeachment in 1640. The charges could not be substantiated and the "inflexibles" in Parliament brought in a bill of Attainder. Wentworth was convicted and executed, the king reluctantly acquiescing in the hope of appeasing Parliament.

Stuart, or Stewart, Charles Edward (1720–88), English prince and claimant to the throne, also called "Bonnie Prince Charlie" and the "Young Pretender". A grandson of the deposed James II and son of James Francis Edward Stuart, he landed in Scotland in 1745 to claim the throne. He was initially victorious at Prestonpans and reached the city of Derby but was persuaded by his commanders to withdraw. A Hanoverian force under the Duke of

---

AD 1950–1952

China's Communist triumph led A to the Korean War.

Arab League blockaded Israel. **US** strengthened defence links with Japan and Formosa. Parsons developed structural functional sociology. The first hydrogen bomb was tested.

Britain saw Health Service charges introduced. Britten wrote traditional opera.

West Indian Fanon analysed

racial repression.

France's Theatre of the Absurd flourished under Ionesco, Genet and Irishman Beckett. Robbe-Grillet and Sarraute developed the "new novel".

Japan's film-maker Kurosawa achieved prominence.

Indian director Ray's films reached the West.

Danish inventor Poulson developed magnetic recording.

Cumberland annihilated his army at Culloden (1746) and he went into exile.

Suez Crisis (1956), Middle East conflict. When Britain and the USA announced that they would not provide financial assistance for Egypt's Aswan Dam project, the President of Egypt, Gamal Abdel Nasser, nationalized the Suez Canal. Israel, denied use of the canal, invaded Egypt. Britain and France then also invaded the canal area. UN intervention ended the crisis, and treaties gave Egypt control of the canal.

Suffragettes, *See* **Pankhurst, Emmeline.**

Sukarno, Achmad (1901–70), Indonesian politican, President from 1947 to 1967. A leader of his country's independence movement, he was jailed by the Dutch and exiled (1933–42). When the Japanese invaded Indonesia during WWII, he cooperated with them and at the end of war became the first President of Indonesia. In 1966 anti-Communist Indonesian military leaders forced a reduction of his powers, and he was deposed in 1967.

Suleiman I, or Süleyman the Magnificent (1494–1566), Ottoman sultan (*r.* 1520–66), son and successor of Selim I. He extended his father's conquests in the Balkans, the Mediterranean and Asia, captured Belgrade (1521), expelled the Knights Hospitallers from Rhodes (1522) and defeated the Hungarians under Louis II at Mohacs (1526). After the death of John I of Hungary (1540) he annexed much of the country. He made an alliance with Francis I of France against the Hapsburgs (1536) and his admiral, Barbarossa, ravaged the coasts of Spain, Italy and Greece. His Turkish fleet was to control the Mediterranean until 1571. It took Tripoli in 1551 but failed to take Malta. His campaigns against Persia completed the conquest of Iraq and the area around Lake Van. He died during the seige of Szigetvar (Hungary) and his son Selim II succeeded him.

Sumerians, inhabitants of Sumer, the most southerly part of ancient Babylonia and the site of an ancient civilization, the origins of which can be traced back to the 3rd millennium

---

AD 1952–1955

French forces withdrew from Vietnam, which divided into north and south. Terrorism started in Algeria. Anouilh's plays emphasized tragi-comedy. **Britain** exploded her first atom bomb and denationalized transport and steel. Terrorism started in Kenya, Cyprus and Malaya. Philosophers Ryle and Austin led the Oxford School of Ordinary Language Philosophy.

USSR opposed Germany's reunification and initiated the Warsaw Pact against NATO. A US senator McCarthy led an anti-Marxist witch hunt. Ellison and Baldwin brought negro writing to prominence. John Cage pioneered music giving freedom to the performer. **Swiss** dramatists Frisch and Durrenmatt emphasized the grotesque.

Sun Yat-sen

BC. The Sumerian language is the oldest written language. The Sumerians developed a remarkably sophisticated artistic culture and technology, which is represented in surviving artefacts and buildings as well as canals and dams. Their religious practices were centred on a pantheon consisting of many deities, each with special qualities.

Sun Yat-sen (1866–1925), first President of the Chinese Republic (1911–12) and revolutionary leader of modern China. After China's defeat by Japan in 1895 Sun became convinced that the Manchu dynasty must be overthrown. In exile (1895–1911), he worked through secret societies and with support from overseas Chinese to bring about his aim. His inspiration eventually brought about the revolution of 1911. He joined in reorganizing the Kuomintang (1912) and became its leader and ideologist.

Supremacy, Acts of, two acts passed by the English Parliament in the 16th century. The first (1534) made the monarch the "supreme head" of the Church of England. It thus made the English Church independent of the papacy and also made it subject to temporal authority. The second act (1559) changed the title from supreme head to "supreme governor", thus signifying that authority was vested, not so much in the person of the monarch as in the Crown-in-parliament.

Taiping Rebellion (1851–64), revolt in China against the Manchu led by a Hakka fanatic, Hung Hsiu-ch'uan, who thought himself to be the son of God. The fighting laid waste 17 provinces of China and resulted in more than 20 million casualties. The Manchus never recovered their ability to govern China with their former authority.

Talleyrand-Périgord, Charles Maurice de (1754–1838), French statesman who was able to follow a successful career throughout the many changes in French politics during his lifetime. Made Foreign Minister under the Directory in 1797, he also served under Napoleon until disagreement over Napoleon's European ambitions led him to help to restore the House of Bourbon in 1814. At the Congress of

---

AD 1955–1958

Europe's Common Market started. **A** USSR's Khrushchev denounced **A** Stalinism, invaded Hungary and split with China. Artificial satellite Sputnik I was launched. **A** Egypt's Nasser sparked off the **A** Suez Crisis, nationalizing the Canal Company.
Britain exploded a hydrogen bomb. The Campaign for Nuclear Disarmament began. Dramatists Osborne, Pinter and Wesker were prominent. Pop art emerged. **US** writer Chomsky revolutionized linguistics. Kelly explored hard-edge art and Calder kinetic art.
France's musique concrète widened musical horizons.
Religion saw Paul Tillich fuse traditional religious values with modern notions of individual responsibility in the *Dynamics of Faith.*

Vienna he skilfully exploited the tensions among the victors to the benefit of France, and as a supporter of Louis Philippe he became ambassador to London from 1830 to 1834.

Tamerlane (Timur i Leng) (1336–1405), Mongol conqueror, claiming to be descended from Genghis Khan. He had brought the area round Samarkand under his control by 1369, extending his conquests to the region of the Golden Horde between the Caspian and Black seas before invading India in 1398. He defeated the Ottoman Sultan Beyazid I in 1402 and died while planning to invade China. Tamerlane gave his name to the Timurid Dynasty.

T'ang dynasty (618–907), Chinese dynasty that ruled during imperial China's most vigorous and creative age. The capital Ch'ang-an (modern Sian) was a cosmopolitan centre of international trade and Chinese political and cultural institutions were at their height. It was the time when Neo-Confucianism became the official ideology and was the golden age of Chinese poetry as well as the period when China re-asserted its suzerainty over much of Central Asia and Korea. The dynasty was threatened in 755 by the revolt of the Turkish military leader An Lu-shan, and never recovered its former power.

Tatars, or Tartars, Turkic-speaking people of central Asia. In early medieval times the name Tatar was given to many different Asiatic invaders of Europe. The Tatar tribe proper originated in E Siberia and, mixed with the Mongols, invaded Europe in the early 13th century under Genghis Khan. They were converted to Islam in the 14th century and, after the collapse of the Mongol empire, the Tatars living in the Crimea (Little Tartary) came under the Ottoman Empire and those in Tartary (Siberia) came under Muscovite control. By the 16th century they had become settled agriculturalists, and many Tatars achieved eminence within Russia. Crimea became part of Russia in 1783. In the mid-20th century there were more than 5 million Tatars.

Tchaikovsky, Peter Ilyich (1840–93), Russian late Romantic composer who studied at the St Petersburg

---

AD 1958–1960

A **France** saw De Gaulle take power because of the Algerian crisis.

A Levi-Strauss developed structuralism in anthropology, Foucault in history. Sartre linked Existentialism and Marxism. The New Wave emerged with the films of Truffaut and Godard.

China's Great Leap Forward ended in chaos when USSR aid was withdrawn.

South Africa alienated world opinion with the Sharpeville Massacre.

A **Cuba** saw Castro take power.

Belgian Congo gained independence.

Britain granted Cyprus independence and joined EFTA. The hovercraft was developed.

US writers Kerouac, Burroughs and Miller developed fiction; Ginsberg and Ferlinghetti poetry. Satellite Explorer I was launched.

Conservatory. He wrote nine operas, four concertos, six symphonies, three ballets, overtures, chamber music and numerous other works. His music includes the orchestral pieces *Romeo and Juliet* (1880) and *Slavonic March* (1876). He also wrote the music for the ballets *Swan Lake* (1876), *The Sleeping Beauty* (1889) and *The Nutcracker* (1892). He died nine days after the premiere of his sixth and most popular symphony, the *Pathétique* (1893).

Telford, Thomas (1757–1834), Scottish civil engineer; builder of bridges, canals, docks, harbours, waterways and roads. Among his many notable achievements are the 177m (580ft) suspension bridge over the Menai Strait, connecting Anglesey with mainland Wales, begun in 1819; the Ellesmere Canal, connecting the English rivers Dee, Mersey and Severn (1793); and the Caledonian Canal in Scotland. He was a founder, and first president, of the Institution of Civil Engineers.

Teutonic knights, German military and religious order, whose Latin name was *Ordo Domus Sanctae Mariae Teutoniconum* (German order of the Hospital of St Mary). The order was founded *c.* 1190 during the Crusades. It transferred its activities to E Europe in 1211, and in 1233 began the conquest of Prussia. The knights became wealthy through engaging in trade, and their power spread to the lands of the E Baltic and into central Germany. Defeated by the Poles and Lithuanians in 1410, the order lost power and territory until its virtual disintegration in 1525, when its grand master accepted the Reformation and proclaimed Prussia's secular duchy.

Thatcher, Margaret Hilda (1925–   ). British politician and leader of the Conservative Party. Elected MP for Finchley in 1959, she was Secretary of State for Education and Science 1970–74, becoming Party leader in 1975. Early in 1979, she became Britain's first female Prime Minister.

Thirty Years War (1618–48), European war involving German Protestant princes together with France, Sweden,

---

AD 1960–1962

Britain saw South Africa leave the Commonwealth over acceptance of decolonization and racial equality. R.D. Laing studied schizophrenia in *The Divided Self*. Bacon's painting showed distorted forms in claustrophobic space. **USSR** built the Berlin Wall and sent Gagarin into space. **US** president Kennedy prompted the Bay of Pigs invasion and provoked the Cuban Missile Crisis. Lasers were developed and weather and communications satellites launched. **Nigerian** writers Achebe and Soyinka described the damage done by colonization. **West Indian** novelist Naipaul wrote of Trinidad's poverty. **Religion** saw the foundation of the Ecumenical movement and the Vatican Council.

England and Denmark against the Hapsburgs and Catholic princes of the Holy Roman Empire. In 1618 Bohemian Protestant princes revolted against the Catholic King Ferdinand (later Emperor Ferdinand II); they were defeated, but the N European Protestant kings of Denmark and Sweden intervened, and the general warfare gave countries such as France the chance to extend their influence. The war left Germany with its lands devastated, its economy in ruins and its population greatly reduced. The Holy Roman Empire fared hardly better, the Hapsburgs losing some of their power. After the war European conflicts arising from religious causes decreased, and the Peace of Westphalia (1648), formally ended the war.

Tiberius (42 BC–AD37), Roman emperor (AD 14–37). He governed Transalpine Gaul and fought in Germany and Illyricum. He was adopted by Augustus, whose heirs had died, and became emperor at Augustus' death. He pursued a peaceful foreign policy and accumulated great wealth. He retired from Rome in AD 26, fearing plots upon his life.

Tito, (1892–), Yugoslav Communist leader, Premier from 1945, and President 1953 b. Josip Broz. As a Croatian soldier in the Austro-Hungarian army in WWI, he was captured by the Tsar's troops (1915) but released by the Communists after the Revolution (1917). Returning to Yugoslavia, he helped organize the Yugoslav Communist Party and, as one of its key members, served a jail term after it was outlawed (1923–34). In WWII he led the partisan resistance forces in Croatia, discrediting his rival Draza Mihajlović, who led the Chetnik guerrillas in Serbia, and became so powerful that he was able to establish a Communist government in 1945 that achieved international recognition. Russian efforts to control Yugoslavia soon led to a split between Tito and Stalin, who expelled the nation from the Communist bloc in 1948. Tito then became an important figure to many Third World countries. Internationally, Tito has gained world respect through Yugoslavia's policy of non-alignment.

AD 1963

A US saw Kennedy, after supporting a civil rights march on Wash-
A ington, assassinated. Johnson passed civil rights bills and
A sent troops to the Vietnam War. With USSR and Britain, US signed the Nuclear Test Ban Treaty. Jewish writers Bellow, Roth and Mailer were prominent. Pop art developed through Lichtenstein and Warhol. Integrated circuits were developed.

German postwar society was described by novelists Böll and Grass.

Britain granted independence to Kenya. Artist Bridget Riley, in op art, studied the effect of optical illusions.

United Arab Republic was formed by Egypt, Syria and Iraq.

A **India's** Nehru requested US aid against China.

Tolstoy, Count Leo Nikolaievich (1828–1910), Russian novelist and philosopher. While serving in the army he wrote his trilogy *Childhood, Boyhood and Youth* (1852–57). He took part in the defence of Sebastopol in 1854, descriptions of which appeared in the journal *Contemporary* and were noted for their unvarnished picture of the war. He left the army and lived on his estate and in St Petersburg, where he wrote *War and Peace* (1865–69) and *Anna Karenina* (1875–77). In 1879 he underwent a spiritual crisis which culminated in his conversion to the Christian doctrine of love and non-resistance to evil. These beliefs are reflected in his later works, such as *The Death of Ivan Ilyich* (1886) and *Resurrection* (1899).

Tone, Theobald Wolfe (1768–98), Irish revolutionary leader. Tone, who wanted the Irish to sink religious differences and unite for political independence, founded the United Irishmen in 1791, and promoted the Catholic Relief Act in 1793. After visiting America in 1795, Tone masterminded an abortive French invasion of Ireland in 1796. He committed suicide after being captured in 1798.

Toussaint l'Ouverture, Pierre Dominique (*c.* 1744–1803), Haitian independence leader. He joined the Negro rebellion in 1791 to free the slaves, drove the British and Spaniards from the island and by 1800 controlled all of Hispaniola. When Napoleon sent troops to re-establish French authority, Toussaint was captured and died in prison in France.

Trafalgar, Battle of (1805), naval engagement in the Napoleonic Wars fought off Cape Trafalgar, Spain. Nelson, the British admiral, divided his 27 ships into two squadrons and broke the Franco-Spanish line of 33 ships under Admiral de Villeneuve. Nelson, on board HMS *Victory*, was killed, but the battle established British naval supremacy in the 19th century.

Trajan (*c.* AD 52–117), Roman emperor (*r.* 98–117) under whom the frontiers of the empire reached their greatest extent. He was born in Spain and was adopted by his

---

AD 1964

A **US** under Johnson sent a communications satellite into space. Marcuse wrote *One Dimensional Man*. Experimental composer Terry Riley wrote *In C*.

A **USSR** under Kosygin sent a three-man mission into space. **China** exploded her first nuclear device. **Malawi** gained independence.

A **Tanzania's** Julius Nyerere tried to weaken Western influence by political non-alignment, village socialism and African nationalism. **Zambia** gained independence

A under Kenneth Kaunda. **Britain and France** designed the supersonic jet Concorde. **Hungarian** artist Vasarely pioneered op art. **German** composer Stockhausen widened the scope of the 12-note system with his avant-garde compositions.

---

predecessor Nerva; he was the first emperor from the
provinces. Trajan maintained good relations with
traditional Roman institutions such as the Senate. In
campaigns of 101–102 and 105–106 he conquered Dacia, N
of the Danube, and from 113 to 116 campaigned against the
Parthians and added Mesopotamia to the empire. In later
years his reign was seen as the summit of Roman power, but
some authorities believe that his conquests strained the
military resources of the empire. He was succeeded by
Hadrian.

Trent, Council of, *See* **Counter-Reformation.**

Trotsky, Leon Davidovitch (1879–1940), Russian
Bolshevik leader. Chairman of the St Petersburg Soviet, he
was prominent in the 1905 revolution, after which he was
tried and escaped abroad. He returned to Russia in time for
the March 1917 revolution. As head of the Military
Revolutionary Committee of the Petrograd Soviet he was in
charge of its defence, resulting in its seizure of power. As
commissar for foreign affairs (1917–18) he negotiated for
peace at Brest-Litovsk, but resigned after the treaty was
concluded. As commissar for war (1918–25) he created and
led the Red Army in the civil war. After Lenin's death he
was ousted from power by Stalin. Trotsky was expelled from
the Party in 1927 and from the country in 1929 as a leader of
the left opposition. He was murdered in Mexico in 1940,
probably by an agent of Stalin. Fiercely independent, he was
a brilliant polemicist and a fiery speaker.

Trudeau, Pierre Elliott (1919–), Canadian politician. He
was elected a Liberal member of Parliament in 1965 and
was appointed Minister of Justice and Attorney General in
1967. He succeeded Lester Pearson as party leader and as
Prime Minister in 1968, and during his administration he
promoted economic and diplomatic independence for
Canada. He recognized the People's Republic of China in
1970 but in that year had temporarily to impose martial law
to combat French separatist terrorism. The Liberal Party
lost its majority in 1970, but Trudeau continued to govern

AD 1965

US civil rights leader Martin
A Luther King was increasingly
opposed by such militants as
Eldridge Cleaver and the Black
Power movement. Hallucinatory
drugs and rock music interested
the young. Mariner 4 sent back
A pictures of Mars. Johnson out-
lawed the Ku Klux Klan.
USSR did the first space walk.
India and Pakistan went to war
over Kashmir.

A Zimbabwe under Ian Smith declared itself independent. Economic pressure from Britain and
A the United Nations failed to
reestablish constitutional
government.
Chinese sculpture *Rent Collection
Yard* depicted the miseries
of the empire.
Mexican poet Octavio Paz
rose to prominence.
Britain condemned racism.

Truman, Harry S.

with the aid of the small New Democratic Party. In 1974 he was re-elected Prime Minister with Liberal support alone.

Truman, Harry S. (1884–1972), 23rd President of the USA (1945–53). He took office in April 1945, just before the end of WWII and faced the problems of post-war readjustment, when he succeeded Pres. Franklin D. Roosevelt. The decisions he took are still controversial: he ordered the first atomic bombings of Japanese cities and effectively ended the war with Japan; he introduced the Truman Doctrine, the Marshall Plan, the North Atlantic Treaty Organization and organized the NATO Berlin airlift – all intended to challenge the real or imagined threat of Soviet Communism. The Cold War pervaded his two terms in office and, at home, Americans watched the witch-hunting trials instigated by Sen. Joseph McCarthy on their television sets. Truman's last years in office were occupied with the Korean War.

Tutankhamen (*r.c.*1348–1340 BC), one of the last pharaohs of the 18th dynasty of Egypt. He married the daughter of Akhenaton at the age of 10. During his eight-year reign the god Amon was restored to prominence and the capital was moved from Akhetaten back to Thebes. The discovery of his tomb in 1922, still containing most of its royal burial equipment, has made him one of the best known Egyptian pharaohs.

Tyler, Wat, *See* **Peasants' Revolt.**

Tyndale, William (*c.* 1494–1536), English religious reformer and Bible translator. He started printing an English version of the Bible in Cologne in 1525 but, because of harassment, had to complete it in Worms. Despite opposition from Thomas More and others, he maintained an output of vernacular scripture and also wrote numerous Protestant works. He was eventually captured and burned at the stake near Brussels.

Ulbricht, Walter (1893–1973), Communist leader of East Germany. A founder of the German Communist Party, he fled to Moscow in 1933 but returned with the Soviet army in 1945. He became Secretary-General of the Party in 1950

AD 1966

A China began its Cultural Revolution, to weaken bureaucracy and strengthen public will.
US increased its military activity in Vietnam to no avail.
A Borlaug led research resulting in the Green Revolution.
Indonesia's abortive Communist coup led to the army cutting
A Sukarno's power.
USSR landed a spacecraft on Venus.

France was reluctant to commit itself militarily to NATO in protest against American strength in Europe.
Britain's realism in painting was exemplified by the works of Lucian Freud and David Hockney.
Religion saw the first formal relation between the Church of England and Catholicism
A when Paul VI met the Archbishop of Canterbury.

---

and leader of East Germany, becoming Chairman of the Council of State in 1960.

Umayyads, or Ommayads, first great Muslim dynasty of Arabian Caliphs, which ruled from 661 to 750. It was a merchant family of Mecca. The house had two ruling branches, the Sufyānid (*r.* 661–84) and the Marwānid (*r.* 684–750).

United Nations (UN), international organization set up to enable countries to work together for peace and mutual development. It was established by a charter signed in San Francisco in June 1945 by 50 nations; in 1977 the UN had 148 members.

Vandals, ancient Germanic people. Their existence in E Europe is recorded during the 1st century AD; early in the 5th century they crossed the Rhine to escape the Huns. They passed through Gaul and Spain, and invaded N Africa in 429. From there they raided the W Mediterranean, briefly capturing Rome in 455. They were Arian Christians, hostile to the Catholic Church. In 533 a Roman army sent by Justinian destroyed their kingdom.

Van Gogh, Vincent, *See* **Gogh, Vincent Van.**

Verdun, Battle of (Feb.–Sept. 1916), the longest and one of the bloodiest engagements of WWI. On 21 Feb. 1916 the Germans launched a massive offensive against the fortress of Verdun in NE France. A British offensive on the Somme relieved German pressure and by December the French had recovered most of the ground lost. Over 2,000,000 men were engaged at Verdun; and there were more than 600,000 casualties.

Versailles, Treaty of (1919), chief among the five peace treaties that formally terminated WWI. The leading figures at the conference were Woodrow Wilson for the USA, David Lloyd George for Britain, Georges Clemenceau for France and Emanuele Orlando for Italy. The treaty represented a compromise between Wilson's Fourteen Points and the demands of Britain, France, Italy and other Allies for reparations from Germany. It demilitarized Germany and

---

AD 1967

Nigeria underwent civil war after Biafran secessionist claims.
Israel defeated the Arab states
A in the Six Day War, taking the Sinai desert and Jerusalem.
US saw the anti-war movement grow, in some ways connected with Flower-Power, based on communes and free love. Musician Jimi Hendrix produced the most powerful and imaginative solos since Charlie Parker.

Bob Dylan rose to fame.
Britain's Beatles group produced *Sergeant Pepper*.
France set up the Rance estuary power station, harnessing tidal power.
A Cyprus saw the United Nations attempt to avert war over the island between Turkey and Greece.
South Africa saw the first heart transplant operation.

Vespasian

created a triple defence alliance against her. Former
German colonies were made mandates of the League of
Nations, which was created by the treaty; Poland received a
corridor to the Baltic; and Yugoslavia was awarded the port
of Rijeka (Fiume). The treaty was never ratified by the USA
because the high reparations contradicted Wilson's
programme.

Vespasian (AD 9–79), Roman emperor (r. 69–79), founder
of the Flavian dynasty. He commanded the army in
Germany (42) and England (43), served as governor of
Judaea under Nero and conducted the war against the Jews
from 40 to 68. His soldiers proclaimed him emperor when
Nero died. He instituted a period of peace, improved
Rome's financial state and started the building and inspired
the Romanization of England.

Vichy Government, regime set up in the town of Vichy to
rule those parts of France and the French overseas empire
not occupied by the Germans after the France-German
armistice of 22 June 1940. Its prime minister was Marshal
Pétain, a hero of WWI, but its most important member was
the deputy prime minister, Pierre Laval. From November
1942 German troops occupied all of France, and the Vichy
regime lost all but the shadow of power. After the Allied
invasions of 1944, the highest officials of the right-wing,
authoritarian Vichy regime moved east with the Germans,
and the Free French movement of De Gaulle became the
dominant political organization.

Victoria (1819–1901), Queen of Great Britain and Ireland
(r. 1837–1901) and Empress of India (r. 1876–1901). She
was the daughter of Edward, Duke of Kent (the fourth son
of George III), and of Mary Louisa Victoria of Saxe-
Coburg-Gotha, and was the successor to William IV. Her
reign was the longest in English history. On her accession to
the throne she allowed Lord Melbourne, the Whig Prime
Minister, to become her adviser. She married her first
cousin, Prince Albert of Saxe-Coburg-Gotha in 1840, and
had nine children. He taught her devotion to, and neutrality

AD 1968

France saw a serious student revolt reflected in Europe.
USSR invaded Czechoslovakia to counter Dubcek's liberali-zation programme. Solzhenitsyn caused a literary stir with *The First Circle* and *Cancer Ward.*

US had growing violent opposition to the Vietnam war coalescing into a movement demanding individual liberation from the constraints of capitalism, influenced by Marcuse and Che Guevara. Senator Robert Kennedy was shot dead.
Britain introduced immigration control.
Columbian writer Gabriel Garcia Marquez rose to fame.
Religion saw Paul VI condemn artificial methods of birth control, causing concern, especially in Latin America.

---

in, political work. On Albert's death in 1861, she retired to private life at Balmoral for three years, during which time her popularity declined; but with Benjamin Disraeli as Prime Minister after 1868 she took a new interest in politics. In her later years her dislike of William Gladstone was to influence affairs, especially his policy of Irish Home Rule. Her reign was important at home in winning respect for the monarchy in an increasingly parliamentary age and abroad for extending British influence.

Vietnam War, military conflict between South Vietnamese government forces, aided by the USA, and the Communists (Viet Cong), supported by North Vietnam. A civil war aimed at reunification of Vietnam following its partition in 1954 into North (Communist) and South (non-Communist) rapidly developed into a major conflict. In the early 1960s the USA became militarily involved and by 1968 there were more than 500,000 US troops in South Vietnam. North Vietnam received aid from the USSR and China. Despite US intervention, the South Vietnamese were unable to defeat the Viet Cong and North Vietnamese. By the late 1960s pressure developed within the USA for the withdrawal of US troops. Efforts towards a negotiated peace were begun in 1969 and a peace treaty was signed in January 1973 by South Vietnam, the USA, North Vietnam and the National Liberation Front (the Communist provisional revolutionary government in South Vietnam). It provided for an end to hostilities and for the withdrawal of US forces. Fighting between South Vietnamese and Communists continued, however, and in April 1975 the South Vietnamese government fell to the Communists.

Vikings, Scandinavian marauders and invaders also called Norsemen and in E Europe Varangians. They were skilled shipbuilders and sailors, and raided areas of continental Europe and the British Isles from the 9th to the 11th centuries. In some areas they established colonies, exerting considerable influence on the history of Europe by encouraging the growth of the Feudal System.

AD 1969

A **France's** De Gaulle resigned after a referendum defeat.

A **US** astronaut Neil Armstrong was the first man on the Moon. Space research facilitated invisible light astronomy and assisted meteorology. DDT was banned as harmful.

Britain sent troops to Northern Ireland to control growing violence in Belfast, and to Anguilla to reestablish control there. Richard Long developed Land Art, using actual landscapes. A politically committed documentary style arose with the films of Loach and Garnett. **Irish** writer Samuel Beckett was awarded the Nobel Prize. **Mexican** shaman Don Juan was immortalized in Carlos Castaneda's study of him, a work which increasingly influenced philosophy.

Wagner, Richard

Wagner, Richard (1813–85), German composer. His works consist entirely of opera, for which he provided his own libretti. It was with Wagner's work that German Romantic music received its fullest expression. His early operas include *Rienzi* (1842), *The Flying Dutchman* (1843)) and *Tannhäuser* (1845). With *Tristan and Isolde* (1865) and *Ring of the Nibelungs* (1851–74) the genius of Wagner is fully displayed. The innovations that he introduced to operatic form were vast and served to fuse the elements of music and stage drama as one. Other operas include the *Mastersingers of Nuremberg* (1868) and the sacred stage drama *Parsifal* (1882).

Wallace, Alfred Russel (1823–1913), British naturalist and evolutionist, who developed a theory of Natural Selection independently of but at the same time as Charles Darwin. He wrote *Contributions to the Theory of Natural Selection* (1870) which, with Darwin's *Origin of Species*, comprised the fundamental explanation and understanding of the theory of evolution. He gave his name to Wallace's line.

Walpole, Sir Robert, 1st Earl of Orford (1676–1745), British statesman. He was a Whig member of Parliament (1701–42), led parliamentary opposition to the Tories, and became Chancellor of the Exchequer in 1715. Although he resigned in 1717 after developing the first sinking fund, he restored order after the South Sea Bubble in 1720. He returned as Chancellor of the Exchequer and First Lord of the Treasury (1721–42) and in that capacity was England's leading politician. His financial policies served to encourage trade, but he was forced to resign in 1742 through opposition to his pacific foreign policy. During his long tenure of office, the Hanoverian Succession became firmly established. He is considered to have been England's first Prime Minister.

Warwick, Richard Neville, Earl of (1428–71), English politician and soldier, known as "the Kingmaker". During the Wars of the Roses he helped the Yorkists to victory at St Albans in 1455 and captured Henry VI at Northampton in

---

AD 1970

US invaded Cambodia and resumed bombing in North Vietnam after peace talks and troop withdrawals. Four anti-war student demonstrators were killed by the National Guard. Science fiction writers Kurt Vonnegut and Isaac Asimov were popular. **Jordan** saw Arab commandoes hijack and blow up three airliners, after seizing the passengers as prisoners of war.

Nigeria defeated Biafra. **Tanzania and Zambia** secured Chinese support for a railway linking the copper belt to the sea. **India** was at war with Pakistan. **Japanese** writer Yukio Mishima killed himself at the height of his popularity. **Irish** writer Christy Brown chronicled poverty in Dublin in *Down All the Days*.

1460. Warwick was the real ruler of England from 1461 to 1464, in the first part of Edward IV's reign. Warwick gradually lost power, however, and in 1469 turned against Edward, whom he drove into exile in 1470. Edward returned in 1471 and Warwick was killed at the Battle of Barnet.

Washington, George (1732–99), first US president (1789–97). He was born into a wealthy Virginia family and trained as a surveyor. As a colonel in the Virginia Militia during the French and Indian Wars, he won a reputation as an astute military commander and was chosen to lead the poorly equipped, untrained Continental Army against the British in the War of American Independence. He retired to his estate after the victory but was called back to preside over the Federal Constitutional Convention (1787). When the new country's Constitution was adopted and ratified, Washington was elected President.

Watergate Scandal (1972–74), US political scandal involving the Nixon administration. It arose from an attempted burglary of the Democratic party's national offices by persons working for President Nixon's re-election committee. The administration's efforts to hide the connection provoked investigations by the Senatĕ and Justice Department which ultimately implicated the President. Impeachment proceedings against him were begun in 1973. In August 1974, after being ordered by a Supreme Court ruling to relinquish tape recordings that attested to his involvement in the affair, Nixon resigned. Although Nixon was pardoned by his successor, Gerald Ford, other members of the administration were prosecuted and convicted.

Waterloo, Battle of, final engagement of the Napoleonic Wars, fought on 18 June 1815. Napoleon I led a French army 72,000 strong in an attack on 68,000 men under the Duke of Wellington, who held positions along Mont St Jean near the village of Waterloo, Belgium. French victory would have been certain but for the arrival of Wellington's allies,

---

AD 1971

US, its currency deflated as a result of massive balance of payments deficits, withdrew more troops from Vietnam. Satellites were launched to map the Earth's resources.
China was admitted to the
A United Nations at the expense of the Nationalists.
Pakistan's civil war ended with Bangladesh being set up. A ceasefire was ordered by India.

USSR continued her persecution of Jews. Only 40 out of 3,000 synagogues remained.
A **Religion** saw Paul VI receive
A President Tito, the first communist leader to be seen officially by a pope. The South African Council of Churches admitted 385 black churches represented by the African Independent Churches Association.

the Prussians under Blücher, on the French right. There were eventually 45,000 Prussians engaged. From midday until 8 pm, Wellington's army held out until the French were routed. There were 23,000 allied casualties and the French lost 33,000 men. The battle resulted in the final abdication and exile of Napoleon.

Watt, James (1736–1819), British engineer. He invented the modern condensing steam engine in 1765. In 1782 he invented the double-acting engine. With Matthew Boulton he founded the Soho Engineering Works at Birmingham in 1775 for the manufacture of steam engines. He and Boulton coined the term "horsepower" and the unit of power called a watt is named after him.

Wellington, Arthur Wellesley, Duke of (1769–1852), British general and statesman, commanded allied forces in the Peninsular War (1808–14) and drove the French back over the Pyrenees in 1814, during the Napoleonic Wars. He was created a duke in 1814 and represented Britain at the Congress of Vienna (1814–15). Together with the Prussian Gen. von Blücher, he defeated Napoleon and the French at the Battle of Waterloo (1815). He became a Tory cabinet minister in 1818 and Prime Minister (1828–30). He supported the Catholic Emancipation Act (1829), but opposed parliamentary reform, over which he resigned in 1830.

Wesley, John (1703–91), British theologian and evangelist who founded Methodism. With his brother Charles he founded the so-called Holy Club at Oxford in 1729. In 1735 they went as missionaries to Georgia, where they established the principles of Methodism which spread quickly after John Wesley's return to England, and many lay preachers were enrolled to help. His *Journal* (1735–90) records the great extent of his itinerant preaching, which often brought Christianity to many who had not known it before.

Wilberforce, William (1759–1833), British social reformer, and MP for more than 40 years. In 1784 he was

---

AD 1972

World currency crisis caused floating of many national currencies. Germ warfare was banned.

A **US'** Nixon visited China and won rapprochement with USSR, winning a landslide reelection.

British troops killed 13 people

A in Ulster rioting. IRA later killed 11 people with bombs in Belfast.

Pakistan withdrew from the Commonwealth.

West Germany saw the arrest of Red Army faction leaders as urban terrorists.

A **Eygpt's** Sadat expelled 20,000 Soviet advisers.

Uganda's Amin expelled all non-citizen Asians.

Palestinian guerrillas killed 11 Israeli athletes at the Olympic Games; 300 people were killed in massive Israeli reprisals.

---

converted to Evangelical Christianity. His strong and outspoken opposition to the slave trade led to its abolition in the West Indies in 1807.

William I (the Conqueror) (*c.* 1027–87), King of England (1066–87), and Duke of Normandy. He was the illegitimate son of Robert I of Normandy, and was unwillingly accepted as Robert's heir, succeeding to the Dukedom of Normandy in 1035. Supported initially by Henry I, King of France, he consolidated his position in Normandy against hostile neighbours throughout the 1050s and expanded his territory in 1063. Having apparently been designated Edward the Confessor's successor as King of England, William secured the agreement of Harold, Earl of Wessex, to his accession. Harold's assumption of kingship was the cause of William's invasion of England and the ensuing Battle of Hastings in 1066. He crushed all internal resistance but spent most of his reign in France, returning to England only when necessary. He established stable government through astute land distribution and by instituting the Feudal System in England. The Domesday Book (1086) was compiled during his reign.

William III, or William of Orange (1650–1702), Prince of Orange, King of England, Scotland and Ireland (1689–1702). Born eight days after the death of his father William II, he was prevented from succeeding him as Stadholder of Holland until 1672. From then he devoted his life to opposing the expansion of France under Louis XIV. He married Mary, daughter of the Duke of York (later James II of England), in 1677. Following the Glorious Revolution in 1688, he and Mary replaced James II and ruled jointly until her death in 1694. Using English resources, William carried on his struggle against France, and prepared the alliance which defeated Louis in the War of the Spanish Succession.

William I (the Silent) (1533–84), Prince of Orange and one of the founders of the Dutch Republic. He was one of the great lords of The Netherlands and led a growing opposition

---

AD 1973

World oil price rises and fear of diminishing fuel supplies caused research into alternatives. A campaign aimed at cutting world populations started. **A US** troops left Vietnam. The **A** Watergate Scandal began. Writer Thomas Pynchon produced the masterly *Gravity's Rainbow*. The Conservation Movement produced *The Limits to Growth*, a gloomy forecast of the depletion of resources.

Chile saw Allende killed in a right-wing coup.
Britain entered the EEC with Ireland and Denmark. Heath imposed a three-day week in response to the miners' strike.
Israel beat Arab neighbours in another Middle East short war.
Hong Kong produced a kung fu film industry.

---

to the intolerant Spanish rule, which culminated in the War of Independence from 1568. In the face of immense difficulties, William managed to unite the Calvinist northern provinces and was recognized as the first stadholder in 1579. He was later assassinated by a Catholic fanatic.

Wilson, Sir James Harold (1916–   ), British Labour politician and Prime Minister. He became an MP in 1945 and was appointed President of the Board of Trade in 1947. In 1951 he resigned from Attlee's government over the imposition of medical prescription charges. He was four times Prime Minister (1964–66, 1966–70, 1974 and 1974–76). He established the Open University (1970) and accelerated the growth of the comprehensive system of education. His government re-nationalized the steel industry, introduced measures for rent control and the control of prices and incomes and provided time for the passing of bills to legalize abortion and homosexual acts. He resigned as Prime Minister in 1976, but retained his seat in the House of Commons.

Wilson, Thomas Woodrow (1856–1924), 28th US president (1913–21), who administered the country throughout WWI and then worked uncompromisingly for a just international peace settlement. During his administration legislation was launched to give women the vote and to prohibit the sale of alcoholic liquor; anti-trust laws were passed; the tariff was reduced and labour conditions on board ship and for railway workers were reformed. In foreign affairs, WWI overshadowed his first term and as public opinion against Germany mounted during his second term, the USA declared war (1917). In 1918, Wilson formulated his Fourteen Points, which were to form the basis for the peace; the resulting Treaty of Versailles was not what he had hoped for. Although he played a leading role in establishing the League of Nations his own country was strongly opposed to it.

Wolsey, Thomas (*c.* 1475–1530), English cardinal and

AD 1974

AUS Watergate Scandal forced ANixon's resignation. The Moon Programme ended, releasing scientists for environmental research. Lead pollution from cars was cut and a micro-computer developed. Joseph Heller wrote *Something Happened*, a gloomy, closely written account of executive life. The disaster movie was popular, with *Earthquake* and *Towering*

Inferno successful examples. **Portugal's** coup displaced Caetano and its colonies sought independence. **Turkish** troops invaded Cyprus. **USSR's** abstract artists tried unsuccessfully to exhibit. **Greek** military junta ended. **Religion** saw the Catholic Church reaffirm its stand against divorce in an unpopular statement from Paul VI.

---

politician. He served as papal legate (1518–30) and Lord Chancellor of England (1515–29). The son of a butcher, he was an ambitious man who rose quickly in Church affairs, becoming Henry VII's chaplain and then Dean of Lincoln (1509). Appointed a Privy councillor in 1511 by Henry VIII, he was soon one of the most important men in England. He became Archbishop of York and Bishop of Lincoln in 1514, and a cardinal in 1515. His failure to obtain Henry VIII's divorce from Catherine of Aragon brought his ruin.

World War I (1914–18), European conflict of unprecedented extent and ferocity, known also as the Great War. Although it was centred in Europe, hostilities also took place in the Middle East, the Far East and Africa. European territorial and economic rivalries had been intensified by the growing power of the German Empire and the conflict was precipitated by the assassination of Archduke Franz Ferdinand of Austria-Hungary (Germany's close ally) by a Serbian nationalist fanatic in 1914. The countries of Europe aligned themselves into two camps: the Allies, comprising Great Britain, France, Russia, Serbia, Montenegro, Japan and later Italy, Romania, Greece and the USA; and the Central Powers, consisting of Germany, Austria-Hungary, Bulgaria and the Ottoman Empire. In France and Belgium (the Western Front) the German schemes for rapid victory (the Schlieffen Plan) failed, and the conflict soon degenerated into a war of attrition, both sides digging trenches and erecting fortifications. In the east, the huge manpower of Russia was savaged by the better trained and equipped German army. The outbreak of the Russian Revolution (1917) effectively removed Russia from the war and peace between Germany and Russia was signed (1918) at Brest-Litovsk.

Meanwhile, in 1917, the USA had entered the war on the Allied side and began ferrying troops to Europe. Early in 1918 the Germans launched a massive attack on the Western Front. It was frustrated by stubborn Allied

AD 1975

World feminism received a boost from the United Nations decision to make 1975 International Women's Year.
Vietnam was entirely taken over by Communist forces, as was Cambodia.
Britain confirmed its membership of the EEC with its first-ever referendum. Anthony Powell completed his Proustian novel sequence *A Dance to the Music*

of *Time* with *Hearing Secret Harmonies*.
USSR space probe took pictures of Venus. A Soyuz spacecraft linked with an Apollo one, ending the space race.
Egypt reopened the Suez Canal to shipping.
Angola's civil war started, involving trained Cuban guerrillas and numerous British mercenaries.

resistance and the exhausted German army, and a starving
civilian population, were not capable of further effort. An
armistice was signed on 11 November, 1918 and the ensuing
Treaty of Versailles (1919) imposed humiliating terms on
Germany.

World War II (1939–1945), most extensive conflict in
human history. After Adolf Hitler had assumed absolute
power in Germany, he rebuilt the German armed forces and
during the 1930s annexed considerable areas in central
Europe. At the same time the Fascist Italy of Benito
Mussolini conquered Ethiopia (1935). Britain and France
sought to appease the dictators but when Germany and the
USSR (hitherto implacable foes) united to attack Poland (1
Sept 1939) a European conflict could not be avoided.

Poland soon succumbed to the German Blitzkrieg and
was partitioned between Germany and the USSR. In April
1940 the German army rapidly overwhelmed Norway,
Holland and France. British forces were evacuated from
Dunkirk and German invasion of England was prevented
only by the RAF's Battle of Britain. In June 1941 Hitler
invaded the USSR. His troops came within sight of Moscow
but were halted in December by the early onset of a
particularly harsh winter. In that same month the war
became a global conflict. On 7 December the Japanese,
determined to secure control of East Asia, bombed Pearl
Harbor, destroying much of the US Pacific fleet. Thereafter
they rapidly overran the Philippines, Indonesia, Malaya,
Burma and many of the Pacific islands. They were not
stemmed until the summer of 1942, when the US navy won
victories at Coral Sea and Midway. In Europe the British
drove the Germans and Italians from North Africa and
then, together with US forces, invaded Sicily and then Italy,
which surrendered in September 1943. Meanwhile, the
Russians had inflicted a crushing defeat on the Germans at
Stalingrad and had begun their advance into Europe. On 6
June 1944 Allied forces landed in Normandy. Germany was
now fighting on three fronts and was finally completely

AD 1976

A US under Carter sent a Viking
probe to photograph Mars.
China had a moderate coup,
A backed by the army, after Mao
Tse-tung's death. Hundreds of
thousands died in earthquakes.
Lebanese capital Beirut was
the scene of bitter fighting.
A **Britain** saw IRA terrorism
extended to London with many
bombings. A Bacon painting
fetched £89,000.

Portugal held its first elections since the 1920s.
Zimbabwe's guerrilla war against
A the Smith regime continued.
Israel rescued hijack victims
in a raid on Entebbe's airport.
Religion saw the continuation
of the Tridentine Mass controversy when Archbishop Lefebvre
was summoned to Rome and
reprimanded, not entirely
A effectively, by Paul VI.

occupied and forced to capitulate in May 1945. In the Pacific, Japanese forces were gradually driven back, the Allies advancing from island to island. On 6 and 9 August 1945 the USA dropped atomic bombs on the Japanese mainland, which brought about Japanese surrender. Perhaps as many as 45,000,000 people, civilians and armed servicemen together, were killed during WWII which radically altered the balance of power with the USA and USSR in positions of supreme power.

Wren, Sir Christopher (1632–1723), English architect, mathematician and astronomer. After the Fire of London in 1666 he made a plan for the reconstruction of the city, but it was not used. He did, however, design 52 new churches in the city of London, the greatest of which is St Paul's Cathedral. Among his many other works are Chelsea and Greenwich hospitals in London.

Wright, Frank Lloyd (1869–1959), US architect. His first independent designs were for domestic houses, which he built with low, horizontal lines in his "prairie" style; the Robie house, Chicago (1908) is the most famous. He attempted to combine new mechanical methods and materials with organic architectural design, and to create open planning and free-flowing internal space.

Wright brothers, Wilbur (1867–1912) and Orville (1871–1948), US aviation pioneers. They used their bicycle factory as a laboratory for assembling their first aircraft and experimented with gliders to learn wing control and lateral balancing. The rolling sand dunes and fairly constant winds at Kitty Hawk, North Carolina, allowed them to test gliders (1900–02). Orville made the first piloted flight in a power-driven plane at Kitty Hawk in 1903.

Wycliffe, John (c. 1328–84), English religious reformer. He studied and taught at Oxford University and was vicar of Fillingham (1361) and Ludgershall (1368) and rector of Lutterworth (1374). In the 1370s he acted to protect the interests of the national Church against the Papacy, and came under the patronage of John of Gaunt. In 1378 he

---

AD 1977

A **Egypt's** Sadat's peace initiative bore little fruit, but paved the way for Arab recognition of Israel.

Somalia and Ethiopia were at war, resulting in tens of thousands of deaths.

West German terrorists of the Baader-Meinhof group allegedly killed themselves in their cells, provoking much anti-governmental speculation.

Britain hosted a European Summit Conference. An art sale at Mentmore Towers fetched £6.4 million. Scientists discovered the complete genetic structure of the virus. Reggae consolidated its popularity with "dub" expressing Rastafarianism.

US author Patricia Highsmith wrote *Edith's Diary* and Hubert Selby *The Demon*, both works of powerful pessimism.

Xerxes I

began a series of works attacking Church practices and beliefs, especially Transubstantiation and the secular ambitions of many churchmen.

Xerxes I (*c.* 519–465 BC), King of Persia (*r.* 486–465 BC). His achievement was to bring Egypt back under Persian rule (484 BC). He launched a campaign to conquer Greece in 480 BC, marching through Macedonia and burning Athens. His fleet was destroyed by the Athenians at Salamis, however, and he returned to Asia; the following year, the Persian army in Greece was defeated. Xerxes was later assassinated by his own bodyguard.

Ypres, Battles of, three WWI battles at Ypres, France. The first (12 Oct–22 Nov 1914) stopped the German "race to the sea". There were more than 50,000 British killed. The second (22 April–25 May 1915) failed to gain Germany control of the Ypres salient. There were 59,000 British killed. The third (31 July–4 Nov 1917) was a British offensive which gained the Allies most of the salient. There were 245,000 British killed.

Zoroaster, or Zarathustra (*c.* 628 BC–*c.* 551 BC), Persian religious reformer, founder of Zoroastrianism. Zoroaster is believed to have been born in western Persia. Unable to convert the petty chieftains of his native land, Zoroaster travelled to the East, where in Chorasmia (now in Khorasan province in NE Iran) he converted the royal family, including King Vishtaspa. By the time of Zoroaster's death, his new religion had spread to a large part of Persia. Parts of the Avesta, the holy scripture of Zoroastrianism, are believed to have been written by Zoroaster himself.

Zulu War (1879), war in southern Africa between the hirtherto unconquered Zulus and the British. Prompted by a fear that the Zulus might attack Natal, the British demanded that the Zulu leader, Cetewaya, disband his army. The Zulus refused, and defeated a British army sent against them, but they were halted at Rorke's Drift and finally defeated at Ulundi, in July 1879. Zululand became a British protectorate in 1877.

AD 1978

Europe saw the Council of Europe united in its determination to counter terrorism.

A **US** President Carter initiated Middle East peace talks at

A Camp David involving Sadat and Begin. Other Arab countries refused to recognize the relevance of the meetings.

Cambodia and Vietnam went to war, causing many refugees to flee the country.

Britain saw the birth of the first test-tube baby. David Hare's play *Plenty* and Tom Stoppard's drama were popular. Iris Murdoch's *The Sea, the Sea* won the Booker Prize. Disco was the musical craze.

Religion saw Paul VI and his successor both die. The World Council of Churches was criticized for supporting the Patriotic Front in Zimbabwe.

Tables

The following eight pages contain easy-access information about the more prominent countries of the world: their location, populations in 1976 and past and present rulers. Dynasties and rulers appearing in the A-Z section have been marked A.

Australia (SW Pacific; Pop: 13,640,000)
Prime Ministers (Commonwealth)
Edmund Barton (1901–03)
Alfred Deakin (1903–04; 1905–08; 1909–10)
John Watson (1904)
George Reid (1904–05)
Andrew Fisher (1908–09; 1910–13; 1914–15)
Joseph Cook (1913–14)
William Hughes (1915–23)
Stanley Bruce (1923–29)
James Scullin (1929–31)
Joseph Lyons (1931–39)
Sir Earle Grafton Page (1939)
Robert Menzies (1939–41; 1949–65)
Arthur Fadden (1941)
John Curtin (1941–45)
Francis Forde (1945)
Joseph Chifley (1945–49)
Harold Holt (1965–67)
John McEwen (1967–68)
John Gorton (1968–71)
William McMahon (1971–72)
Gough Whitlam (1972–75)
Malcolm Fraser (1975–   )
Austria (Central Europe; Pop: 7,500,000)
Monarchs (Duchy)
Ottokar II (1251–76)
Rudolf of Hapsburg (1276–91)
Holy Roman Emperors (1291–1740)
Monarchs of Austria-Hungary
A Maria Theresa (1740–80)
Joseph II (1780–90)
Leopold II (1790–92)
Francis II (1792–1835)
Ferdinand I (1835–48)
Emperors of Austria and Kings of Hungary
A Francis Joseph I (1848–1916)
Charles I (1916–18)
Presidents (First Republic)
Karl Seitz (1919–20)
Michael Hainisch (1920–28)
Wilhelm Miklas (1928–38)
Presidents (Second Republic)
Karl Renner (1945–50)
Theodor Koerner (1951–57)
Adolf Schaerf (1957–65)
Franz Jonas (1965–74)
Rudolf Kirchschläger (1974–   )

Canada (N America; Pop: 23,140,000)
Prime Ministers (Federal Union; Constitutional Monarchy
Sir John A. Macdonald (1867–73; 1878–91)
Alexander Mackenzie (1873–78)
Sir John J.C. Abbott (1891–92)
Sir John S.D. Thompson (1892–94)
Sir Mackenzie Bowell (1894–96)
Sir Charles Tupper (1896)
Sir Wilfrid Laurier (1896–1911)
Sir Robert L. Borden (1911–20)
Aurther Meighen (1920–21; 1926)
W.L. Mackenzie King (1921–26; 1926–30; 1935–48)
Richard B. Bennett (1930–35)
Louis S. St Laurent (1948–57)
John Diefenbaker (1957–63)
Lester B. Pearson (1963–68)
A Pierre Elliott Trudeau (1968–)
China (Asia; Pop: 852,130,000)
Chairmen (People's Republic)
A Mao Tse-tung (1949–54; 1968–76)
Liu Shao-ch'i (1954–68)
Hua Kuo-feng (1976–)
France (W Europe; Pop: 52,920,000)
Monarchs (Kingdom)
Bourbons
A Henry IV (1589–1610)
A Louis XIII (1610–43)
A Louis XIV (1643–1715)
A Louis XV (1715–74)
A Louis XVI (1774–92)
Louis XVII (1793–95)
The Republic
National Convention (1792–95)
The Directory (1795–99)
The Consulate (1799–1804)
First Empire
A Napoleon Bonaparte (1804–15)
Restoration
Louis XVIII (1814–24)
A Charles X (1824–30)
Louis Philippe (1830–48)
The Second Republic
Louis Napoleon (1848–52)
Second Empire
A Napoleon III (1852–70)
The Third Republic
Louis Adolphe Thiers (1871–73)
Marshall MacMahon (1873–79)
Jules Grévy (1879–87)
Marie François Sadi Carnot (1887–94)
Jean Casimir-Périer (1894–95)
François Félix Faure (1895–99)
Emile Loubet (1899–1906)
Armand Fallières (1906–13)
Raymond Poincaré (1913–20)
Paul Deschanel (1920)
Alexandre Mulerand (1920–24)
Gaston Doumergue (1924–31)

Paul Doumer (1931–32)
Albert Lebrun (1932–40)
A *Vichy Government*
A Henri Philippe Petain (1940–44)
Provisional Government
A Charles De Gaulle (1944–46)
Félix Gouin (1946)
Georges Bidault (1946)
Léon Blum (1946)
Fourth Republic
Vincent Auriol (1947–54)
René Coty (1954–59)
Fifth Republic
A Charles De Gaulle (1959–69)
A Georges Pompidou (1969–74)
Valéry Giscard D'Estaing (1974–   )
Germany, West (N Europe; Pop: 61,500,000)
Kings of Prussia
Frederick I (1701–13)
A Frederick William I (1713–40)
A Frederick II the Great (1740–86)
Frederick William II (1786–97)
Frederick William III (1797–1840)
Frederick William IV (1840–61)
William I (1861–71)
Emperors of Germany
William I (1871–88)
Frederick III (1888)
William II (1888–1918)
Weimar Republic
Friedrich Ebert (President) (1919–25)
A Paul Von Hindenburg (President) (1925–34)
A Adolf Hitler (Fuhrer & Chancellor) (1934–45)
Presidents
Theodor Heuss (1949–59)
Heinrich Lubke (1959–69)
Gustav Heinemann (1969–74)
Walter Scheel (1974–   )
Chancellors
A Konrad Adenauer (1949–63)
Ludwig Erhard (1963–66)
Kurt-Georg Kiesinger (1966–69)
A Willy Brandt (1969–74)
A Helmut Schmidt (1976–   )
India (S Asia; Pop: 610,080,000)
Presidents (Republic)
A Rajendra Prasad (1950–62)
Sarvepalli Radhakrishnan (1962–67)
Zakir Husain (1967–69)
Varahagiri Venkata Giri (1969–77)
Neelham Sanjiva Reddy (1977–   )
Prime Ministers
A Jawaharial Pandit Nehru (1947–64)
Lal Bahadur Shastri (1964–67)
Indira Gandhi (1967–77)
A Morarji Ranchodji Desai (1977–   )

Ireland (W Europe; Pop: 3,160,000)
Prime Ministers (Republic)
A William T. Cosgrave (1922–32)
A Eamon de Valera (1932–48; 1951–54; 1957–59)
  John A. Costello (1948–51; 1954–57)
  Sean Lemass (1959–66)
  Jack Lynch (1966–73; 1977–)
  Liam Cosgrave (1973–77)

Netherlands, The (NW Europe; Pop: 13,770,000)
Princes of Orange, Stadtholders
A William I (1579–84)
  Maurice (1587–1625)
  Frederick Henry (1625–47)
  William II (1647–50)
  Jan De Witt, Grand Pensionary (1653–72)
A William of Nassau (1672–1702)
  William IV (1747–51)
  William V (1751–95)
Monarchs (Kingdom)
  Louis Bonaparte (1806–10)
  Willem Frederick (William I) (1815–40)
  William II (1840–49)
  William III (1849–90)
  Wilhelmina (1890–1948)
  Juliana (1948–)

New Zealand (SW Pacific; Pop: 3,140,000)
Prime Ministers (Constitutional Monarchy)
Henry Sewell (1856)
William Fox (1856; 1861–62; 1869–72; 1873)
Edward Stafford (1856–61; 1865–69; 1872)
Alfred Dommet (1862–63)
Frederick Whitaker (1863–64; 1882–83)
Frederick Weld (1864–65)
George Waterhouse (1872–73)
Julius Vogel (1873–75; 1876)
Daniel Pollen (1875–76)
Harry Atkinson (1876–77; 1883–84; 1884; 1887–91)
George Grey (1877–79)
John Hall (1879–82)
Robert Stout (1884; 1884–87)
John Ballance (1891–93)
Richard Seddon (1893–1906)
William Hall-Jones (1906)
Joseph Ward (1906–12; 1928–30)
Thomas Mackenzie (1912)
William Massey (1912–25)
Francis Bell (1925)
Gordon Coates (1925–28)
George Forbes (1930–35)
Michael Savage (1935–40)
Peter Fraser (1940–49)
Sidney Holland (1949–57)
Keith Holyoake (1957; 1960–72)
Walter Nash (1957–60)
John Marshall (1972)
Norman Kirk (1972–74)
Wallace Rowling (1974–75)
A Robert Muldoon (1975–)

Union of Soviet Socialist Republics
(Europe/Asia; Pop: 256,670,000)
Chairmen of the Presidium of the Supreme Soviet
Mikhail Kalinin (1923–46)
Nikolai Shvernik (1946–53)
Kliment Voroshilov (1953–60)
A Leonid Brezhnev (1960–64; 1977–)
Anastasi Mikoyan (1964–66)
A Nikolai Podgorny (1966–74)
A.P. Shitikov (1974–77)
Premiers
A Vladimir Ilyich Lenin (1917–24)
A Joseph Stalin (1924–53)
Georgi Malenkov (1953–55)
A Nikita Khrushchev (1955–64)
A Aleksey Kosygin (1964–)
United Kingdom (W Europe; Pop: 55,930,000)
England- Monarchs
A *Saxons*
Egbert (828–39)
Ethelwulf (839–58)
Ethelbald (858–60)
Ethelbert (860–66)
Ethelred I (866–71)
A Alfred the Great (871–99)
Edward the Elder (899–924)
Athelstan (924–39)
Edmund I (939–46)
Edred (946–55)
Edwy (955–59)
Edgar (959–75)
Edward the Martyr (975–78)
A Ethelred II the Unready (978–1016)
Edmund II Ironside (1016)
A *Danes*
A Canute (Cnut) (1016–35)
Harold I Harefoot (1035–40)
Hardicanute (1040–42)
A *Saxons*
A Edward the Confessor (1042–66)
Harold II (1066)
House of Normandy
William I the Conqueror (1066–87)
William II Rufus (1087–1100)
Henry I Beauclerc (1100–35)
House of Blois
Stephen (1135–54)
House of Plantagenet
A Henry II (1154–89)
A Richard I Lionheart (1189–99)
A John Lackland (1199–1216)
Henry III (1216–72)
A Edward I Longshanks (1272–1307)
A Edward II (1307–27)
A Edward III (1327–77)
Richard II (1377–99)
House of Lancaster
Henry IV (1399–1413)
A Henry V (1413–22)

Henry VI (1422–61; 1470–71)
House of York
A Edward IV (1461–70; 1471–83)
Edward V (1483)
A Richard III (1483–85)
House of Tudor
A Henry VII (1485–1509)
A Henry VIII (1509–47)
Edward VI (1547–53)
A Mary I (1553–58)
A Elizabeth I (1558–1603)
Scotland- Monarchs
Malcolm II (1005–34)
Duncan I (1034–40)
Macbeth (1040–57)
Lulach (1057–58)
Malcolm III Canmore (1058–93)
Donald Bane (1093–94; 1094–97)
Duncan II (1094)
Edgar (1097–1107)
Alexander I (1107–24)
A David I (1124–53)
Malcolm IV (1153–65)
William I the Lion (1165–1214)
Alexander II (1214–49)
Alexander III (1249–86)
Margaret, Maid of Norway (1286–90)
Interregnum (1290–92)
John Balliol (1292–96)
Interregnum (1296–1306)
Robert I the Bruce (1306–29)
A David II (1329–71)
House of Stewart (Stuart)
Robert II (1371–90)
Robert III (1390–1406)
James I (1406–37)
James II (1437–60)
James III (1460–88)
James IV (1488–1513)
James V (1513–42)
A Mary Queen of Scots (1542–67)
James VI (1567–1625)
United Kingdom- Monarchs
A James I (VI of Scotland) (1603–25)
A Charles I (1625–49)
Council of State (1649–53)
A   Oliver Cromwell (1653–58)
Richard Cromwell (1658–59)
A Charles II (1660–85)
A James II (1685–89)
Mary II (1689–94)
A William III (1689–1702)
A Anne (1702–14)
House of Hanover
A George I (1714–27)
A George II (1727–60)
A George III (1760–1820)
George IV (1820–30)

William IV (1830–37)
A Victoria (1837–1901)
House of Saxe-Coburg
Edward VII (1901–10)
House of Windsor
A George V (1910–36)
A Edward VIII (1936)
A George VI (1936–52)
A Elizabeth II (1952–)
Prime Ministers of Northern Ireland
Sir James Craig (1921–40)
John Andrews (1940–43)
Sir Basil Brooke (1943–63)
Capt. Terence O'Neill (1963–69)
Maj. James Chichester-Clark (1969–71)
Brian Faulkner (1971–72)
Direct Rule (1972–)
First Lords of the Treasury
Charles Montagu (1714–15)
Charles Howard (1715)
A Robert Walpole (1715–17)
James Stanhope (1717–18)
Charles Spencer (1718–21)
Prime Ministers
A Robert Walpole (1721–42)
Spencer Compton (1742–43)
Henry Pelham (1743–54)
Thomas Pelham-Holles (1754–56; 1757–62)
William Cavendish (1756–57)
John Stuart (1762–63)
George Grenville (1763–65)
Charles Watson-Wentworth (1765–66; 1782)
A William Pitt (1766–68)
Augustus Fitzroy (1768–70)
Frederick North (1770–82)
William Petty (1782–83)
William Bentinck (1783; 1807–09)
A William Pitt the Younger (1783–1801; 1804–06)
Henry Addington (1801–04)
William Grenville (1806–07)
Spencer Perceval (1809–12)
Robert Jenkinson (1812–27)
George Canning (1827)
Frederick Robinson (1827–28)
A Arthur Wellesley (1828–30)
Charles Grey (1830–34)
William Lamb (1834; 1835–41)
A Robert Peel (1834–35; 1841–46)
A John Russell (1846–52; 1865–66)
Edward Stanley (1852; 1858–59; 1866–68)
George Gordon (1852–55)
A Viscount Palmerston (1855–58; 1859–65)
A Benjamin Disraeli (1868; 1874–80)
A William Gladstone (1868–74; 1880–85; 1886; 1892–94)
Robert Cecil (1885–86; 1886–92; 1895–1902)
Archibald Primrose (1894–95)
A Arthur Balfour (1902–05)

Henry Campbell-Bannerman (1905–08)
A Herbert Asquith (1908–16)
A David Lloyd George (1916–22)
Andrew Bonar Law (1922–23)
A Stanley Baldwin (1923–24; 1924–29; 1935–37)
A Ramsay Macdonald (1924; 1929–35)
A Neville Chamberlain (1937–40)
A Winston Churchill (1940–45; 1951–55)
A Clement Attlee (1945–51)
A Anthony Eden (1955–57)
A Harold Macmillan (1957–63)
Alec Douglas-Home (1963–64)
A Harold Wilson (1964–70; 1974–76)
A Edward Heath (1970–74)
A James Callaghan (1976–   )

United States of America (N America; Pop: 215,120,0(
Presidents (Federal Republic)
A George Washington (1789–97)
John Adams (1797–1801)
A Thomas Jefferson (1801–09)
James Madison (1809–17)
A James Monroe (1817–25)
John Adams (1825–29)
A Andrew Jackson (1829–37)
Martin Van Buren (1837–41)
William Harrison (1841)
John Tyler (1841–45)
James Knox Polk (1845–49)
Zachary Taylor (1849–50)
Millard Filmore (1850–53)
Franklin Pierce (1853–57)
James Buchanan (1857–61)
A Abraham Lincoln (1861–65)
Andrew Johnson (1865–69)
A Ulysses Grant (1869–77)
Rutherford Hayes (1877–81)
James Garfield (1881)
Chester Arthur (1881–85)
Grover Cleveland (1885–89; 1893–97)
Benjamin Harrison (1889–93)
A William McKinley (1897–1901)
Theodore Roosevelt (1901–09)
William Taft (1909–13)
A Woodrow Wilson (1913–21)
Warren Harding (1921–23)
Calvin Coolidge (1923–29)
Herbert Hoover (1929–33)
A Franklin Roosevelt (1933–45)
A Harry S. Truman (1945–53)
A Dwight Eisenhower (1953–61)
A John Kennedy (1961–63)
A Lyndon Johnson (1963–69)
A Richard Nixon (1969–74)
Gerald Ford (1974–76)
A James Carter (1976–   )